The End of
EURASIA

Advance praise for *The End of Eurasia*

"A rare example of a scholarly work that covers challenges facing Russia from the Baltic Sea to the Far East, this book offers a splendid description of how Russia's former fortress-like borders have turned into frontiers and makes a contribution to the understanding of how Russia's difficult democratic devolution influences foreign policy."

—**Mauno Koivisto**, former President of Finland

"Dmitri Trenin's book serves as a reminder of the peril that geopolitical realities can lead mankind directly to disaster. This is a book about the 20th century, which has witnessed nightmares turn into reality, and about Russia, a country that has passed through great temptation and terrible ordeals. *The End of Eurasia* can help people both in avoiding further suffering and also in keeping their hopes alive."

—**Vladimir Ryzhkov**, member of the Russian State Duma

"As both an idea and a physical reality, Eurasia is dead, argues Trenin. It was destroyed by the definitive collapse of the Russian empire, by the rise of viable new states (many of which will merge into either Europe or Asia), and by new anti-imperial imperatives such as globalization. Because Eurasia offers no refuge for Russia in its quest for a new identity, Russians need to move on toward Europe. There Russia belongs, Trenin contends, for spiritual as well as practical reasons—notwithstanding the difficulties ahead, including those created by Russia's internal passage. Trenin makes these points clear in an exceedingly sophisticated exploration of the interaction between space and identity in Russian history and the challenges facing Russia as it deals with its new neighbors on all three sides. This work is both the best and the most thought-provoking book on Russian foreign policy around, written by a Russian who is ahead of his time and the vast majority of his countrymen."

—*Foreign Affairs*

The End of EURASIA

Russia on the Border Between Geopolitics and Globalization

Dmitri Trenin

Carnegie Endowment for International Peace
Washington, D.C., and Moscow

Carnegie Endowment for International Peace
1779 Massachusetts Avenue, N.W., Washington, D.C. 20036
202-483-7600 www.CarnegieEndowment.org

The Carnegie Endowment for International Peace normally does not take institutional positions on public policy issues; the views and recommendations presented in this publication do not necessarily represent the views of the Carnegie Endowment, its officers, staff, or trustees.

To order, contact Carnegie's distributor:
The Brookings Institution Press
Department 029, Washington, D.C. 20042-0029, USA
1-800-275-1447 or 1-202-797-6258

Printed in the United States of America

Library of Congress Cataloging-in-Publication Data

Trenin, Dmitriæi
    The end of Eurasia : Russia on the border between geopolitics and
    globalization / Dmitri Trenin.
        p. cm.
Includes bibliographical referneces and index.
    ISBN 0-87003-190-2 (pbk. : alk. Paper)
    1. Russia (Federation)—Politics and government—1991- 2. Geopolitics—Russia (Federation) I. Title.

DK510.763.T74 2002
327.47—dc21   2001006591

3rd Printing 2005

Contents

Foreword

Ten years after the end of the Soviet Union, Russia's international identity still remains largely unresolved. In recent years, Moscow has pursued an erratic foreign policy, veering between cooperation with the West and alienation from it. Moreover, for much of Russia's ruling elite, nineteenth-century style geopolitics has replaced Marxism-Leninism as the guiding light for foreign policy.

Books by Russian authors on their country's international role and security strategy tend either to be reactive and anti-Western or to ignore geopolitics altogether, thus vacating the field well before the battle. This book is different. The author, a convinced supporter of Russia's integration with the West, seeks to make his case on geopolitical grounds.

Dmitri Trenin believes that a geopolitics of "multipolarity" is a bad idea for Russia. He contends that Russia lacks the resources to act as a pole, and thus risks being torn among the real centers of power positioned along its three fronts: the West, a southern tier of nations where Islam is the most powerful factor, and the Far East. Instead, he argues, political instability on Russia's southern flank and China's growing might to the east make it imperative for Russia to join the West by becoming integrated with the European Union and building an alliance with the United States.

Besides making a case for integration, the book analyzes post-Soviet territorial arrangements along Russia's land border of more than 10,000 miles. It delineates the political, economic, demographic, religious, and strategic challenges that Russia faces in relation to neighboring countries—in Eastern Europe, along the Baltic Sea, around the Caspian Sea, in Central Asia, and in the Far East. Trenin also describes the internal territorial structure of the Russian state and its links to both the political regime and the country's ethnic groups.

The volume's title reveals its thesis that Russia's time as the region's hegemon is over and that Russia and Eurasia are no longer geopolitically coterminous. Even before the terrorist attacks of September 11, 2001, vast Eurasia, with its many territorial conflicts, was becoming the main focus of concern for U.S. national security. Now, new developments in the world call for new alignments and make Trenin's analysis even more timely. A post-imperial, Europe-oriented Russia will be an important factor in structuring a security system that can respond to current and future challenges.

JESSICA T. MATHEWS
President
Carnegie Endowment for International Peace

Acknowledgments

This book is the result of over two years of my work at the Carnegie Moscow Center. I would not have been able to undertake this project without the encouragement and close support of the Center's outgoing director and my personal friend, Alan Rousso. As a serious student of Russia, he took on the great effort necessary to read the manuscript very closely, and provided me with a detailed, fair, and very honest critique of its content, for which I am very much indebted to him. Alan also ironed out many problems related to the publication process, never an easy thing, to say the least. Throughout, he gave me steady and sound advice.

I also received support and encouragement from the senior leadership of the Carnegie Endowment for International Peace—its president, Jessica T. Mathews; executive vice president, Paul Balaran; vice president and director of studies, Thomas Carothers; vice president for communications, Carmen McDougall; director of the Russian-Eurasian program, Andrew Kuchins, and the former vice president for the Russian-Eurasian Program, Arnold Horelick.

Very special thanks to the reviewers of the book. Thomas Graham, my former colleague at the Carnegie Endowment in Washington, D.C., and among the very top experts on Russia anywhere, gave extremely insightful comments on the manuscript which allowed me to improve it in important ways. Anatol Lieven, my partner in the Foreign and Security Policy project at Carnegie, and someone whose experience as a journalist, analyst, and now a scholar specializing in certain key parts of Eurasia is truly unique, managed to be both frank and friendly in his appraisal of my work. I am also greatly indebted to Rene Nyberg, Finland's very able ambassador to Moscow and a friend of many years, for his detailed and shrewd observations. Last, but by no means least, I am grateful to Professor Vladimir Baranovsky, Deputy Director of the Institute of World Economy and International Relations in Moscow and one of the truly great lights of the Russian academic scene, whose comments stimulated me to both broaden my outlook and deepen my analysis.

As anyone who attempts to write in a language that is not one's mother tongue, I badly needed someone who would turn my English into proper English. I was very fortunate to find Michael Kazmarek, a former editor of the *Moscow Times*, who invested much time and energy into making the text more readable.

I was enormously assisted in preparing the manuscript for publication in Moscow first by Ekaterina Shirley, the Carnegie Center's most able assistant director for communications, and later by her successor, Natalia Kirpikova. At the Endowment's offices in Washington, I could safely rely on the good sense and efficiency of Trish Reynolds and Sherry Pettie. I was lucky to be able to rely throughout the project on the prompt and ever-effective support of Dmitri Basisty, our computer wizard and layout designer. I am indebted to Helen Belopolsky, the Center's exceptionally able intern, who shepherded the text in the final stages before it was sent to the presses. I am also very grateful to Sergei Psurtsev, program assistant, and Tania Keefe, the Center's intern, for their contribution to the production of this book.

Last but not least, it must be mentioned that this book grew out of a short essay I did for an East-West Institute volume on Russia and the West, edited by the star *troika* of Alexei Arbatov, Karl Kaiser, and Robert Legvold.

This is a prolonged way of saying that I fully share with my colleagues and friends whatever strengths the book has; all its weaknesses, however, are totally mine.

DMITRI TRENIN
Moscow
December 2001

To Vera, Pyotr, and Andrei

Introduction

CHURCHILL: I want to raise only one question. I note that the word "Germany" is used here. What is now the meaning of "Germany"?
TRUMAN: How is this question understood by the Soviet delegation? . . .
STALIN: Germany is, as we say, a geographical concept. . . . Let us define the western borders of Poland, and we shall be clearer on the question of Germany.
The Potsdam Conference, Second Sitting, July 18, 1945.[1]

This book raises the question of the meaning of "Russia" today, its place in the world, and the possible evolution of both. For Russia, at the start of the third millennium, is very much a country whose identity is changing. Like Germany, Russia has also traditionally been a geographical concept. Its external borders have defined its cultural and international identity, and its internal territorial organization has been intimately linked with the nature of the country's political regime. To cite one of the most frequently paraphrased lines by the poet Yevgeny Yevtushenko, "a border in Russia is more than a border."

The nominal subject of the book is therefore Russia's borders. Toward the end of the 20th century the tide of history began to turn. As Germany became reunited, the Soviet Union disintegrated, changing a centuries-old pattern of international relations on the continent of Eurasia. While most people celebrated the end of Soviet communism, some analysts held the view that the resulting collapse of the U.S.S.R. threatened to end in nothing less than a world geo-

1

political catastrophe. Despite its central position as a heartland, Russia, they argued, was no longer in the position of holding the world in geopolitical balance. They believed that a chain reaction would ultimately follow.[2]

The worst-case scenario has not happened—at least, not yet. However, since the fall of the U.S.S.R. and the end of communism ten years ago, the Russian Federation has been unsure of its new role, place, and identity. The political elite and the public view their country as the successor state of both the U.S.S.R. and the Russian Empire. Today's Russia encompasses just about 50 percent of the Soviet population, 60 percent of its industrial capacity, and 70 percent of the land mass. The latter is of key importance. Generations of Russians have formed their conception of their country simply by looking at a map, which shows it to be the world's biggest by far. A tsarist-era school primer cites Russia's "bigness" as its natural defining quality: Russia is big. Even after 1991, it appeared that Russia had simply been trimmed at the margins. Having preserved most of the Soviet Union's territory, the Russian Federation was almost naturally cast in the geopolitical role of the U.S.S.R.—only to discover that it was impossible to act like its predecessor.

The notion of "Eurasia" as used in this book should not be confused with the entire continent of Eurasia (which, of course, will continue to exist). What we are referring to is the traditional Russian state—the tsardom of Muscovy, the empire, the Soviet Union. These used to be synonymous with Russia. Not any longer. The present-day Russian Federation still includes major elements of the traditional Russian state—Greater Russia itself, Siberia, the Far East, and the North Caucasus. It is still located in Europe and in Asia. But it has lost its former quality as the center of gravity on the continent.

The process of fundamental change is not complete. Questions abound. Will Belarus survive as a separate country in the next ten years? What will happen to Ukraine in the long term? Will Kazakhstan ever be able to achieve internal cohesion, and what could be the likely consequences of its failure to do so? Will Russia be able to distinguish between Muslim revival and Islamic extremism, and then cope with either of them? What will happen to the Russian Far East, which is rich in natural resources, but has a miniscule population, and shares a long border with China? Will Russia itself recentralize, become a loose confederation, or find a way to balance regionalism and central authority in some yet-to-be devised form of federalism? Lastly, how will Russia fit into the outside world: as an island, a bridge, or part of some larger construct? These are the kinds of questions that will be dealt with in this book. It uses the notion of the border not so much as a way to discuss territorial arrangements, however important these may be, but rather as an analytical tool, as a prism through which some clues to the answers to the questions cited above can be found.

The book argues that the recent changes in the shape and nature of Russia's borders are of a qualitative nature. The end of the Soviet/Russian Empire is the result of a long process of self-determination, not the product of mistakes, greed, or crimes. Post-imperial Russia faces new and very different challenges along its European, Central Asian, and Far Eastern borders. The method of response and the options chosen will help shape its new international identity. By the same token, the way the Russian government deals with the issue of internal borders will help define the nature of the political regime in Russia. It will be rough sailing between the Scylla of fragmentation and the Charybdis of stifling recentralization. Whatever options are pursued and whatever choices are made in the future, the era during which Eurasia was synonymous with Russia is over. In the 21st century, these notions, while continuing to exist, will no longer be blurred together.

* * *

Books on geopolitics are popular in Russia. In the West, on the contrary, the subject is often treated as largely irrelevant, and with good reason. It is argued that in the age of globalization the issue of state borders is obsolete or archaic. The traditional world of nation-states is becoming an international community. Borders, it is said, are being blurred, and will ultimately wither away. There is even a telling comparison between state borders and the medieval city walls that were torn down when the feudal era came to an end. [3] Most post-industrial states have abjured territorial expansion as a worthy policy goal, having concentrated instead on attaining economic prowess, technological sophistication, the capacity for innovation, or wide cultural outreach. [4] Since the end of the Cold War, European integration has made great strides. The signing of the Maastricht Treaty in 1992 established a truly common market; the Schengen Agreement of 1995 did away with border controls within a space now covered by ten countries; and the introduction in 1999 by 11 member states of the European Union of a common currency, the euro, was closely followed by the emergence of a common foreign and security policy. In North America, a free trade area was created in 1993, bringing not only Canada but also Mexico into ever closer integration with the United States. Despite the 1997 Asian financial crisis and the turmoil in Indonesia, ASEAN continues to act as a pole of attraction. Integrationist projects, such as MERCOSUR, are bringing together many Latin American nations.

None of these trends has eliminated the essential role that the state plays in the world economic arena. What is striking, however, is that in many parts of the world, borders have ceased to be barriers and are increasingly becoming a place for cooperation and integration. Indeed, cross-border interaction has become a new motor of economic growth. The erasing of borders has fostered greater environmental cooperation, huge flows of capital, and a vast exchange of information in a borderless global environment that is virtually outside the control of national governments. Border conflicts excepted, the only serious recent example of a state pursuing the traditional policy of territorial annexation is the famously unsuccessful attempt by Saddam Hussein's Iraq to take over Kuwait.

The counter-argument to this, of course, is that state borders are now being challenged from within rather than from without. Liberated from the straightjacket of the Cold War, separatism has become a major issue in most parts of the world. The collapse of the former Yugoslavia has led to a decade of war in the Balkans, and to a chain reaction of territorial fragmentation. Likewise, the break-up of the Soviet Union has resulted in several armed conflicts, most of which are frozen but none of which is resolved. Out of 12 states making up the post-Soviet Commonwealth of Independent States (CIS), four—including Russia—do not control the whole of their territory, with at least four unrecognized political entities[5] claiming independence from central governments and acting as autonomous players. Similar processes of state fragmentation, in different forms, are at work in other parts of the world, from Africa to Indonesia.

Even perfectly orderly devolution, as in the United Kingdom, is raising important issues of identity.[6]

Another kind of challenge comes from the international community. In 1975, the Helsinki Final Act of the Conference on Security and Cooperation in Europe (CSCE) elevated human rights in Europe to a legitimate topic of international concern. In 1992, the CSCE agreed that a consensus on human rights issues need not include the country immediately affected, thus further expanding the international *droit de regard* inside state borders.

International military actions such as NATO's intervention in Kosovo fundamentally challenge the principle of territorial sovereignty and the sanctity of international borders. Conversely, Russia's military action in Chechnya, India's fight against separatist rebels in Kashmir, and China's insistence that Taiwan is a domestic political issue to be resolved by whatever means considered appropriate by Beijing, are all instances that defend the principle as rigorously as it is being challenged, if not more so. There is a serious disagreement between, in Samuel Huntington's phrase, "the West and the rest" as to who can use force across internationally recognized borders for the lofty cause of preventing humanitarian catastrophes and protecting human rights, in what circumstances, and under whose mandate. Similarly, there is disagreement over the limits of the use of force to preserve territorial integrity. An even more contentious issue is the right to, conditions for, and modalities of secession.

Whereas in much of the post-industrial world, though by no means everywhere,[7] borders are not a relevant issue any longer, in other parts of the world this is not the case. Border conflicts remain among the factors most likely to set off wars. (Didn't Romulus kill Remus for crossing a boundary line he had drawn?) From the Caspian Sea to the Indian subcontinent to East Asia, inter-state territorial disputes can have potentially dramatic implications far beyond the immediate conflict areas. Ironically, globalization, with its emphasis on cross-border contacts, has once again brought the importance of borders to light for the countries seeking to protect themselves from its undesirable effects, such as international crime, illegal immigration, and illicit drugs and arms trade.[8]

There is a broader notion of a border as a line identifying a political community, a military alliance, or an economic union. Even as countries that are sometimes called post-modern join forces economically, politically, or militarily, and borders between them blur and lose their former significance, emphasis is increasingly laid on their common *external* perimeter. NATO enlargement, which brought new countries into the Transatlantic security community, has at the same time provoked a palpable increase in the level of anxiety, if not tension, among the "would-be ins," and a crisis of confidence between the expanding alliance and Russia, a likely permanent outsider. The enlargement of the European Union could ultimately draw a real and durable dividing line between the integrated Western and Central Europe and the non-integrated eastern periphery of the continent, which, ultimately, could also be only Russia (with Belarus).

Apparently rejected by the West, at least for now, as a candidate member of many western institutions, Russia has been trying to reorganize the post-Soviet space to suit its interests. There has been an early attempt to carve out a sphere of influence, or a zone of vital (or "special") interests in the territory of the former U.S.S.R. Irredentists predictably used the concept of the near abroad and the external borders of the CIS as a means of staking out their Monroe Doctrine-type claims. They did not get their way, and questions remain about the nature, meaning, and prospects of the CIS.

At the global level, the end of the Cold War division of the world into the "capitalist," "communist," and "third" (non-aligned) parties has given prominence to affinities within civilizations. The territorial domains of Western Christianity, Islam, Confucianism, and other civilizations (including that of Orthodoxy, with Russia as its core state) were proclaimed to be the building blocs of the post-Cold War world.[9] Even if one does not accept the notion of the clash of civilizations, it is clear that borderlines between civilizations, which are inherently blurred, have often turned into principal zones of tension and conflict in the post-Cold War world.[10]

The notion of territory is intimately tied with the concept of borders. Friedrich Ratzel called them "a peripheral organ of the state, a testimony of its growth, strength, weakness and changes in its organization."[11] For centuries, Russia saw itself as a world unto itself, a new ("third") Rome, a self-contained and largely self-sustained universe—almost a minor planet sitting on planet Earth. Territorial politics, from geographical expansion to tight border controls, was key both to the vaunted Russian Idea (which was basically that of a universal empire), Russia's perceived mission in the world, and the political and economic organization of the Russian state. After 1945, the steady territorial expansion of the world socialist system was elevated to the level of a law of history. The end of the Soviet Union meant that this firmament, once so solid, began moving, causing confusion and even despair.

Thus, at the start of the new millennium the composite picture of the world struggling to restructure itself along new lines is very complicated. Globalization proceeds alongside fragmentation. Even as states lose power over their subjects, they show their capacity to survive and even multiply. Borders do wither away, but not everywhere; they emerge where they have never existed in the past; and, where associations of states are concerned, the lines between them are being reconfigured, and new constellations of international actors spring up. Caught between the post-modern reality of globalization and the European Union at its doorstep, on the one hand, and the modern structure of the present-day Russian policy and the pre-modern state of some of its regions, such as Chechnya on the other, Russia is not only deeply implicated in many of these processes, but is a key testing ground for the outcome of such processes. Thus, the way it performs geopolitically will be of extraordinary importance for others. Simply put, geopolitics is too important a factor to abandon it to its adepts.

* * *

It has long been accepted that the problem of state territory, or space, is intimately linked with the more fundamental problem of identity. A country's fate is determined by its geography, Napoleon observed. He definitely meant this in a broader context. Dramatic losses of territory can lead to a fundamental change of identity. In this sense, Russia's present case is hardly unique. Within two decades after the end of World War II, Britain and France lost their vast colonial empires, which had been built over centuries of relentless expansion. Having thus lost the status of world powers, both have found it hard, though not impossible, to redefine themselves as part of an increasingly integrated Europe. The process is not complete, but the trend is clear and probably irreversible. More to the point, after World War I, having lost their possessions, the Austro-Hungarian and the Ottoman empires, both traditional multinational states with contiguous territory (as is Russia), ceased to be "great powers" in name as well as in reality, and thoroughly recast their identity as small or medium-sized, ethnically homogeneous, and modern nation-states. In a more complicated and brutal fashion, the same result was achieved in Poland. Having ceased to exist for 125 years, it was reconstituted as a multinational state, lost its independence again, and eventually was restored, minus its Lithuanian, Ukrainian, and Belarussian provinces. It received compensation in the form of former German lands, without the Germans, who were resettled to the west, and finally emerged as one of the most cohesive and stable European nation-states. Such a neat end result was achieved, one shouldn't be shy to admit, thanks to the Allied plan of ethnic cleansing. After World War I, borders had to move to reflect ethnic settlement patterns; after the second, peoples were moved around to satisfy geopolitical exigencies.

After the end of the Cold War, the peculiarity of the Russian case is not the nature but the size, complexity, and potential implications of the problem. For centuries, a mere sight of their country on the world map helped shape—and distort—many a Russian generation's view of their country, and of their own identity. Russia's long borders were a traditional and very powerful argument for keeping a strong army. Even the rump post-Soviet Russia with its 17.1 million square kilometers, almost as big as the United States and Canada combined, continues to be a geographical superpower, stretching across 11 time zones, from the southern Baltic coast to the Bering Strait. It is impossible for Russian leaders and the public alike *not* to see their country as a great power, but it is extremely difficult for them to come to terms with the huge and growing discrepancy between the country's geographical size and its currently negligible economic and trade weight and the low "social status" among the nations of the world.[12]

Suffice it to examine the following table.[13]

Territory	Share of the world's land surface	Share of the world's population	Share of the world's GDP (Purchasing Power Parity)
Russian empire, 1913	17%	9.80%	9.40%
Present-day RF territory, in 1913	13%	5.30%	5.10%
Russian Federation 1999	13%	2.50%	1.60%

In one way, this discrepancy could be overcome, of course, if present-day Russia were to go the way of the U.S.S.R. and break up itself.[14] This would effectively mean that Russia itself ceases to exist, for unlike the British or French empires Russia has no island, no distinct *patrimoine* to return to. A "Muscovy" (i.e., European Russia minus its Muslim republics) would be *Russian, but not Russia*. In the foreseeable future, the probability that Russia will break up is not high.[15] After all, four fifths of its present population is ethnic Russians who are traditionally wedded to the concept of a big state, but the uncertainties abound. As Zbigniew Brzezinski put it, "the disintegration late in 1991 of the world's territorially largest state created a 'black hole' in the very center of Eurasia. It was as if the geopoliticians' 'heartland' had been suddenly yanked from the global map."[16] This sudden meltdown caused despair among many Russians. Using the 1867 sale of Alaska to the United States as a precedent, suggestions—although not very serious ones—have been made for a similar sale of Siberia.[17] Ironically, it was the acquisition of Siberia in the 17th century that was seen as the event marking the transition from tsardom to empire.[18] Of course, Russia's demise, if it indeed comes to pass, will be much messier and bloodier than the remarkably orderly dismantlement of the U.S.S.R. in 1991.

The Russian case is further compounded, in comparison to the Franco-British one, by the fact that since the mid-1980s the country has been in the throes of a profound and extremely complex transformation that fundamentally affects its economy, government, society, culture, and foreign relations. In short, Russia was trying both to rediscover and, as much as possible, to reinvent itself. Even under ideal circumstances, this project can only be partially successful. As it enters the 21st century, Russia is still a work in progress whose success or failure will have far-reaching consequences for its vast neighborhood in Europe and Asia.

As part of this monumental effort, the issue of space and identity is either underrated or overemphasized. More than many other countries around the world, and certainly more than Germany in the summer of 1945 when Stalin made his comment quoted at the beginning of this introduction, Russia, as a historically imperial and multi-ethnic state, is defined by its borders. Russia *is* a geographical concept, until recently commonly accepted to be on par with—or at least next to—Europe and Asia. One is routinely using phrases like "relations between Russia and Europe," or, more recently, "economic crisis in Asia and Russia."

When one talks about "France and Europe," one addresses relations between a part and a whole; in the Russian case, the implication has been, traditionally, of a horizontal-type relationship. Such diverse countries as Armenia, Estonia, or Tajikistan did not only *belong* to Russia, as India and Ireland once belonged to the British Empire; for centuries or many decades they were an integral part of it. Now that Ukraine (or "Little Russia," with its capital Kiev, the "mother of Russian cities") and Belarus (literally, "White Russia") are also independent, the question arises as to what remains of Russia (in the old sense) and, much more importantly, *what is Russia today*. (Europe, of course, is also changing profoundly. The emerging relationship between the two will have a decisive impact on the nature of each other's "end state.")

When, after the break-up of the U.S.S.R., the official name of the principal successor was being decided, most ethnically Russian regions opted for "Russia," whereas the non-Russian regions insisted on the "Russian Federation." The final decision was in favor of the Russian Federation as the full name, and Russia as the shortened one, with both enjoying equal status and used interchangeably. This may have been an acceptable compromise at the time, but the deeper problem is anything but resolved.

Currently, the Russian Federation excludes places like the Crimea and Northern Kazakhstan, where the ethnic Russian population, language, and culture predominate; but it includes Dagestan, Ingushetia, and other North Caucasian republics, which are ethnically, linguistically, and culturally infinitely more alien to Moscow than Kiev or Minsk. Unable for years to put down Chechen separatism, the Russians have been, nevertheless, consistently refusing to grant the Chechens formal independence, for fear of unleashing a chain reaction and compromising the unity of the federation. At least in part, the Russian position in the Kosovo crisis in 1998-1999 was governed by the parallels between Kosovo and Chechnya, which were obvious to the Russian public. Since then, the war in Dagestan has again raised the possibility of Russia's actually losing the North Caucasus, and the new war in Chechnya has evoked the prospect of ending secessionist revolt by military means—though in the guise of an antiterrorist operation. This leads eminent Western scholars to conclude that "Russian identity is still predicated [more] on the geographical extent of the old empire than on any notion of a modern state."[19] This, however, is precisely the problem: the Russian Federation cannot exit from the "old empire" without risking its territorial integrity, and not just in the borderlands.

Now that Russia has allowed German reunification to happen and let loose former Warsaw Pact nations, taken the lead in dismantling the U.S.S.R., and withdrawn some 700,000 troops from Central and Eastern Europe and the Baltic States, the political elite and public have dug in their heels. They have grown increasingly reluctant to resolve the seemingly marginal territorial dispute with Japan about four islands roughly 4,000 square kilometers in area. The 1991 border treaty with China, which re-established the norm of setting the border along the main shipping channel of the river and not the Chinese bank as in the previous 60 years, provoked backlash in Russia several years later. The ratification in 1999 of the treaty with Ukraine aroused influential forces that continue to hold that the Crimea or in any case Sevastopol must belong to Russia. The treaty was eventually ratified, but irredentism, and not necessarily limited to Ukraine, has become established in Russia, at least as a minority view. By the same token, since 1997, the proposed merger with Belarus has become a perennial issue of principle in the struggle about the future direction of Russian politics.

The other side of the "Russian question" concerns people. The Russian national community was formed and defined by the state's borders. Historically, Russia has never been a melting pot. Rather, the Russian community is akin to a salad mixed by the authoritarian regime, and, under Stalin, a layered cake with each ethnic group assigned its own territory and status within a clearly defined hierarchy. This community was bound not so much by ethnicity as by religion (until the 18th century) and the Russian language (in the more modern times).[20] The language has become a mother tongue and a vehicle of modernization for millions of non-Russians, who consider Russian culture as their own. Actually, in Russia the word *russky* for ethnic Russian is paralleled by the word *rossiisky,* which refers to Russia as a country or a state. In German, this difference is reflected in the words *russisch* and *russlaendisch.*[21]

Will the new Russia be able to integrate the population within the country's borders and forge a new community of citizens of Russia (*rossiyane*)? With the new emphasis on "Russianness" and recurrent instances of anti-Semitism and chauvinism originating on the communist and nationalist flanks of the political spectrum, the final answer is difficult to give. It is equally unclear how Moscow will relate to the Russian diasporas in the newly independent neighboring countries.[22] So far, comparison between Russia and most of the other former empires is rather in favor of the Russian Federation, which in one stroke and with apparent ease let go of former provinces and borderlands, including the core areas of Ukraine and Belarus. However, the "process" of post-imperial readjustment is far from over. The comparatively smooth way the process has gone along so far may mean that more trouble is in store for the future.

Thus, simply speaking, the fundamental twin questions on the national agenda at the start of the 21st century are: *What is Russia?* and *Who is Russian?* In other words, the problem of space is inseparably linked to and compounded by the problem of identity. Answers to these questions are bound to have far-reaching implications not only for those living in that largest former Soviet republic, but for a number of countries in both Europe and Asia.[23]

It may be argued, of course, that the answers were already given back in 1991, when the Soviet Union was carefully dismantled with Moscow's active participation, if not under its enthusiastic leadership. True, there is a formal and solemn recognition by the Russian Federation of the inviolability of the boundaries with the former Soviet republics, and there is a law on citizenship primarily based on a person's permanent residence in the Soviet era. Despite the fears that Russia will return to its "historical rhythm" of imperial restoration,[24] these commitments are still being honored. But in this period of momentous change, the viability of the new boundaries, international and domestic, and the prospects for the integration or assimilation of some 25 million ethnic Russians and an equal number of other former Soviet ethnic groups into the new nations are too often taken for granted. It could well be some time before final answers are given and accepted.

At a different level of analysis, one would conclude that Russia is undergoing a more profound structural transformation than ever before in its history. Ever since the present red brick Kremlin was built (in the 1480s) Russia has been a centralized state, the ruler of the Kremlin (or, for two centuries, the owner of the Winter Palace in

St. Petersburg) being the unquestioned master of a vast land. Ever since Kazan was conquered (1552) Russia has been a continental-size empire, uniting diverse nations, collectively known to the outside world as "Russians." Russia was a world unto itself, a universe that was self-contained and largely self-sustained. At the close of the 20th century, both these 500- and 400-year old traditions came to an end. Russia simply cannot continue as before, either in its internal organization or in its relations with other countries. In order to survive, it has to reinvent itself. Where will Russia's center of gravity be?

This has not been fully realized. The domestic Russian debate on "geopolitics" has been dominated by *Realpolitik* conservatives, nationalists, and those who can be described as "nativists."[25] The internationalist/idealist school of Gorbachev and Shevardnadze, which used to reject geopolitics altogether, has been marginalized. In the midst of the politicized debate, several more scholarly volumes have appeared.[26] Translations of foreign, mainly American authors, have been published, demonstrating the publishers' and the public's preferences.[27] Russia's liberals,[28] on the other hand, have paid the issue scant attention. They appear content to leave "retrograde" geopolitics to their opponents, so that they themselves can deal with more forward-looking issues such as economic reform, democracy building, and globalization. On the one hand, many of Russia's original liberals shied away from anything that smacked of patriotism, which was dismissed either as neo-imperialism or nationalism. On the other hand, the surviving liberals of the late 1990s, surprisingly, turned into latter-day geopoliticians. This inability to come to terms with the new realities is potentially serious. So far, Russia's adaptation to fundamentally changed geopolitical realities has been remarkably smooth, but it may not continue in the same fashion indefinitely, unless the very real and difficult issues that are rooted in the past are properly identified, carefully studied, and consistently dealt with. "It's geopolitics, stupid!" is a patently wrong answer; but mere economics is clearly not enough.

* * *

Borders are superficial by definition. However, they are a useful prism that can offer interesting insights. For a post-imperial country such as Russia, the issue of borders is intimately linked to the nature of the political regime, the structure of the state, and the pattern of its foreign relations. Russia's integration within a broader world cannot be achieved without dealing with the practical issues related to space and identity. Where does Europe stop? What is the scope of the Euro-Atlantic community? What is the present political meaning of Eurasia, if any? How relevant are the terms *post-Soviet space* and the *former Soviet Union*? Where does *Russia itself* start? Fitting Russia into both Europe and Asia is a Herculean task, but one that cannot be avoided if the goal is Europe's security and Asia's relative stability. Finally, devising a new Russian national identity is a sine qua non for domestic stability in the country.

Russia's attitude to the new borders, no less than anything else, will help define its identity, role in the world, and relations with its neighbors. Consider, for example, Zbigniew Brzezinski's two famous dictums to the effect that: (a) Russia can be either a democracy or an empire; and (b) Russia minus Ukraine can't be an empire.[29] True, Russia without Ukraine is certainly a very different Russia. If Russia also loses its Far Eastern provinces because of failures on the part of the state or foreign expansion or domination, it will again be a very different Russia. The global dimension will have been lost forever.[30] Whether Russia could have become a democratic empire is a question linked to the broader question of whether Gorbachev's perestroika could have succeeded. This author's view is that, under the circumstances prevailing at the turn of the 1990s, it was already too late. But even without its former "sister" republics, the Russian Federation includes non-Russian enclaves and the question persists, albeit in a different form: can Russia become a democratic federation?

Despite its poor governance and backward economy, Russia is essential to the international system by virtue of its unique geographic position in Eurasia. Thus, how Russia will organize itself within its current borders will have a significant impact on the domestic Russian regime and indirectly on the international system. The region of the world to watch most closely in the early- and mid-21st century is certainly Eurasia. This Eurasia, however, will no longer be just another name for Russia.

* * *

This book is a study in contemporary Russian and Eurasian geopolitics. It does not, however, treat geopolitics as an end in itself or some supreme science of statecraft, as is now fashionable in Russia. Nor does it deny its importance. Geopolitics will remain relevant as long as individual states and their associations continue to be the principal actors on the world arena. Rather, the book attempts to place geopolitical processes within a broader context of Russia's post-communist, post-imperial transformation, especially as it impacts on its search for a new national and international identity.

This book is a piece of policy research rather than an academic study. The author was more interested in policy implications than in methodology. As such, the book is meant for a fairly broad audience, including not only academics, but also foreign policy experts, journalists, and students still interested in Russia and what is referred to here as the *former* Eurasia.

The book is organized into three parts and a total of seven chapters.

Part One is devoted to Russia's historical experience, both imperial (before 1991) and post-imperial (after 1991). Within it, Chapter 1 discusses the historical patterns of Russian territorial state formation and their relevance for any future attempt to restore the imperial territory. Chapter 2 is devoted to the implications of the break-up of the Soviet space, which is viewed as a break in continuity and a reversal of a 500-year-old trend. It examines the role of the Commonwealth of Independent States (CIS), and looks into the cause of failure of a Eurasian Union. It also analyzes the evolution of Moscow's "border policy."

Part Two is regionally oriented. It seeks to define the challenges and opportunities that Russia faces along its three geopolitical fronts. Chapter 3 deals with the West/Europe, Chapter 4 with the South/Muslim world, and Chapter 5 with the East/Asia. All chapters closely examine the link between borders and ethnicity.

Finally, Part Three is made up of two chapters. Chapter 6 deals with the territorial organization of Russia itself, looking in particular at the prospects for both recentralization and further regionalization. It addresses the potential for Russia's further disintegration and assesses stabilizing and destabilizing factors at work. Chapter 7 examines the link between borders, security, and identity. Discussing the various options for "fitting Russia" into the wider world, it addresses the implications for Russia of the enlargements of NATO and the EU, the challenge of Islamic militancy, and the rise of China.

NOTES

[1] *The Tehran, Yalta and Potsdam Conferences. Documents,* Progress Publishers, Moscow, 1969, pp. 161-162.

[2] See, for example, E.A. Pozdnyakov, in *Vneshnyaya politika i bezopasnost sovremennoi Rossii,* A Reader, Vol. 1, Book 1, pp. 20, 34.

[3] François Denieul, "Frontières et territoires," in *Les nouvelles frontières d'un monde sans frontières,* Plain-Sud, Cahiers No. 2, Editions de l'Aube, Marseilles, 1997, p. 10.

[4] This does not mean, of course, that even the post-industrial states take the issue of borders lightly. As recently as 1982, Britain fought a war defending its claim to the Falkland Islands, and was prepared to suffer losses of over 200 men killed in the action. Even within the United States, interstate boundaries are occasionally disputed. Ironically, the state of New Hampshire uses the text of the 1905 Russo-Japanese Peace Treaty to support its claim to a few tiny islands off Portsmouth, which are also claimed by the neighboring state of Maine.

[5] Abkhazia and South Ossetia which broke away from Georgia; Nagorno-Karabakh, which declared independence from Azerbaijan; Transdniestria, which separated from Moldova.

[6] See, for example, Ian Buruma, "What England Means to the English," *Time,* May 10, 1999, p. 36.

[7] Suffice it to recall the secessionist movements in Canada (Quebec), the United Kingdom (Northern Ireland), Italy (the idea that the richer northern provinces should form a state of their own, "Padania," and leave the poorer cousins in southern Italy to their own devices), etc.

[8] The Schengen Agreement is a good example of this situation. Even as movement of people becomes easier within the European Union, it is getting harder for outsiders, especially from the poorer countries of the east

and the south, to find their way into the Union. The United States, for its part, despite the NAFTA agreement has not dropped its efforts to stem illegal immigration from Mexico.

9   See Samuel Huntington, *The Clash of Civilizations and the Remaking of World Order*, Simon and Schuster, New York, 1996.

10   Look at Bosnia-Herzegovina, Nagorno-Karabakh, or Chechnya.

11   Quoted by E.A. Pozdnyakov, op. cit., p. 33.

12   Vladimir Putin, in his first major article published on the Internet and reprinted by *Nezavisimaya gazeta* of December 30, 1999, had to concede that Russia held 71st place among the nations of the world in terms of its standard of living. Yet, at the same time he joined in the call for the restoration of Russia's great power status. The realization of their country's backwardness vis-à-vis the West, on the one hand, and the awareness of the abundance of resources, on the other, has been the traditional incentive for reform in Russia, from Peter the Great to Stalin to Gorbachev to Putin.

13   Source: Institute of Economic Analysis (Moscow). See Andrei Illarionov, "Rossiya na sovremennoi karte mira," *Izvestia*, April 28, 1999.

14   Ibid. The above-mentioned report by IEA argues that "should the trend toward degradation of demographic and economic potentials continue," the "disproportions" that result will eventually be "'adjusted,' as a rule, through the loss of territory."

15   However, such a prominent Russian intellectual as Sergei Karaganov, chairman of the Council on Foreign and Defense Policy, does not rule out Russia's disintegration within 10 to 15 years (*Obshchaya gazeta*, New Year's issue, December 1999/January 2000).

16   Zbigniew Brzezinski, *The Grand Chessboard: American Primacy and Its Geostrategic Imperatives*, Basic Books, New York, 1997, p. 87.

17   In 1992, Walter Mead suggested a price of $2.3 trillion (Alaska was purchased for $7.5 million). In 1999, a Moscow State University scholar proposed turning Siberia into a "limited liability company" with America, Japan, Korea, Germany, China, and Russia as its principal "shareholders." See Sergei Lopatnikov, "Strategicheskuyu ugrozu my pochti promorgali," *Noviye izvestia*, May 27, 1999, p. 4.

[18] See Pavel Milyukov, *Istoriya russkoi kultury*, Progress, Moscow, Vol.1, Part 2, 1993, p. 488.

[19] Dominique Moïsi, "The Last Gasp of a Former Superpower," *Financial Times*, October 25, 1999, p. 15.

[20] As Anatol Lieven aptly observed, in the 18th and 19th centuries it was possible for an unconverted German nobleman to own thousands of Russian serfs.

[21] In Soviet times, there was a widespread use of the words *Soyuz* and *soyuzny*. In 2000, an Israeli immigrant from Uzbekistan in a conversation with the author even used the phrase *soyuzny alphabet* when he was actually referring to the Russian alphabet.

[22] Vladimir Putin claimed in January 2000 that the presence of ethnic Russians in former Soviet republics was a prime rationale for the existence of the CIS.

[23] Russia, of course, is not unique among the former Soviet republics to face a similar problem. In Ukraine, Kazakhstan, Latvia, Estonia, and some other countries the issue of building citizenship-based nations is no less relevant.

[24] See, for example, Henry Kissinger, *Diplomacy*, Simon and Schuster, New York, 1994, p. 25. A critique of this point of view is given notably by Steven Sestanovich in "Giving Russia Its Due," *National Interest*, Summer 1994, pp. 3-12.

[25] See, Gennady Zyuganov (leader of the Communist Party), *Geografiya pobedy*, Moscow, 1997; Alexei Mitrofanov ("shadow foreign minister" of Zhirinovsky's Liberal Democratic Party), *Shagi geopolitiki*, Russki Vestnik, Moscow, 1997; Alexander Dugin (a scholar with good connections to the Russian military), *Osnovy geopolitiki*, Arctogaia, Moscow, 1997; second edition, 1999.

[26] K.S. Gadzhiev, *Vvedeniye v geopolitiku*, Logos, Moscow, 1998.

[27] Zbigniew Brzezinski, *Bolshaya shakhmatnaya doska* (The Grand Chessboard), Mezhdunarodnye otnosheya, Moscow, 1999; Henry Kissinger, *Diplomatiya* (Diplomacy), Ladomir, Moscow, 1997; Samuel P. Huntington, "Stolknoveniye Tsivilizatstyi I pereustroistvo mirovogo poryadka (ot ryvki iz knigi)," *Pro et Contra*, T. 2. Moscow, 1997.

28 Andrei Kozyrev, *Preobrazheniye*, Mezhdunarodniye Otnosheniya, Moscow, 1995. The best book on the subject by a liberal academic-turned-politician is Alexei Arbatov's *Bezopasnost Rossii*, Moscow, 1999; the most interesting scholarly study is Igor Yakovenko's *Rossiiskoye gosudarstvo: natsionalniye interesy, granitsy, perspektivy,* Sibirsky Khronograf, Novosibirsk, 1999. One could also point to *Kto soyuzniki Rossii* by Vadim Makarenko, Stradiz FI-AMR, Moscow, 2000.

29 Much depends on the definition of an empire. The Russian Federation within its present borders is arguably an empire, which includes not only the North Caucasus, but also Tatarstan, Bashkortostan, and, in a yet broader sense, Siberia and the Far East.

30 This doesn't apply to Russia alone: in its present borders, Kazakhstan is perhaps the only genuinely "Eurasian" state, but the secession of the northern provinces, if this occurred, would make the rest firmly "Asian."

Part One

A FAREWELL
TO THE EMPIRE

A Farewell to the Empire

In a poll of Moscow high school students about the country's frontiers conducted in the spring of 2000, at about the time of Vladimir Putin's election as president of Russia, over half the respondents said they favored the restoration of the Russian Empire within either the pre-revolutionary or the Soviet-era frontiers. Although this certainly does not mean that students are nostalgic for the Soviet internal order (only 12 percent of those polled wanted a return to the old regime), the desire for territorial revanchism among the youth is a serious warning signal.

Those who have grown up in the Soviet Union are equally aware of all of its facets: space launches as well as the Gulag, great power ambitions as well as shortages of basic foodstuffs. Not everyone would agree with Ronald Reagan's description of the U.S.S.R. as an evil empire, but both the evil and the empire are deeply engraved in their memory. To some in the younger age group, with no direct adult experience of the Soviet Union, which was buried a decade ago, the U.S.S.R. was just an empire and a state that was feared, and therefore respected worldwide. The Russian Federation, with its third-rate world status and almost Third World living standards, is despised and disparaged. No wonder that the remedy that many propose is to become big again. In other words, back to the U.S.S.R., or better still, to the Russian Empire.

Nostalgia for the Russian Empire is evident in the pomp of Kremlin ceremonies, in the popularity of Nikita

Mikhalkov's film *The Barber of Siberia*, and in the quotation from Alexander III displayed on the wall of the General Staff Academy (formerly the Voroshilov Academy) in Moscow: "Russia has only two true friends in the world, its army and its navy." As a cultural phenomenon, this nostalgia is not a cause for worry. When, however, it has an impact on the world view of decision-makers, it can raise concern. If such nostalgia is translated into a policy program, difficult international problems will emerge.

For a country searching for its new identity, the value and relevance of historical experience are of prime importance. The book starts with the discussion of the patterns of territorial growth and contraction in Russian history and their implications, but the real questions concern long-term trends. In other words, what is the *correlation of forces* between historical continuities and discontinuities in Russia's territorial status at the beginning of the third millennium?

CHAPTER 1

The Spatial Dimension of Russian History

History is usually what people make of it. In Russia, with its Soviet tradition of constantly rewriting history, this rings more true than elsewhere. The way people read history has an impact on their collective behavior. Often, factual reality is overtaken by a parallel reality of perceptions. This chapter examines the importance of territory and territorial acquisitions in Russian history. It attempts to define the models of territorial enlargement and discuss their relevance for the future, while asking the question: "Will history repeat itself?" No less important is the history of Russia's territorial contraction, which is far less known and is generally regarded as "negative." The central problem here is: can Russia hold itself together and develop as a non-empire?

Ever since Friedrich Ratzel developed his theories of political geography, traditional geopolitics has regarded states as living organisms aspiring to "natural" borders. In the Russian tradition, there has always been something sacred about the country's territory and borders. According to the philosopher Ivan Ilyin, Russia was "an organism of nature and spirit,"[1] and in the words of another philosopher, Konstantin Leontiev, was "doomed by history to grow, even *despite itself*."[2] Hence its territory was considered as the "terrestrial habitat of national spirit," and a "historically given and accepted spiritual pasture of the people,"[3] and a "sacred space."[4] Consequently, while growth was natural, any dismemberment of the composite whole, Russian theorists constantly warned, was not only unnatural or tantamount to sacrilege, but bound to have catastrophic consequences. This "organism" was held to be coterminous with *Eurasia*—a vast area in the north-central part of the continent ruled from Moscow or St. Petersburg.[5]

West European countries have traditionally looked with suspicion, sometimes mixed with awe, at the territorial expansion of the Russian state, which they perceived as an enormous geographical overhang. "For centuries," Henry Kissinger wrote, "imperialism has been Russia's basic foreign policy as it has expanded from the region around Moscow to the shores of the Pacific, the gates of the Middle East and the center of Europe, relentlessly subjugating weaker neighbors and seeking to overawe those not under its direct control."

"Torn between obsessive insecurity and the proselytizing zeal," Kissinger wrote elsewhere, "Russia on the march rarely showed a sense of limits; thwarted, it tended to withdraw into sullen resentment."[6] This expansion, of course, was not unique to Russia: other European empires grew at the same time and, like Russia, they stopped when they encountered strong opposition. Moreover, like America in pursuit of Manifest Destiny, Russia also marched to the Pacific, moving its border eastward until it reached the water's edge.

Historically, Russia was an archetypal continental empire, having virtually no overseas possessions, with the exception of Alaska, which lay only 90 miles away from the Chukotka shoreline.[7] This contiguity of the territory is often used to stress the "special" and "natural" character of the Russian Empire. This argument is traditionally supported by several instances of the "voluntary accession" of various territories to Russia. Some historians have found cases of aggression and annexation to be extremely rare in Russian history,[8] and have portrayed even outright conquests as driven, essentially, by Russia's need for security and for "settling in."[9] Others argue that the Russian people have never oppressed others; instead, they populated wastelands, peacefully assimilated other ethnic groups, and offered them military protection.[10]

In this chapter we will first explore the factors, both geographical and cultural, behind the movement of Russia's borders, and then will examine the many historical models of Russian expansion and contraction. We will pose the question of whether Russia suffers from territorial obsession and whether the emerging Russian idea is, like the old myths about Russia's mission, inextricably linked to a certain shape of the country's borders.

Factors Behind the Territorial Enlargement

Geographical Factors

In a strictly geographical sense, Russia as a country has always lacked clear boundaries. The landscape of its European portion is a vast monotonous plain, lacking mountain ranges or other natural barriers that would divide it into distinct sectors or set it apart from neighbors. This has had important consequences. When Russia was weak, nature offered it little protection; but when it grew strong, there were few geographical barriers to stop it from projecting its power in virtually all directions.

Traveling from Russia to the heart of Europe meant crossing forests and fording rivers and avoiding marshes whenever possible. The distances involved were substantial, but the obstacles were rather few. The lack of good roads and the severity of the climate, rather than wide streams or mountain ranges, were factors that set Russia apart. In modern times, most of the invasions that Russia experienced came from the west. The Poles in the 17th century, the Swedes in the 18th, the French in the 19th, and the Germans in the 20th all posed credible threats to Russia's independence. The historic memory of almost falling into enemy hands—in 1610-1612, in 1812, and finally in 1941, when the Germans were within 20 kilometers of Moscow before they could be turned back—lives on as a warning to Kremlin leaders.

Russia looks toward Asia across its steppes, which in the Russian language are usually defined as "boundless," *beskrainiye*. The classical Russian historians regarded the steppe as an "Asiatic wedge that extends deep into Europe."[11] From the Huns to the Mongols, these steppes offered a broad corridor for Asian hordes en route to Europe. Asian invaders kept Russia captive for almost 250 years, and even after that continued to threaten Moscow for another century.[12] The memory of these historically more distant threats is also present in the Russian collective psyche.

Due to the absence of natural barriers of protection, it made strategic sense to meet the enemy as far from the core territory as possible. Territorial expansion was originally mandated by the sheer need for survival. In the words of Ivan Ilyin, "one either had to perish as a result of perennial raids or rebuff them, pacify the plain through armed force, and [then] develop it."[13] Since the 15th century, the requirement "to win space" and thus deny it to a potential adversary has become "an axiom."[14] Thus, the Russians have learned to compensate for their initial geographical vulnerability by means of territorial expansion.

Over time, this "strengthening of borders" became a euphemism for acquiring more and more land—in the name of self-defense, but for the purposes of an eventual counteroffensive or simple offensive. Since potential adversaries were all around, the Russians had to organize a circular defense. In doing so, the Russian state followed the pattern of the city of Moscow, where the Kremlin is the nucleus of a concentric system of fortifications (Kitai-Gorod, Bely Gorod, now the Boulevard Ring, and Zemlyanoi Gorod, now the Garden Ring). Thus, each new circle of fortresses and monasteries represented a "new success in the counteroffensive of Greater Russia."[15] This pattern of expansion is by no means unique to Russia: take, for example, France in the 15th-17th centuries. What is different is the scale and quality of the process.

To most Russians—at least the bulk of the nation living on the wide easternmost periphery of Europe—the geographical boundary between Europe and Asia running along the Ural Mountains carries little meaning. Russian territorial expansion did not stop for long at the Ural Mountains. At the highest point, the mountains reach 1,894 meters, but in the central part of the range, near the city of Yekaterinburg, most areas lie between 300 and 500 meters above sea level, and thus are fairly easy to cross. Less than 50 years separate the takeover of Kazan on the Volga (1552) from the annexation of the Siberian khanate on the Irtysh (1598), 500 miles east of the Urals.

The Russians were bewildered by the phrase crafted in the early 1960s by President Charles de Gaulle of "Europe from the Atlantic to the Urals." They were heartened by the implication that their country was regarded as European, and they never doubted that Central Asia and much of the Caucasus lay outside the sphere of European culture, but they couldn't see why Siberia and the Russian Far East were to be separated in any meaningful way from European Russia. What to West European eyes looked like a natural barrier at which to stop was to the Soviets the geographical center of their country. Nikita Khrushchev at about the same time was playing with the idea of moving the capital of the Russian republic from Moscow to Sverdlovsk, now (again) Yekaterinburg.

Geography makes Russia Eurasian. This description has important implications. To many a European, this means "not one of us." Czech President Vaclav Havel, for example, uses this characteristic to argue that Russia can never belong to Europe. To virtually all Asians, there is no question of regarding Russia as an Asian country. To a number of Russian traditionalists, however, this special position gives Russia a license to pursue a "third way," neither European nor Asian. The question of borders naturally becomes a question of political, economic, and social orientation. Geography is not enough, it must be supplemented by a discussion of cultural links.

Cultural Factors

In many a debate on Russia's identity, geopolitics and civilization become mixed up. From a common Russian point of view, either Europe stretches all the way to the North Pacific (which would be most Russians' preference) or, alternatively, Asia begins east of Poland. Since both propositions are equally difficult to sustain, and the philosophical "eternal question" of Russia's place in the world is likely to

34

continue to provoke debate for quite some time, many pragmatic Russians have adopted the notion of Russia as a "land bridge" between the "real" Europe, meaning Western Europe, and the "genuine" Asia of the Far East. This is deemed to be the geographical foundation of the theory of Russia's very own "third way" in world affairs, neither fully European nor Asian, but offering a unique amalgam. But what about non-Western Europe, Central Asia, and the Caucasus?

It has become commonplace to lay emphasis on the uniqueness of Russian culture and civilization and believe that the country's mission is to unify the entire Eurasian landmass.[16] This has been the underlying ideology of the Russian Empire since Peter the Great. The goal was almost achieved in the early 1950s when the Soviet Army stood on the Elbe and the Danube, and China was briefly affiliated with the Soviet bloc. After the demise of the U.S.S.R., however, the uncertainty of Russia's position has again come to the fore.

Some would go as far as to call Russia a gigantic borderland,[17] which could shift either way—to the east or to the west. Though the country clearly originated, under the first Kievan princes, as the easternmost advance of European Christendom, it later served—for example, during the 240 years of Mongolian rule—as Asia's bridgehead in Europe. The craving to be admitted to Europe, on very special terms, accompanied by the threat to join forces with the powers of Asia was, if not accepted by the West, the underlying theme of post-communist Russia's approach to Europe.

Of course, both "Europe" and "Asia" are above all mental constructs, but the conscious self-identification of Russia's political elite with Europe or Eurasia has defined the practical policies of the Russian state.[18] In reality, the predominance of European elements in Russian culture and civilization is hardly in question; it is equally clear that, in geopolitical terms, Russia is located in both Europe and Asia. A way out of the apparent dilemma would be to distinguish between the cultural and the geographical. In other words, to stress Russia's Europeanness and at the same time to highlight its position in Asia. Again, Russia is not unique: take, for instance, Turkey in its relations with Europe or Australia and its links to Asia. A European country in Europe and Asia is not the same thing as a Eurasian country. Eurasianism is a dead end: a pretentious neither-nor position erects an unnecessary barrier on the Russian-European border, while doing nothing to strengthen Russia's position in Asia, or even the greater Middle East.

Before we deal in Chapter Two with the implications of the collapse of the Soviet empire, we need to analyze briefly the ways the empire was created, or, to put it differently, historical models of the inclusion and integration of various territories within the expanding Russian state. These models are of more than historical interest: as we will demonstrate, from the perspective of various Russian political forces they can and do serve as examples to emulate in the future.

The Models of Expansion

The Collecting of Lands Model

This most ancient model has traditionally applied to Russian and eastern Slav territories. It has gone through three phases, which can be regarded as three distinct historical drives:

(a) the 14th-16th centuries;

(b) the 17th-18th centuries;

(c) the 1930s-1940s.

The first phase was the formation of the Great Russian State. Within 200 years, from the early 14th century through the early 16th, the Moscow princes, and later grand dukes, managed to "collect the Russian lands." They bought up, annexed through armed force, or otherwise acquired the territory of fellow Russian principalities.[19] As a result, the whole of northeastern Russia, heretofore fragmented, was unified, with Moscow as its capital (see map, p. 38). This created a new identity. From the late 15th and especially the 16th centuries, the word "Russia" became commonly used. The first phase of the consolidation of Russian lands was an essential part of the process of building a centralized monarchy, which was common to many other countries in Europe.

The second phase concerned the western and southwestern parts of ancient Kievan Rus (see map, p. 39). The tsars, who were endowed with a keen—and self-serving—sense of history, and saw themselves as the direct heirs of the Kievan princes, were set on restoring their forefathers' possessions. This was made possible through many wars with Poland in the 17th century and finally its partitioning three times in the second half of the 18th. It is important to note, however, that the new territorial acquisitions were not regarded by Russia as annexations, but rather as the tsars' "coming into what was theirs" and were popularly characterized as acts of liberation of fellow Orthodox Ukrainians and Belarussians from Catholic Polish rule. The decision in 1654 by a Ukrainian Cossack Rada to seek the protection of the Moscow tsar was symbolic for Russia and later marked the reunification of Ukraine with Russia.

Collection of Russian Lands, 14th-16th Centuries

Legend:
— western border of the Russian State, early 17th century
▬ western border of the Russian Empire, 1795
Ukrainian and Belarussian lands annexed
by Russia in the 17th-18th centuries

Collection of Kievan Rus Lands, 17ᵗʰ-18ᵗʰ Centuries

TALLINN
Leningrad
ESTONIAN SSR
BALTIC SEA
(Soviet Russian Republic)
RIGA
LATVIAN SSR
R S F S R
LITHUANIAN SSR
MOSCOW
R S F S R
VILNIUS
MINSK
BELARUSSIAN SSR
Byalystok Grodno
Visla
WARSAW
Brest
POLAND
West Bug
KIEV
Przemysl
UKRAINIAN SSR
Lvov
Dniepr
CZECHOSLOVAKIA
Uzgorod
Dne str
Chernovtsy
MOLDAVIAN SSR
HUNGARY
Prut
CHISINAU
ROMANIA
BLACK SEA

— USSR Western border, Sept. 1., 1939. — USSR Western border, Sept. 1., 1945.

Belarussian and Ukrainian Soviet Republics (joined USSR in 1922)

Western Belarus and Western Ukraine (annexed by USSR in 1939)

Western Bukovina (annexed by USSR in 1940)

Carpathian Ukraine annexed by USSR in April 1945

Byalystok and Przemysl areas annexed by USSR in 1939 and ceded to Poland in August 1945

Collection of Russian Lands, 20th Century

The fourth partition of Poland resulted from a narrow-minded strategic pact between Hitler and Stalin in 1939 that trampled on the sovereignty of weaker states. Nonetheless, this led to a de facto reunification of Ukrainian and Belarussian lands within the U.S.S.R., whose western border now followed the ethnically based Curzon line, proposed by the British twenty years earlier. In Western Ukraine, or Galicia, Stalin followed in the footsteps of Nicholas II, whose army occupied the province at the start of World War I and held it until 1915. With the annexation of northern Bukovina in 1940 and Ruthenia in 1945, the "collecting of Ukrainian lands" was complete (see map, p. 40). Ironically, the political unity of the Ukrainian nation is a lasting legacy of Josef Stalin.

It is interesting to note that this model was limited to the areas populated by the eastern Slavs. The apparently strong arguments in favor of building a pan-Slavist empire were never translated into actual policy-making. Pan-Slavism remained a tool of imperial foreign policy looking for spheres of influence, but never became an ideology for territorial acquisition.

This most ancient model of Russian territorial statebuilding has not lost its appeal entirely. Those traditionalists and nationalists in Russia who recognize the impossibility or the undesirability of a full restoration of the U.S.S.R. believe that "collecting Russian lands" is still feasible. As early as 1990, the Nobel Prize–winning author and thinker Alexander Solzhenitsyn publicized a plan of a "Russian Union" that would include the Russian Federation, Ukraine, Belarus, and Russian-populated provinces of Northern Kazakhstan. In the first week after the dissolution of the Soviet Union, the CIS functioned as a pact among three republics, Russia, Ukraine, and Belarus. The rest were not immediately invited to join. This idea, more often described as a "Slav Union," still has many adherents.[20] In a more practical way, continuing attempts to achieve a full state fusion between Russia and Belarus are seen as a first step in crafting such a union of Slavs. There are those who argue that should Russia bring its house in order, relaunch its economy, and reach a moderate level of prosperity, Ukraine, or at least the four-fifths of it that existed before 1939, will gravitate toward Russia. According to the same logic, Kazakhstan, or at least its northern part, will move in the same direction. The strengths and weaknesses of this argument will be discussed in Chapter II. As to Pan-Slavism, it has, interestingly, resurfaced as a rhetorical figure of speech rather than a policy proposal in the calls made at the height of the war in Kosovo for a union of Russia, Belarus, and Yugoslavia.

The Moving of Borders (Colonization) Model

This model was in operation from the 16th through the 19th centuries, and applied to Siberia and the Far East, northern Kazakhstan, and the Don-Kuban area (see map, p. 43). The history of Russia, the Russian historian Vassily Klyuchevsky wrote, is a history of a country in the process of colonization.[21] This predominantly peasant colonization was the equivalent of the settlement of North America. Although originally spontaneous, migrations were soon fitted into the Russian state policy.

It is true that Russia acquired more land area through relatively peaceful colonization than through outright conquest.[22] It is enough to look at the vast expanses of Siberia and northern Russia. From the very beginning of Russian history, there has existed a fundamental distinction between

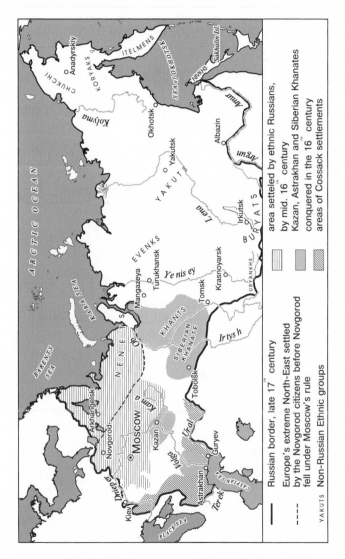

The March of Russian Colonization

	area settled by ethnic Russians, by mid. 16th century
	Kazan, Astrakhan and Siberian Khanates conquered in the 16th century
	areas of Cossack settlements

Russian border, late 17th century

Europe's extreme North-East settled by the Novgorod citizens before Novgorod fell under Moscow's rule

YAKUTS   Non-Russian Ethnic groups

Russia's borders in the west, on the one hand, and the south and east, on the other. The border with European countries was a more or less clear line: Vassily Klyuchevsky observed that "everything a Russian sees in Europe imposes on him a concept of a border, a limit, a clear finality."[23] In contrast to that, there could be, of course, no clear lines drawn through the nomad-populated steppe or very sparsely populated taiga. Thus, the typical border in the south and the southeast was a wide stretch of land, subjected to the ebbs and flows of nomadic invasions. As a result, whole districts in the southern and southeastern parts of Russia were regarded as insecure borderlands.[24] This readily reminds one of the 19th-century American frontier or the pattern of the Spanish and Portuguese advance in South America.

In the south, Russian peasants fleeing the oppression of their landlords from the second half of the 16th century established free Cossack settlements along the Don, the Kuban, and as far south as the Terek rivers. The Russian government soon concluded that it could defend itself against the Crimean tatars' devastating raids only if the local population of the borderlands was prepared to defend itself. Hence, the essence of Cossack culture was peasants in peacetime, warriors when attacked.

In the east, toward the Urals and beyond, there was virtually no border of any kind, only the current limit of Russian peasant colonization. After the annexation of Kazan and the defeat of the much weaker Siberian khanate, from 1600 on, Russia encountered no organized states in the eastern direction until the Russian advance reached the Chinese-dominated territories along the Amur and Argun rivers. The clash at Albazin in 1688-1689, where the Russians were defeated by the Manchus and the Chinese, set a temporary limit to the Russian expansion.

Still, the result was grandiose. Within less than 100 years, Russian settlers crossed Siberia and reached the shores of the Pacific Ocean.[25] To many, however, expansion across Siberia all the way toward the Pacific and North America (Alaska) *looked* very much like Russia's exercising its manifest destiny. In the early 20th century, under Prime Minister Pyotr Stolypin, the government pursued a coherent and largely successful policy of sponsoring mass migration from the European provinces of the empire to Siberia and the Russian Far East.

The Soviet regime continued and intensified this effort, but on a less voluntary basis. Hundreds of thousands of people were invited or ordered to the Far East, Siberia, and the Virgin Lands of Northern Kazakhstan. It also extended the settlement drive in a northern direction, all the way to the Arctic and the North Pole. Cities were built north of the Polar circle, and the Northern Sea Route from Murmansk to Vladivostok became operational, relying on a fleet of icebreakers to clear the way. The settlement of the north for economic and military purposes became one of the Soviet Union's first heroic sagas. In 1926, the Soviet government lay claim to a vast sector of the Arctic as the "polar possessions of the U.S.S.R." This is not dissimilar from the claims made roughly in the same period by several countries, including Britain, Australia, and Chile, to large chunks of Antarctica.

At present, this model cannot be repeated. Not only are there no free territories to move into but given the declining birth rate among Russians and the collapse of the Soviet-era industrial and social infrastructure, a reverse process has set in. Russia finds it extremely difficult to maintain a presence in the northern and eastern outposts of the former empire. Many northern settlements, too costly to maintain, have been abandoned. Fast depopulation and general decay are destroying the fruits of the efforts of Stolypin and the Soviet Union. Unless the Russian government devises a way to manage the situation, bearing in mind that the resource base has become much narrower than under the tsarist or Soviet regimes, the frontiers may move again, this time in the opposite direction. This predicament will be discussed in more detail in Chapters 2 and 5.

The Strategic Borders Model

The Russian Empire, its one-time Prime Minister Sergei Witte wrote, was "essentially a military empire."[26] As briefly discussed above, the strategic borders model, in its broader sense, was a *leitmotif* throughout Russian history; it is singled out here as a separate model to describe Russian acquisitions in the west and the south from the 16th through the 20th centuries.

On all fronts and in all periods of its history, Russia has resorted to annexations for purely strategic reasons. Once it finally threw off the Mongol ("Tatar") yoke in 1480, it moved to annex the successor states of the Golden Horde, Kazan (1552), Astrakhan (1556), and finally the Crimea (1783) in order to remove residual threats, stamp out the sources of predatory raids into Russia,[27] and free avenues for further Russian political and economic expansion.

A virtually landlocked country along its western frontier, 16th- and 17th-century Russia strove to gain access to the seas, so as to lift the de facto blockade by Sweden, Poland, and Ottoman Turkey and enter into direct contact with Europe. This task was completed in the course of the 18th century when the Russian state assumed full control over the entire length of all the great rivers that originate in the Great Russian plain, down to their estuaries. Through its control of the eastern shores of the Baltic and the northern and eastern shores of the Black Sea, Russia established its powerful presence in both of these bodies of water.

At the same time, Russia sought access to the southern seas. Having secured Russia's gains in the Baltic, Peter the Great embarked in 1722 on a conquest of northern Persia. The two exercises, one quite successful and the other not, were part of a single project. Eventually, in the 19th century, the Caspian virtually became a Russian lake. However, the Caspian was only of marginal importance, and the outlet to the Black Sea was controlled by the Ottomans. Displacing them has become a long-standing Russian obsession. From Catherine the Great's 1780 "Greek project" of creating a neo-Byzantine empire with a Russian tsarevich for an emperor to Stalin's 1946 demands on Turkey (which ultimately drove it into NATO's arms), Russia has been trying, unsuccessfully, to control the Straits.

As a powerful traditional empire, Russia has had to deal, again and again, with the concept of buffer states, spheres of influence, and the like. Some of these geopolitical buffers were incorporated into the realm; others were allowed nominal freedom. The first group included the territories that were deemed to be of vital importance. Finland was annexed by the empire in 1809 as a buffer against Sweden, thus effectively putting St. Petersburg out of reach of the potential enemy. The Transcaucasus, annexed between 1801 and 1829, became a similar buffer against Turkey and Iran, and Bessarabia, annexed in 1812, performed the same function vis-à-vis the Ottomans on the Balkan flank. Much of Central Asia was included in the Russian Empire in the second half of the 19th century in the course of the Great Game with Britain, which was also becoming highly active at the time in India and the Middle East.

The second group included territories whose importance to Russia was considered to be less than vital, or more difficult to incorporate. While Kokand in the Fergana Valley was annexed, the Empire allowed Bukhara and Khiva to carry on as nominally independent states. In the late 19th and early 20th centuries, Russia and Britain agreed to treat Afghanistan as a neutral buffer between the two empires and divided up Iran into respective spheres of influence. Iran and Afghanistan retained their role as buffers throughout the Cold War until 1978-1979.[28] The perceived threat of Afghanistan's being turned over to the U.S.-controlled "zone" was probably the one decisive factor in favor of Soviet military intervention there in December 1979. Stalin sought, through aid to local pro-Communist forces, to create buffer zones in northern Iran and eastern Turkestan (Uighuristan, Xingjiang). In the Far East, the Russian sphere at the turn of the 20th century included Manchuria, Mongolia, and the Uryanhai territory (now Tuva).[29] In the 1930s, nominally independent Mongolia served as a Soviet buffer against Japan, which then ruled Manchuria (Manchukuo). After Japan's defeat, the Soviet Union used its military presence in Manchuria to arm the Chinese Communist forces, which successfully used the province as a base for the takeover of the entire country (1946-1949).

After the Bolshevik Revolution, the *cordon sanitaire* was regarded as a hostile pro-Western buffer, but the neighboring states, especially Poland and Romania, though designated by the Soviet General Staff as likely adversaries, did not represent an overwhelming military threat. The *cordon* was still more of a defensive wall than a marching ground for a large-scale invasion. It was the momentous geostrategic shifts of

1938-1939 in Europe that made Stalin look for more secure borders. Instead of relying on anti-Soviet buffers to hold out against German pressure, a mission impossible by any account,[30] he preferred to advance Russia's own defenses in a secret agreement with Germany carving up Eastern Europe (the Molotov-Ribbentrop pact of August 1939 and the Soviet-German treaty of September 1939).

In mid-September 1939 the Soviet troops marched into eastern Poland, already under attack from the Wehrmacht. In late November 1939, also under the secret agreement with Hitler, Stalin launched an attack on Finland after the Helsinki government had refused a Soviet offer of territorial exchange that would have put Leningrad outside of the range of artillery fire from Finland.[31] The bitter Winter War followed, in which the Red Army suffered 250,000 casualties but made Finland agree to a transfer of even more territory (eastern Karelia and the isthmus) to the U.S.S.R. with no compensation. Yet, Finland as a nation defended its right to exist, which set it apart from the Baltic States. In 1940, Stalin proceeded to occupy and then Sovietize Estonia, Latvia, and Lithuania because he could not trust them as allies in the coming conflict with Germany.

Tragically but also ironically, carving up Eastern Europe with Hitler in 1939-1940 did not buy the Soviet Union more security. Having gotten rid of the buffer states and having received instead a 1,500 km long common border with Germany and its satellites, Stalin placed the U.S.S.R. in danger of a potentially massive, surprise German attack, which indeed occurred on June 22, 1941. At that time, there was no longer a Poland to take a little *blitz* from the German *krieg*.

After the end of the war, Stalin drew some lessons from his past mistakes. At the conferences with the Western allies, he successfully insisted that the forward base of the potential German advance toward the east, East Prussia, be eliminated altogether, its population totally removed, ethnically cleansed—in the end-of-the-century phraseology—and the territory divided between the U.S.S.R. and Poland.[32] He further prevailed on the issue of the German-Polish border, which was moved hundreds of kilometers west to the Oder-Western Neisse line. Thus, Poland was compensated for accepting the Curzon line in the east, which was then internationally recognized. A solid buffer state was erected between the Soviet Union and the defeated Germany. With one-third of Poland's post-1945 territory previously German-held, Warsaw was turned into an automatic member of any future coalition to contain a resurgent Germany.

Stalin took similar precautions vis-à-vis the other former adversaries. Finland lost its access to the Arctic (Petsamo, which became Russian Pechenga), and had to lease out the Porkkala naval base to the U.S.S.R. Romania lost the strategically situated Snake Island in the Black Sea. Japan was to cede southern Sakhalin and the Kuril Islands, and Port Arthur on the Yellow Sea once again (as in 1898-1905) became a Russian naval base. These sovereign bases and naval outposts were to become instruments of a Soviet forward presence in the Cold War, which was about to start. Expanding the strategic *Vorfeld*, Stalin sought to make the Soviet fortress impregnable, and escape a new surprise attack.

After these territorial changes, the Soviet Union was generally satisfied with its borders, both in terms of its sovereign territory and in terms of the actual political control that it now exercised. The "hostile encirclement" of the inter-war period had now been broken through.[33]

Interestingly, Stalin did not insist on Finland's or Poland's reincorporation into his realm. International disapproval was not the only reason for his moderation. The stubborn resistance offered by the Finns on the Karelian Isthmus during the Winter War of 1939-1940 and again in July 1944[34] and the fervor of Polish nationalism in the latter persuaded the dictator that they would serve Soviet interests better as external buffers rather than as imperfectly integrated provinces. His judgment on the Baltics, however, must have been just the opposite, with all the attendant consequences.

The Sovietization of the historical *Mitteleuropa*, the area between Germany and Russia, where "borders have flowed back and forth like rivers over flood plains,"[35] had as its primary motive creating a strategic defensive buffer against a possible future clash with Germany, and later with the United States and its NATO allies. Communist ideology was initially utilized as a means toward this end, and became more important only with the advent of the Cold War confrontation with the United States. Throughout the 40 years of that confrontation, it was the Warsaw Pact and the Soviet military presence in Eastern Europe, rather than the trade and economic association of COMECON and "socialist economic integration," that was the linchpin of the Soviet-led system. The borders of the "socialist community" essentially marked the strategic perimeter of the U.S.S.R.

Stalin's fear of a German nationalist resurgence based on the post-Versailles experience must have been his motive in 1945 when he rejected Western plans for dismemberment of the German state. It was enough for Germany to be truncated, deprived of the territories east of the Oder-Western Neisse line, and especially of East Prussia, which was seen as a "nest of German aggression against the Slavs." A permanent division, he feared, could become counter-productive, breeding a German nationalist revival. Or else, it would turn Western Germany into the premier U.S. military base on the continent of Europe. Ironically, Stalin's policies helped bring about the latter result. After the Prague coup of February 1948 and the Berlin blockade of 1948-1949, he could be called, together with Harry Truman, a founding father of NATO. However, even when Germany and Berlin actually became divided with the start of the Cold War, the Soviet policy oscillated between the option of German unification (on the sine qua non condition of its neutralization) and the consolidation of Eastern Germany. The second option finally prevailed, but only by 1961, when the Soviet Union decided to build the Berlin Wall.

With the advent of confrontation between blocs in Europe, the Soviet Union discovered the usefulness of neutral buffers. In a 1948 treaty, Finland received confirmation of its sovereignty in exchange for "friendly neutrality" vis-à-vis the U.S.S.R. Moscow finally agreed in 1955 to withdraw its forces from Austria, which was reconstituted as a neutral state, and prohibited from joining Germany. The withdrawal of Western forces from Austria also meant that NATO would be unable to use it as a land bridge between its forces in central Europe (Germany) and southern Europe (Italy). Baltic independence however was not restored; once incorporated into the U.S.S.R., there was no way out.

Elsewhere, Stalin attempted, albeit half-heartedly and unsuccessfully, to pursue the tsars' unfulfilled or unconsolidated agenda—from Ardahan and Kars and the Turkish Straits and beyond to the Mediterranean, where at one point he pressed for a UN mandate for Libya. Aiding pro-Communist revolutionaries and using or abandoning them as he saw fit, he sought to create buffer zones in northern

Iran (Iranian Azerbaijan), Uighurstan (Xinjiang), and Manchuria. As Stalin was an opportunist, a change in circumstances would usually turn a defensive buffer zone into a staging area for new expansion.

Along the southern perimeter, the strategic borders were less precise. Throughout most of the Cold War, Iran and Afghanistan, to Moscow's general satisfaction, were classic buffer states between the U.S.S.R. and the West. The change in their geopolitical status in 1978-1979 came as a result of internal developments in those countries, which took both Cold War adversaries, Washington and Moscow, by surprise.

Most Soviet leaders, including Brezhnev and Prime Minister Alexei Kosygin, were quite happy with Afghanistan as a buffer, and only a minority, represented by the chief ideologue, Mikhail Suslov, and his associate Boris Ponomaryov favored extension of the socialist community toward the Middle East. Moscow's blundering decision to intervene in Afghanistan in 1979 was prompted not so much by an urge to seize upon an opportunity to project its power southward and put its tactical air force within reach of the Strait of Hormuz, as Western media speculated at the time, as by the reports that the Afghan pro-Communist leader at the time, Hafizulla Amin, was allegedly about to change sides and, as a token of his new allegiance, welcome the U.S. missile launch monitoring stations that Iran had just closed down. That consideration tilted the balance in favor of intervention.

The territorial satisfaction expressed by the Soviet leadership concerning their own country's borders was genuine: after 1945, the U.S.S.R. borders remained stable until the country's breakup in 1991. For the first time, the Soviet Union felt safe from a conventional attack across its borders, and for good reason. These borders were now in a deep rear area. The lines of confrontation were drawn on foreign territory: Germany, Eastern Europe, Korea, and Vietnam. Stalin's successors broadened the horizons of Soviet foreign policy and effectively extended the country's strategic boundaries even further afield. Khrushchev not only consolidated the Soviet Union's power position in Europe, using brutal methods as he saw fit (in East Germany in 1953, and Hungary and Poland in 1956), he also managed to break the U.S.S.R. free from Eurasia, which had been the tsars' and Stalin's habitat. In the 1950s and 1960s, for the first time in history, the Soviet Union established its presence and influence in countries as far away as Egypt, India, Indonesia, and Cuba.

Like the medieval city of Moscow, the Soviet Union had several defensive rings. The U.S.S.R. itself, as sacrosanct as the Kremlin, was essentially secure. The inner ring, running along the borders of the socialist community countries, had maximum protection, assured by powerful Soviet forces: in East Germany, Poland, Czechoslovakia, and Hungary. The Brezhnev Doctrine clearly stated that Communist regimes (i.e., Soviet strategic gains) were irreversible, and demonstrated that in Czechoslovakia in 1968. It was only the outer ring of "socialist-oriented" countries, extending to the Middle East, Africa, and Latin America (with the sole exception of Cuba, over which Khrushchev almost risked a nuclear war with the United States in 1962) that allowed for some ebbs and flows. This elaborate construct required enormous resources, which ultimately made it unsustainable. It was the reluctant decision in 1979 to intervene by force in Afghanistan—in the name of the "historic irreversibility" of the strategic gains that broke the camel's back. Eight months after the completion of the Soviet withdrawal from Afghanistan the Berlin Wall fell.[36]

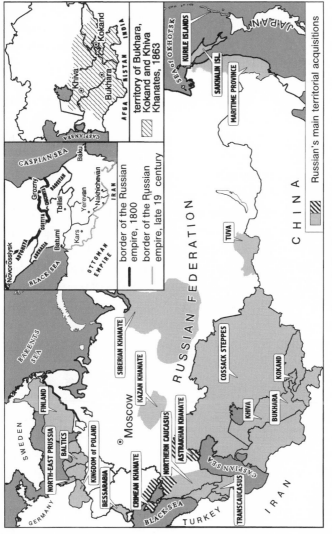

Strategic Borders

This model still appeals to most Russian supporters of a strong state, or *derzhava*. Influential Russian officials regard Russia's keeping its great power status to be in its primary national security interest, which needs to be defended at all cost. The view that Russia should use the Commonwealth of Independent States as a string of buffer countries under the influence of Moscow is the preferred scenario for the bulk of the Russian political elite.

The Restoration Model

Outwardly, restoration is similar to the Collecting of Lands. The difference is that the Soviet restoration at the turn of the century occurred in pretty short order in response to a defeat and the loss of territory. This was the geopolitical equivalent of a military counteroffensive. The logic of the Civil War of 1918-1920 made the revolutionary Soviets into imperial restorationists. To them, the 1918 treaty of Brest-Litovsk, which bought peace with Germany at the price of huge territorial concessions, was "obscene." It is a moot point whether the aborted Red Army invasion of Poland in 1919 was an attempt to export revolution to Germany or to re-establish control over Poland; from the Bolshevik point of view, both were very valid goals. In the next several years, however, the Red Army acted not so much as a vehicle of socialist revolution, as an instrument of restoration of the Russian Empire under a different name. They succeeded brilliantly in Ukraine, the Transcaucasus, and Central Asia, where even the nominally autonomous protectorates of Bukhara and Khiva were taken over. Where the Red Army failed, such as in Poland in 1919, this was not through lack of trying. The Soviet republics, thus formed, immediately entered a political-military alliance with Soviet Russia (formalized in early 1922) and soon thereafter, on December 30, 1922, were fully fused under the name of the U.S.S.R.

Initially, Stalin's socialism in one country was an introvert exercise. In the 1920s and 1930s, the U.S.S.R. established diplomatic relations with all neighboring countries, including those formed on the territory of the former Russian Empire, and had no claims on their territory. Only Bessarabia was shaded on the Soviet maps as Romanian-occupied.

This changed in the late 1930s. Stalin evidently started to view territorial restoration of the Russian Empire as his historic mission, which was almost accomplished by the time he died in 1953—with the sole exceptions of Poland, Finland, and the eastern Turkish districts of Kars and Ardahan. He succeeded in unifying the Ukrainian nation—under the U.S.S.R., of course—through land acquisitions from Poland, Romania, and Czechoslovakia. In a similar fashion, he succeeded in "reunifying" Moldova, which later became split again as a result of the Soviet Union's demise. An attempt to take over Finland failed because of the Finns' stubborn resistance during the Winter War. At Yalta and Potsdam, Stalin explicitly insisted on the return of the territories lost by Russia to Japan in 1905, including Sakhalin and the Kuril Islands, as well as the China Eastern Railway and the lease of the Port Arthur naval base.

Despite the routine pronouncements by Communist Party leaders and Zhirinovsky's supporters, it is difficult to see much interest among the Russian elite in favor of restoring the U.S.S.R. to its pre-1991 form (see map, p. 58). Above all else, in the foreseeable future, such a project would strain all of Russia's resources and would still not guarantee success. The activist version of this model has been finally relegated to history. However, it is worth considering the

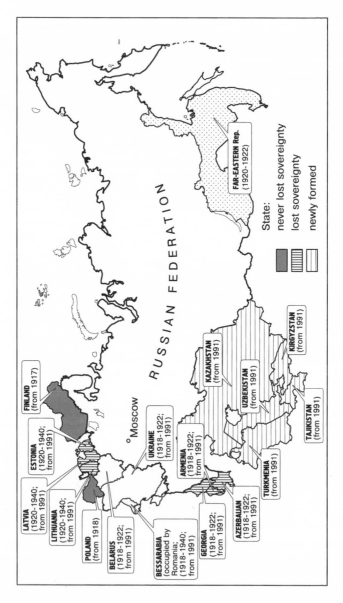

Desintegration, Restoration, and new Desintegration

same argument as that of the Collecting of Lands section. Russia's economic success, should it eventually come, would not only draw Belarus and Ukraine into Moscow's orbit: Russia's gravitational pull would have an impact on the behavior and orientation of the Transcaucasian and Central Asian states. Even if the independence of the CIS states is preserved, their association with Russia might well grow not only in degree but also in kind.

Le Monde Sans Frontières: A Revolutionary Aberration

The Bolsheviks, who as Marxists placed class above nation and initially had little time for inter-state borders, had to deal with major territorial issues almost immediately after seizing power in Petrograd. Lenin, too, at first did not consider borders a priority. The proletariat, he taught before the revolution, was not interested in territory, but rather in a total victory over "world capitalism."

At the outset of World War I, the Bolsheviks called for the military defeat of Russia. Looking for allies in their struggle against tsarism and the international bourgeoisie, they proclaimed the right of nations to self-determination, including secession. This had fateful implications 70 years later, when the Soviet Union entered its terminal crisis.

Once they came to power, the Bolsheviks had to deal with the realities of power politics. Under the March 1918 separate peace treaty with Germany signed at Brest-Litovsk, they agreed to give up Poland, the Baltic provinces, Ukraine, much of Belarus, and the Transcaucasus. In return, the Germans stopped their advance, which threatened the Bolsheviks' power position at home. To the early Soviet Communists, however, Russia was little more than a territorial base for world revolution. As seen by Lenin and his cohorts, the

Soviet government's historical role was to win time before a revolution took place in Germany. By late 1923, however, these expectations were finally revealed as delusions.

They were replaced by the building of socialism in one country and the creation of outposts for a revolutionary movement in the neighboring countries. In the 1920s, the pro-Soviet Mongolia and Tuva were seen as bases for spreading Communist influence to Asia, but already from the 1930s they were turned into a strategic glacis. Interestingly, in 1924, Stalin ordered the creation of the Moldavian Republic in Tiraspol and in 1940 the upgrading of the Karelo-Finnish Republic in Petrozavodsk as way-stations toward the eventual absorption of Bessarabia and Finland. He succeeded in the first instance, and failed in the second.

Having suffered such a crushing defeat, this romanticism never resurfaced in Russia again. "Socialism in one country," for all its internationalist veneer, was based on the idea of the centrality of the Soviet state and the inviolability of its territory. Post-Soviet Communists are even further from their Leninist forefathers. They are openly nationalistic—in the Russian sense, as *derzhavniks*—and proud of it.

Like the Bolsheviks, the leadership of the Russian Republic in 1990-1991 followed a distinctly anti-territorial logic. What was most important for Boris Yeltsin in his struggle against Mikhail Gorbachev was raw power. Yeltsin's secretary of state, Gennady Burbulis, was busy masterminding the power transition; and acting Prime Minister Yegor Gaidar was engineering the start of an economic transition. While pursuing their political interests or ideals, they barely mentioned geopolitics. Borders again became irrelevant. And again, this had important implications.

Patterns of Russia's Territorial Contraction

Throughout Russian history, territorial expansion prevailed. However, occasionally Russia had to cede ground and recoil, and in a few rare cases its territorial integrity was actually threatened (see map, p. 62).

Territorial concessions to neighbors occurred mainly as a result of military defeats, which were very common in the 16th and 17th centuries. The Livonian War (1558-1583), fought in order to expand Russia's access to the Baltics, ended in the loss of the only narrow outlet that it had there. More recently, the most serious military failures were the Crimean War of 1853-1856 and the Russo-Japanese War of 1904-1905. Although both led to relatively small territorial losses, they had a far more serious strategic impact, hemming in Russia on the Black Sea and the Far East, respectively. While different in form, the withdrawal from Afghanistan in 1989 and the Khasavyurt peace of 1996, which de facto recognized Chechen independence, belong in the same category. Humiliating as they were, these defeats have not directly affected the existence of the Russian state.

Territorial deals come in different forms. Selling a province, as Alexander II did with Alaska, was very rare in Russian history. More frequently, territorial withdrawals have been part of a complex political package—such as Khrushchev's agreement to pull back from Austria, his decision to hand over base rights in Finland and China, his promise to return the Habomai and Shikotan islands to Japan (and hold negotiations about the two other South Kuril islands) and Gorbachev's sweeping political-military withdrawal from Central and Eastern Europe. Khrushchev was looking for *détente* and Gorbachev for *entente* with the West. These

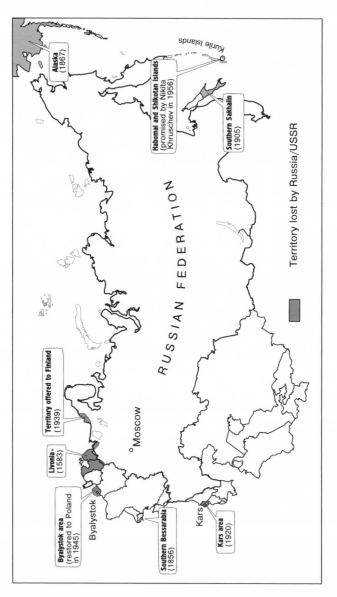

Territorial Concessions

package deals could be more or less successful, as judged by their results, but they did not affect the core of the Russian state body.

At this time, there is only one territorial problem pending that Moscow recognizes and which it will probably have to resolve through a deal, namely the South Kuril islands or, in the official Russian parlance, the issue of the border delimitation with Japan.

Territorial catastrophes are those rare occasions when the very body of Russia has been split. One occurred during World War I, which ushered in the Bolshevik Revolution and the much bloodier Civil War of 1918-1920. The other one was the dismantling of the U.S.S.R. On each occasion, the fundamental principles of state, nation, and international identity were called into question. After its first "clinical death," following the October Revolution, Russia was resuscitated as a great power, albeit at a horrendous cost to its people, and apparently restored in its glory as a result of World War II. However, the seeds of destruction of the traditional imperial model could not be eliminated. Moreover, their growth was accelerated by the fundamental and fatal flaws of the Soviet model, which was placed atop a more traditional imperial structure. The second crisis, coming in 1991, proved to be fatal, and final.

For a country so much wedded to the state as Russia, a catastrophe of that nature and scale has the potential of either sending the nation on an entirely different historical course or, alternatively, destroying it. In reality, both options are present at the same time, and the art of the statesman lies in maximizing the liberating constructive potential of the catastrophe while protecting the nation from self-annihilation.

Implications of the "Spacial Syndrome"

The most important implication of the pattern of moving borders and strategic borders was that Russia did not evolve into a nation-state. Whatever chance there might have existed of that was consciously forfeited in the mid-16th century, with Ivan the Terrible's fateful annexation of the two Muslim khanates on the middle and lower reaches of the Volga, Kazan and Astrakhan, and the concomitant decision to grant the new arrivals a measure of ethnic and religious identity. Early on, ethnicity in Russia became subordinated to the imperial state. If there was a "Russian idea," it was that of a universal Eurasian empire. It was the state that formed the Russian mentality and way of life, rather than a diluted and blurred ethnicity or domesticated Orthodoxy, which had never gone through a reformation phase and had been represented by a church hierarchy subordinate and even subservient to a monarch. According to the political scientist Igor Chubais, the core of the traditional Russian set of values was formed by Orthodoxy and the consolidation of lands, which evolved into imperialism, and peasant collectivism.[37]

Of course, Russia's failure to become a nation-state was owing to reasons other than the borders/identity problem. The most important among them was the lack throughout much of Russian history of a *nation* in Russia. The patrimonial state did not allow for the growth of a vibrant civil society, of a broad social structure that could in fact represent the nation or articulate its views. In post-Communist Russia, democratization is instrumental in nation-building, and setbacks to this process are further delaying the formation of a Russian nation.

However driven, geographical expansion became something approaching a modus vivendi for Russia. Territorial aggrandizement, at the rate of 42,000 square kilometers per year, from the mid-16th through late 17th centuries,[38] which meant permanently moving borders, starting as necessity,[39] eventually came to be seen as part of Russia's *raison d'être*, a source of pride and even legitimacy to the country's rulers. "I saw my task as foreign minister in expanding the borders of our fatherland as far as possible," Vyacheslav Molotov reportedly said.[40] It must be noted that most territorial gains were acquired through peasant colonization, not outright military conquest. Expansion of territory was seen as equaling expansion of national power. The means became the end: the original rationale for gaining access to the Baltic and Black seas and the Caspian and the Pacific coast was easing trade relations with the outside world. The result invariably was the further strengthening of Russia's geostrategic position, but not, at least not to the same extent, as its position as a trading nation.

Eventually, the expansion of Russia's territory and obligations resulted in imperial overstretch. Late 19th-century historians believed that Russia had reached its "natural borders" through a geographic "rounding up" of territory and the achievement of national reunification, meaning the union of Great Russians, Ukrainians (Little Russians, in the official parlance of the time), and White Russians. Of course, the Poles were never really integrated, and were a constant thorn in the side for St. Petersburg. Regular uprisings and revolutions made Russian control of the Vistula provinces tenuous at best. True Slavophiles like Nikolai Danilevsky regarded the annexation of Poland as a mistake, saddling Russia with a powerful and hostile element, never to be truly russified.[41] Finland, a Grand Duchy with a broad autonomy, strong constitutional aspirations,[42] and a monetary system of its own, was another non-integral part of the empire. There was a customs border that protected Finland from the rest of the empire but opened up the Russian market for Finnish goods. It is significant that neither country was reabsorbed into the U.S.S.R. after World War II.[43] In the south the Russians, acting more out of short-term political and strategic reasons, went beyond the natural borders formed by the Caucasus mountain range and the Cossack steppes.[44] These annexations, which led to a serious strain on the country's resources, represented clear early cases of imperial overstretch. Even the natural riches of which the Russians took possession, such as the Baku oilfields, did not fully compensate them for the sacrifice of establishing control over the North Caucasus.

So far, we have been discussing the geographical and strategic nature of Russia's borders. Now let us turn to their political and even psychological meaning.

From *Pax Russica* to the *Soviet Universe*: The Psychological Impact

As Russia gradually developed into a self-contained and almost self-sufficient world, a universe unto itself, the early meaning of border profoundly changed. The core Russian lands became enveloped by ethnically non-Russian borderlands. Borders no longer served as a means of immediate military protection. Instead, they provided Russia with a strategic depth, which itself became one of the principal means of national defense. It is interesting that in 1812 the war of defense against Napoleon's invasion did not become a patriotic war until the *Grande Armée* reached Smolensk, which, lying some 300 miles inland from the border, was the first major Russian city to be overrun by the enemy. One hundred years later, all official attempts to characterize

World War I as a second patriotic war came to naught: the front line, although moving east, still ran, in early 1917, from Riga to the Carpathian mountains, leaving only Poland, Kurland, Lithuania, and the western Belorussian provinces under German occupation. Conversely, when in 1941 Hitler's troops had taken over Ukraine and Belorussia and stood at the gates of Leningrad and Moscow, the war naturally became patriotic independent of Soviet propaganda, which itself had had to shed its Communist jargon and instead made appeals to patriotism.

The Two Worlds Model: Boundaries of the (Soviet) Universe

In the course of the 20th century, the mental image of a border has undergone a dramatic change in Russia. The fact that Russia's borders spread far from the ethnic Russian core made the bulk of the Russian people see those borders as something very distant. Generations of Russians lived and died without ever crossing the country's boundaries. The elite, on the other hand, since the 18th century had adopted a habit of traveling to Europe, and spending much time and money there.

Since the early 1920s, Russia's borders became more than simple inter-state boundaries. Fearful of the spread of a revolution, the Western powers erected a *cordon sanitaire* along the Soviet-European border and treated the U.S.S.R. very much as a rogue state. At the same time, for reasons of the stability of the Communist regime, this same border was made almost impregnable from within. Whereas before 1917 the symbol of a border was a customs post, later it became the border troops organized as part of the secret police. As a result, Russia's international isolation was redoubled. This new quality of Russia's Soviet borders had even more lasting implications than the actual shape of those borders.

The decision to "build socialism in one country" implied that the Soviet Union would have to live indefinitely under conditions of a hostile "capitalist encirclement." Soviet boundaries thus became class battlelines and ideological barriers. They not only marked out the Soviet citizens' habitat. They defined the confines of the world known to them, their "socialist camp." While the means of communication allowed traveling faster and farther and information and ideas spread more easily, restrictions became harsher. Contacts with the outside world were minimized and closely controlled. Soviet citizens became virtually insulated within a continental-sized and largely self-sufficient country. The Soviet border was not merely an ideological but also a civilizational and cultural divide, a wall between "two worlds."[45] Even traditional cross-border contacts were suspended, as between Siberia's Chukchis and Alaska's Eskimos. The famous Soviet song had a line that went: "I don't know another country where a man can breathe so freely." In fact, the vast majority of Soviet people did not know *any other country* but their own.

Not all borders had the same quality and function, of course. The Soviet leadership made a clear distinction between borders with capitalist states (e.g., Norway, Finland), or capitalist-dominated countries, such as Turkey, Iran, royal Afghanistan, on the one hand, and those with "people's republics," or socialist states, on the other. In response, a popular Soviet saying went: *Kuritsa ne ptitsa, GDR* (or Poland, Bulgaria, etc.) *ne zagranitsa* (A hen is not a bird, and the GDR is not abroad). Interestingly, the same attitude exists today, with respect to CIS countries.

When the arguably impregnable Fortress U.S.S.R. imploded, a new concept was officially adopted, which treated borders more as interfaces. The problem, ironically, was that Russia, for the first time in history, lost a contiguous border. Managing that situation was a supremely difficult task. This will be further discussed in Chapters 3, 4, and 5.

Costs of Territorial Expansion

Russia's domestic, economic, and societal progress did not exactly follow the rise in its power as a state, and often, outward expansion was achieved at the price of internal development.[46] Even as new lands were added to the title of the Russian tsar, the development of the country's core areas proceeded very slowly. Under the Communists, a besieged fortress demanded strict discipline, suppression of dissent, etc. In Russia, to the extent its territory expanded and state power grew, the people's internal freedom shrank.[47] In the Soviet period, this discrepancy became especially pronounced.

Not all domestic repression, of course, was directly linked to outward expansion, much less caused by it. Ivan the Terrible fought against the *boyars* to centralize the state; the 19th-century monarchs tried above all to prevent a revolution in Russia itself. However, the need to suppress the Polish uprisings led in the 19th century to domestic reaction; the invasion of Czechoslovakia in 1968 put an end to the timid attempts at reforming the Soviet economy; the conquest of Central Asia by Alexander II distracted the tsar's attention and left many of his reforms incomplete; and the Afghan war one century later aggravated the general crisis of the Soviet system. Both Chechen wars of the

1990s, although technically not expansionist, put the process of democratization in Russia to a severe test.

One obvious cost was the sacrifice of human lives. The four decades of war in the Caucasus in the 19th century left 77,000 Russian soldiers dead (only the Napoleonic invasion demanded a heavier toll).[48] The first Chechen war of modern Russia claimed 3,500 soldiers' lives, and the second one, in its first year, 2,500.

Not disputing these facts, modern "statists" view this as an inevitable price worth paying for ensuring national survival.[49] From a more traditional geopolitical point of view, however, this unchecked expansion was turning Russia "into a gigantic comet with a yet unsolidified European core and a hideous Asiatic tail. In addition to the exhaustion resulting from foreign wars there was added permanent exhaustion from feeding the borderlands."[50] In the Soviet era, the situation was aggravated many times over. Ironically, despite all the victories and annexations, Russia's territorial integrity was never fully assured.

The view from the borderlands, of course, was different. Unlike the Russians, who learned to see Central Eurasia as their historical arena, the indigenous population of the borderlands became cut off from their historical habitats. The notions of "Russia" and "Eurasia" became interchangeable or, at the very least, the two words were hyphenated. Similarly, the Baltic peoples in the U.S.S.R. became separated from the West, of which their elite considered themselves an integral part,[51] Central Asia was separated from the rest of the Muslim world, etc. While the Russians genuinely believed that they "never oppressed other numerically smaller tribes"[52] and that as a result they achieved a unity of spirit and culture, of territory and government, of international and military "fate," of common economic and trade interests,[53] this unity was never perfect, and in many cases, was illusory. To this day, geopolitical thinking remains deeply rooted in the mentality of post-Communist elite in Central and Eastern Europe. One needs to distinguish, however, between the geopolitics of the victims and of the victimizers.[54]

Conclusion

Russian territorial expansion was mandated by geography, historical circumstances, and the particular mentality of Russian leaders, whether they be grand dukes, tsars, emperors, or the Communist nomenklatura. They all saw Russia as essentially friendless in the world, a country that could rely on itself only, and had to be powerful to succeed and big to meet the enemy as far as possible from its vital urban centers. In the celebrated phrase of Alexander III, military force was highlighted as the ultimate foundation of Russian power.[55] Russia's imperial foreign policy was marked by typical dualism. While fully involved in sophisticated diplomatic games in Europe and even occasionally seeking some pan-European order (as with the Holy Alliance and the *Dreikaiserbund*), elsewhere Russia preferred territorial gains or zones of control and influence to any complicated diplomatic balancing. Also, in its push east, Russian expansionism was closely linked to messianic exceptionalism and isolationism. In Central Asia and the Caucasus, Russia was performing its version of *mission civilisatrice*, not dissimilar from that of France, or Britain.

Russia, however, differed from classical West European maritime empires not only because there was no physical separation between the metropolitan territory and the colonies. There was practically no difference in status between the former and the latter. Neither was Russia a mechanical collection of lands and peoples united by a dynasty, as was Austria-Hungary. It achieved a much more intimate kind of assimilation. However, its capacity for assimilating borderlands was limited, and the process detracted from, rather than added to, the development of the core areas.

NOTES

[1] Ivan Ilyin, "Rossiya est zhivoi organism" (1937), in Ilyin (1992), p. 51.

[2] Konstantin Leontiev, *Vostok, Rossiya i Slavyanstvo*, Respublika, Moscow, 1996, p. 158.

[3] Ivan Ilyin, *Put k ochevidnosti*, Exmo-Press, Moscow, 1998, p. 247.

[4] Alexander Dugin, "Prigovoryonnaya rodina," *Zavtra,* No. 1, 2000, pp. 2-3.

[5] The Russians did not create the first Eurasian empire in history; they were preceded by the Mongols who ruled over Eastern Europe, Central and Inner Asia, and China from the 13th through the 14th centuries.

[6] Henry Kissinger, *Diplomacy*, Simon and Schuster, New York, 1994, pp. 24-25.

[7] Alaska was not the only Russian settlement on the American continent. Fort Ross, in the vicinity of San Francisco, was until the mid-19th century the southernmost point of permanent Russian presence in America.

[8] Nikolai Danilevsky, *Rossiya i Yevropa. Vzglyad na kulturniye i politicheskiye otnosheniya slavyanskogo mira k romano-germanskomu*, 6th ed., Glagol/ St. Petersburg University, St. Petersburg, 1995, p. 19. Danilevsky concedes that "only Turkestan, the Caucasus Mountains, five or six districts in Transcaucasus and, perhaps, the Crimea" were actually conquered by Russia

[9] Andrei Nikolayev, *Na perelome: zapiski russkogo generala*, Sovetsky Pisatel, Moscow, 1998, pp.15-18.

[10] Nikolai Danilevsky, op. cit., p. 20.

[11] Vassily Klyuchevsky, *Russkaya istoriya. Polny kurs lektsii*, Mysl, Moscow, Book 1-3, Vol. 1, Lecture III, 1993, p. 35.

[12]   Moscow was first taken by the Mongols and ransacked in 1237; the "Tatar yoke" was shaken off in 1480; the Crimea khan Devlet-Girei burnt down Moscow in 1571, although he was unable to take the Kremlin.

[13]   Ivan Ilyin, "Rossiya est zhivoi organizm," p. 53.

[14]   Vladimir Zolotaryov, *Voyennaya bezopasnost otechestva*, Kanon Press, Kuchkovo Pole, Moscow, 1998, p. 53.

[15]   Fyodor Nesterov, *Svyaz vremyon: opyt istoricheskoi publitsistiki*, 2nd ed., Molodaya Gvardiya, Moscow, 1984, p. 49.

[16]   Alexander Dugin, *Osnovy geopolitiki. Geopoliticheskoye budushcheye Rossii*, Arktogeya, Moscow, 1997, p. 196; Gennady Zyuganov, "Rossiya neodolimaya," interview with *Zavtra* weekly, No. 23, 1999, p. 2.

[17]   Andrei Nikolayev, op. cit., p. 39.

[18]   Thus, it was deemed highly important, especially by outside observers, that Vladimir Putin, born in the country's most "European" metropolis, repeatedly stressed Russia's European and even *Western* origins and vocation. See *Ot pervogo litsa. Razgovory s Vladimirom Putinym*, Vagrius, Moscow, 2000, p. 156.

[19]   The process was completed in the 15th-16th centuries. Moscow acquired Yaroslavl in 1463, Novgorod and Rostov in 1478, Tver in 1485, Pskov in 1510, Smolensk in 1514, and Ryazan in 1521.

[20]   Toward the late 1990s, Solzhenitsyn modified his stance somewhat, allowing for the inclusion of the whole of Kazakhstan within his "Russian Union." See Alexander Solzhenitsyn, *Rossiya v obvale*, Russki put', Moscow, 1998.

[21]   Vassily Klyuchevsky, op. cit., Lecture I, p. 20.

[22]   Nikolai Danilevsky, op. cit., p. 19.

[23]   Vassily Klyuchevsky, op. cit., Lecture IV, p. 56.

[24]   Interestingly, this coincides with the notion of "geopolitical border" as used by Alexander Dugin. He notes that whole countries can form geopolitical borders as buffer states, *cordons sanitaires*, etc. See Alexander Dugin, *Osnovy geopolitiki*, p. 25. A less charitable interpretation of the "bridge idea" is Russia as a "borderland" between Europe and China.

[25] In 1710, the Russian population of Siberia totaled 314,000, but in 1795 it reached 1 million. See *Russkiye*, ed. by V.A. Alexandrov, I.V. Vlasova, N.S. Polishchuk (Series: Peoples and Cultures), Nauka, Moscow, 1999, pp. 30, 32.

[26] Sergei Witte, *Vospominaniya*, Skif-Alex, Tallinn-Moscow, 1994, Vol. 2, p. 476.

[27] The Crimeans were particularly successful in reaching deep into Russia. They burned down Moscow in 1571, and in the first half of the 17th century enslaved some 200,000 Russians. See *Sovetskaya istoricheskaya entsiklopediya*; Sovetskaya entsiklopediya, Moscow, 1965, Vol. 8, p. 209.

[28] In 1941, Soviet forces entered Iran from the north and the British from the south, in order to prevent the Shah's tilting to Germany.

[29] Russia kept an entire army corps, complete with cavalry and artillery, in Manchuria. These forces were disguised as railroad police and *border guards* (sic!). See Vladimir A. Sukhomlinov (War Minister and Chief of the General Staff), *Vospominaniya*, Russkoye Universalnoye Izdatelstvo, Berlin, 1924, p. 243.

[30] In the summer of 1939, the Poles feared a Soviet expeditionary force to protect them from the Germans as much as the Germans themselves, which was not unreasonable in light of the Baltic States' experience in the ensuing months.

[31] The Soviet-Nazi agreement did not call for Finland's re-incorporation into the U.S.S.R. Stalin's actions were motivated by purely strategic reasons: had the Finns promptly agreed to the proposed territorial exchange, the war could have been prevented. Stalin, however, was in a hurry.

[32] Stalin argued his case by emphasizing the necessity for the U.S.S.R to have an ice-free port on the Baltic (Königsberg), but the strategic implications of the annexation of East Prussia were much greater. Interestingly, Stalin attached most of the Soviet portion of East Prussia to the Russian Federation, which had no common border with the province, while returning the port of Memel (Klaipeda) to neighboring—and now again Soviet—Lithuania, which had held it in 1923-1939.

[33] "Never in all its history has our Motherland had such fair and well organized state borders," said senior Politburo member Georgy Malenkov in November 1949. The consolidation, by that time, of the Soviet sphere of in-

fluence in Eastern Europe and the victory of China's Communist Party in the civil war against the Kuomintang must have contributed heavily to the "good feeling" in the Kremlin. See Georgy Malenkov, *32nd Anniversary of the Great October Socialist Revolution*, Moscow, 1949, p. 5.

[34] In July 1944, the Soviet offensive into Finland ground to a halt due to the stubborn Finish resistance, which made Stalin drop any plans of a military occupation of Finland. In the end, he opted for a political solution.

[35] *The Economist*, December 19, 1998, p. 20.

[36] For a study of how the U.S.S.R overstretched itself, see Hannes Adomeit, *Imperial Overstretch*: *Germany in Soviet Foreign Policy from Stalin to Gorbachev*, Nomos, Baden Baden, 1998.

[37] Igor Chubais, "Russkaya ideya bez Pinocheta," *Izvestia*, May 5, 2000, p. 3.

[38] Colin S. Gray, *The Geopolitics of the Nuclear Era*, Crane, Russack and Co., New York, N.Y., 1977, p. 35. Gray quotes Richard Pipes's article: "Détente: Moscow's Views."

[39] Pierre Gallois, in his discussion of the Russian geopolitical experience, notes: "L'adversaire était partout. . . . C'est aux quatre points cardinaux qu'il fallait lutter pour grandir, sous peine de périr" (Pierre Gallois, *Géopolitique. Les voies de la puissance*, Plon, Paris, 1990, p. 410).

[40] Feliks Chuyev, *Sto sorok besed s Molotovym*, Terra, Moscow, 1991, p. 14.

[41] Stalin reportedly shared this view, referring to the Poles as people unlikely to embrace communism.

[42] In reality, Finland's "constitution" consisted of an oath by the Emperor and Grand Duke to respect the autonomy and privileges of Finland. Upon ascending the throne all emperors repeated the formula which Alexander I used back in 1809 before the finnish Estates. Alexander III interfered with the autonomy, but real Russification started only under Nicholas II.

[43] The Baltic States, though re-incorporated into the territorial body of Russia, were allowed to keep a measure of cultural autonomy, symbolized by the Latin alphabet, which was not abolished (as in Moldova).

[44] Vassily Klyuchevsky, op. cit., Vol. 3, Lecture LXXXII, p. 361.

[45] For a description of the Stalinist concept of a socialist border at that time, see *Rodina*, Molodaya Gvuardia, Moscow, 1939, p. 22.

[46] The Russian émigré thinker Georgy Fedotov deplored the emanciation of the historical nucleus of the Russian state in the 19th century: "Greater Russia was growing weaker, giving its blood to the borderlands, which now imagine that she was exploiting them" (Georgy Fedotov, "Budet li sushchestvovat Rossiya?", 1929, quoted from *Novoye Vremya*, No. 10, 1992, p. 57.

[47] Vassily Kyuchevsky, op. cit., Vol. 2, Lecture XLI, p. 129.

[48] Colonel General Yury Baluyevsky (Chief, Main Operational Directorate, Russian General Staff), "Kavkazskaya liniya: istoriya, politika, uroki, " *Krasnaya Zvezda*, May 16, 2000, p. 1.

[49] Andrei Nikolayev, op. cit., p. 25.

[50] General Obruchev's words are quoted in Vladimir Zolotaryov, op. cit., p. 253.

[51] Of course, before World War I, as Anatol Lieven aptly notes, the German elite in the Baltic provinces maintained very close contacts with the West, and the indigenous population was at least spared the fate of total extinction, which might have awaited them in the German empire.

[52] Ivan Ilyin, "Osnovy borby za natsionalnuyu Rossiyu" (1938), in Ilyin (1992), p. 62.

[53] Ibid, p. 62.

[54] Paul Latawski, "The Russian Geopolitical Trap," in *International Geopolitical Colloquium on Euro-Atlantic Security. Conference Report. 12-15 November 1995*, George C. Marshall Center, Garmisch-Partenkirchen, p.10.

[55] Reference to the Emperor's phrase about the army and navy as Russia's only two true friends. The U.S.S.R leadership's reliance on military force was even stronger.

CHAPTER 2

The Break-Up of the U.S.S.R.:
A Break in Continuity

Russia's new borders result from its double failure as a global, albeit one-dimensional superpower and as a historical empire. Throughout its history, Russia has experienced several periods of state failure, followed by chaos. It is enough to recall the Time of Troubles at the beginning of the 17th century and the revolutionary turmoil at the beginning of the 20th. In both cases, the change in the domestic regime led to political confusion, foreign intervention, and the loss of territory. In both cases, Russia managed to get back on its feet, recover lost ground, and eventually become bigger and more powerful than before. For some in Russia and many in the West, the parallels are too obvious. These people like to quote Ivan Ilyin: "With each attempt to divide [Russia] and after each disintegration it restores itself again by the mysterious ancient power of its spiritual identity (*bytiya*)."[1] The optimistic fatalists of this kind apparently believe in a "phoenix model," although some concede that Russia's chances of rebirth are dwindling fast.[2] Although this view is firmly rooted in Russian historical experience, the phoenix model pays scant attention to the new developments, and unduly favors continuity over discontinuity. But are the factors that in the past led to reconstitution of Russian territory available now? Will they appear in the future?

This chapter argues that the demise of the U.S.S.R. was owing to natural causes. The break-up of the country was not fortuitous, and cannot be ascribed to a domestic or foreign conspiracy or fatal ineptitude. It was not only mounting difficulties and Soviet policy failures that were sapping the unity of the multinational union, but Soviet successes as well, which were slowly preparing the constituent republics for independence. Ironically, the only part of the U.S.S.R. that was left out of the process of gradually becoming sovereign was the Soviet Russian Republic. This chapter will examine the effect of the Soviet Union's break-up on the Russian Federation and the attitude that is often summarized in a popular phrase: He who does not regret the passing of the U.S.S.R. has no heart; he who wants to restore it has no head.[3]

Why Did the U.S.S.R. Break Up?

To most Russians, and most Soviet people at the time, the break-up of the U.S.S.R. was like a sudden, brief, and fatal disease. Just two or three years before, Moscow had controlled a truly world system of client states, which included several zones: the *socialist community* (Eastern Europe, Mongolia, Cuba, and Vietnam), the *socialist-oriented countries* of Asia, Africa, and Latin America—roughly 20 states from Angola to Nicaragua to South Yemen—and *geopolitical allies* such as Iraq. This led to acute imperial overstretch, as Moscow had to heavily subsidize more than two dozen allies and clients in all corners of the world.[4]

Having reached the peak of its outward expansion in Afghanistan, and having been rebuffed, the U.S.S.R. started a fast de-escalation, first from Kabul, then from Berlin, and eventually breaking up itself—all within about 30 months.

Why did the Soviet leadership give up? Why did the Russian people not follow the Serbian example and turn nationalist? Why this global and largely graceful retreat of a major power without a world war, followed by voluntary abdication of its traditional role, and ending in self-destruction, which is without parallel in modern history?

The explanations differed depending on the general philosophical position of those concerned. To the radical liberals of the Democratic Russia movement, such an outcome was of course inevitable. Communism was doomed. All colonial empires break up. Post-Communist Russia was simply the last one to do so. By contrast, to the liberal patriots and moderate nationalists, this voluntary dismantling of the "thousand year-old" state was sheer stupidity, a clear case of ineptitude.[5] To the Communist opposition in the Duma, the conduct of the authorities, first under Gorbachev and later under Yeltsin, was high treason deserving presidential impeachment.

All unhappy nations, like all unhappy families, are unhappy in their own way. In Russia, conspiracy theories abound. One can say that it is bad to be defeated, but it is worse to be defeated in a way that is not obvious to all. As in many similar cases in modern history, there is a temptation to present the break-up of the Soviet Union as a result of a colossal betrayal, a conspiracy, a stab in the back, etc. Disturbingly but predictably, a Russian version of Germany's 1918 *Dolchstosslegende*, or stab-in-the-back theory, was born and is still popular with part of the elite and the public.

As for the decolonization argument, it cannot be dismissed, but should be nuanced. It is true that in some respects, Russia's experience was not dissimilar to that of the classical European empires. Like Britain, Russia had to give up what it had gained in the Great Game (i.e., the Transcaucasus, Central Asia, and most of the Caspian); like France, it chose to fight a long and dirty war to keep what it regarded as part of its sovereign territory (i.e., Chechnya). Like Britain in the 1950s, it "has lost an empire and not found a new role"; like France in the 1960s, it insists on its continuing "grandeur" even though much of the outside world regards this as pure self-indulgence. However, Russia differed from both of these empires in several important ways, which had an impact on the way de-colonization was carried out:

(1) Given that Russia is a continental rather than a maritime power, its "colonies" were actually its borderlands, i.e., a direct continuation of the national territory;

(2) In the cases of Ukraine and Belarus, colonization certainly does not apply (and hence the de-colonization argument is also irrelevant). This is rather the result of self-differentiation within a family of ethnically and (for the most part) religiously very close groups of peoples;

(3) The Russian Empire included both Asian and European borderlands. Russia's possessions in the west, such as Poland, Finland, and the Baltic provinces, were often more economically, politically, and culturally advanced than the Russian core lands;

(4) Russia's patchwork state structure was held together by a huge army and pervasive government bureaucracy, rather than by commercial interests;

(5) Even within the core territory there existed non-Russian territorial enclaves retaining their cultural and religious identity (e.g., along the Volga River);

(6) All subjects of the tsars were equal in the sense that they enjoyed few rights, and ordinary Russians, as distinct from the generals and the government offi-

cials, were hardly regarded as a dominant race by the others;

(7) The local colonial nobility were co-opted into the core imperial elite, and were allowed, if not encouraged, to take high positions in the military and civilian sections of government; the non-Russian population was being progressively assimilated; and

(8) The Soviet Communist regime was quite unlike any of the colonial ones in its ideology, claims, and global pretensions.

In fact, Russia had more in common with the more traditional Austro-Hungarian and especially the Ottoman empires than with either the British or the French overseas ones. This contiguity of territory made it easier to keep the empire going longer, but once the imperial era was over, the Russians had no safe haven to return to. Instead, they had to draw new borders where there had been none for centuries. Still, even within the borders of the Soviet Russian Republic, the Russian Federation carries a major imperial legacy.

The British and French experience of exiting from the empire is relevant for Russia, but only to a certain extent. Post-imperial Austria (and Hungary) and Turkey offer Russia two other options. In the more extreme case, *Deutsch-Oesterreich* in 1918 had to settle for a small state option, giving up any pretense to even a regional role. The Austrian Germans, however, had the big German state as their neighbor, and a feeling of national solidarity with the Germans (logically leading to an *Anschluss*) was winning over their imperial habits. Turkey, for its part, managed to carve out a medium-sized, ethnically homogeneous nation-state from the former multinational empire.[6] Even this, however, required the expulsion of the Greeks and Armenians from Asia Minor and drastic measures against the emergence of a Kurdish identity.

Given Russian conditions, an "Austrian solution" would reduce Russia to the size of the pre-1540s Grand Duchy of Muscovy. This rump state would probably be compact and homogeneous enough to fit into a "Europe" as its ultimate eastern borderland. Faced with Muslims and, as some fear, the Chinese on its borders, this European Russia would strive to integrate into European institutions, and would probably be acceptable to them as a natural but a very long-shot candidate to membership. This option, however, is an invitation to intense competition for the lands to be abandoned, such as the Urals, Siberia, the Russian Far East, the North Caucasus, and the lower and middle reaches of the Volga. Such a solution, needless to say, is regarded by virtually all Russians as totally unacceptable.

The "Turkish option," by contrast, would either mean creating an ethnic Russian republic (shaped like a Swiss cheese to take account of the numerous landlocked non-Russian enclaves) or, more likely, fully, and probably forcefully, russifying the present federation. Neither model has elite or popular support. And Russia has no Ataturk.

Most Russians see the Russian Federation as the successor state of both the U.S.S.R. and the Russian Empire. To them, celebrating June 12 as "Independence Day" (which since 1992 has replaced November 7, the anniversary of the Bolshevik Revolution, as the main national holiday) raises a baffling question—independence from whom?[7] Thus, unlike all other post-Soviet states, most people in present-day Russia regard their country not as a new state (like West Germany after 1949), but a truncated one—thrown back to its 16th century borders in the west and the south (and thus, more like post-1919 Weimar Germany).

Thus, if one interprets the Soviet Union's break-up as a process of decolonization, one should guard oneself against drawing parallels too closely with the more recent cases of decolonization involving West European maritime empires. The Russian case is more complex, again inviting comparisons with Austria-Hungary and the Ottomans. The geographical proximity and the much more involved relationship between the core country and the borderlands also suggest that, however much the bonds within the former empire may be dramatically loosened, they are likely to stay, and could be reactivated in the future.

With hindsight, it can be claimed that the end of the Soviet world empire started on March 15, 1989 when the last Soviet troops left Afghanistan. This represented a formal recognition of its first major political-military defeat since the end of World War II. The alternative, however, would have been sending in a 500,000 strong army, with the uncertain prospect of forcibly pacifying a country that had rejected the Soviet-supported regime. Moscow had to cede territory simply in order to cut its growing losses.

Within the six months that followed, the Soviet government again consciously let the Warsaw Pact countries choose their own form of government ("Do it your way," in the famous phrase of Gorbachev's spokesman, Gennady Gerasimov) and, by implication, a different foreign policy course. To their critics, Gorbachev and his foreign minister Eduard Shevardnadze had thus committed high treason. But with the Cold War over and Communist ideology in decline, Eastern Europe, where Moscow's interest had been primarily strategic, political, and ideological, came to be regarded as an unnecessary burden.[8]

Where the Kremlin did eventually lose control was over dealing with the drive for sovereignty on the part of the constituent republics of the U.S.S.R. But this was largely because Moscow itself stood as a house divided, with the Kremlin incumbents challenged by the Russian republican leadership, which for political reasons had allied itself with the pro-independence forces in the other republics.

The Soviet "outer" empire could not have been sustained. It actually lasted too long, and was a major drain on resources that ought to have been spent instead on domestic development projects. The problem was not whether to withdraw from its outer empire, but when and how. In several cases, there was inept handling of the withdrawal by Moscow, but the withdrawal itself was both necessary and eventually salutary for Russia. In the case of the Soviet Union itself, the failure of Marxism and the inefficiency of the Soviet economy had predictable consequences. The Soviet myth started to give way in the mid-1950s and the 1960s, and it was only a matter of time before the forces of liberation would prevail over the ossified Soviet structures. These forces could not have failed to have a national dimension—including in the Soviet Russian Republic itself. Ethnic Russians started to move back to "the old country" already in the 1970s. Thus, it is pure speculation to discuss the outcome of the process of creating a confederacy, which was opened up by Gorbachev in 1990 in a failed attempt to create a more perfect union. The chances for keeping even the bigger republics—Russia, Ukraine, Kazakhstan, Belarus—together were constantly dwindling, and the attempted coup in August 1991 reduced them to nil.

A Long Decline

This is not the place to theorize about imperial decline. Paul Kennedy's seminal book, *The Rise and Fall of the Great Powers*, provides a very sophisticated argument about imperial overstretch as the prime cause of imperial decline. What was unusual about the U.S.S.R. was the fact that it collapsed in peacetime, not as a result of a war. (Neither the Cold War nor the war in Afghanistan could be seriously considered as causes for Soviet break-up.) Soviet internal contradictions were many,[9] but the chief Soviet strength, its mobilization capacity, turned out to be its principal weakness, when tensions with the outside world were eased. Undefeated in war, the Soviet Union died of weariness. The famous phrase from Russian history, *Karaul ustal,* "The guard is tired," which spelled the end of the Constitutional Assembly in January 1918, dispersed by the Red Guards, and ushered in more than 70 years of Communist rule, can be fully applied to the circumstances of 1991. The U.S.S.R. was drowning, that was clear, but at the critical moment there was no one who cared to try to save it. This weariness was a direct product of half a century of overstretch. Thus, a combination of factors sapping Soviet strength had been formed a long time before the empire was allowed to run its course. Some of them are briefly summarized here:

1. The economic decline that started in the mid-1970s as the Soviet Union failed to carry out economic reform and missed out on the computer revolution and has been worsening ever since. The resource base was shrinking fast. The economy was being grossly mismanaged, with pervasive militarization reaching a level that the U.S.S.R. was simply unable to afford.[10] Gorbachev's attempt to revitalize the system only showed that it couldn't be reformed. Perestroika only accelerated its end by a few years. The central government was increasingly unable to cope with its role as the provider and distributor of most goods

and services. This led the regional elites in the republics to believe that they would be better off if they broke with the center and managed their resources independently.

2. The crisis of the Communist Party's system of governance. The highly centralized party apparatus was unable to cope with the increasingly complex tasks of day-to-day governing of the vast country. It was equally unable to set strategic goals. This inefficiency of the central party leadership both frustrated the party organizations in the republics and offered their leaders a chance to concentrate more de facto power at the regional level. Later, the political paralysis at the center pushed the regional elites to the fore.

3. The demise of Communist ideology, facilitated by glasnost, but begun decades before Gorbachev's arrival to power. The bankrupt Communist ideology, no longer capable of serving as a basis for legitimizing the regime in the eyes of both the elite and the public, was being displaced by nationalism. Not only anti-Communist forces but also the Communist elites themselves embraced nationalism in the intensifying struggle for power.[11] The central leadership genuinely believed that the nationalities issue in the U.S.S.R. had been successively resolved,[12] and was totally unprepared for the nationalist upsurge after seven decades of Soviet internationalism.

4. The very success of Soviet national policy that helped the non-Russian borderlands, especially in the Muslim republics, on their way toward sovereignty and independence. The Soviet Union not only provided the formal trappings of sovereignty to its constituent parts, but also an economic base and educated na-

tional elites. When these elites became conscious of their own role, they started to look for their own way in the world.

5. The religious revival that was gaining strength in the atmosphere of glasnost underlined and strengthened the differences within the Soviet Union, mainly between the Christians and the Muslims.

6. The evolution of the demographic situation in the U.S.S.R. was rapidly undermining the dominant position of the Slavs, and especially the Russians. In 1989, the latter constituted a bare majority in the country, which they were going to lose in the 1990s. The Muslims, on the other hand, were on the rise. This made some ethnic Russian elites look for ways to separate the Russian Republic from its Muslim counterparts.

7. The fiasco of Soviet foreign policy, which squandered resources in various adventurous projects. The inability of the Soviet Union to hold Afghanistan dealt a heavy blow not only to the morale of the armed forces, but to the overall confidence of the political class and society at large that Soviet advances were irreversible and that its overall strategy was correct. In the ten year long war, the military forces, instrumental in both acquiring new territories and holding them for Moscow, proved to be unable to carry out their usual mission. Once the high-water mark of the Soviet advance was reached, the tide abruptly turned. This was immediately noted by the East Europeans and both Muslims and non-Muslims in the U.S.S.R.

8. Just as the Soviet Union was growing weaker, its neighbors were gaining strength. The U.S.S.R. was no longer facing a weak Europe and a backward Asia. Its "soft underbelly" in the south was developing

excruciating pains, evident in Iran and Afghanistan. The European Union was not only becoming more prosperous, but also more economically integrated. Under Deng Xiaoping, China started its economic reforms in 1978. The Iranian revolution and the Afghan rebels were re-energizing the forces of radical Islam across the greater Middle East. A reversal of the geopolitical dynamic was in the offing.

The process of saving the union by means of a new deal between the center and the republics, launched by Gorbachev in 1990,[13] was moving too slowly. Even then, it raised fears in conservative quarters about the ultimate dismantlement of the U.S.S.R. The timing of the last-ditch effort to save the Soviet system, the so-called August *putsch* of 1991, was provoked by the decision to sign a new union treaty that would have turned the U.S.S.R. into a confederation. After the *putsch,* whatever chance there might have existed for a confederal option was totally destroyed.[14] The Russian republic's determination not to tolerate a strong central government was critical. Ukraine's decision not to join in any new union was a pivotal event. The Ukrainian referendum on independence, held on December 1, 1991, closed the book on the U.S.S.R.

To a classical geopolitician, 1989 became a seminal turning point in the geopolitical dynamic of Eurasia. Five hundred years of heartland expansion ended. The rimland, represented by NATO and the European Union in the west, Islamic forces in the south, and the power of China in the east, started to spread its influence into the rapidly disintegrating "Continent Russia." The heartland was unable to resist the pressure. Russia's borders began moving again—this time inward. The cracks appeared not on the outer perimeter, but within the country itself.

The demise of the Soviet Union was hastened by the domestic territorial dispute between the Armenians and the Azeris over Nagorno-Karabakh, which came into the open in 1988. Inter-ethnic tension was rising elsewhere from Moldova to Kyrgyzstan. When the Soviet Union came apart three years later, however, this largely happened in an ostensibly orderly and largely smooth fashion, complete with many legal procedures. The inviolability of the borders existing between republics-turned-sovereign states was immediately confirmed by all leaders and explicitly codified in the documents establishing the Commonwealth of Independent States.[15] The Russian law of 1993 on the border explicitly defines the territory of the Russian Federation as lying within the boundaries of the pre-1991 Russian Soviet republic. It was critically important that even before the end of the U.S.S.R., the Russian Republic had concluded bilateral treaties with other members of the union, which included mutual recognition of borders.

A Phoenix Redux? What Role for the CIS?

In the initial shock that accompanied the dissolution of the U.S.S.R., the new situation was seen by many as probably catastrophic, but transient, paving the way for some sort of a rebound. For a few years, illusions were kept alive, by those who refused to believe that the Soviet Union had died a natural death, that a new and better union, meaning, in fact, a state of "normalcy," would in the end be restored.[16] At the height of the 1996 presidential election campaign in Russia, the Communist/Nationalist–dominated State Duma passed a resolution that pronounced the Belovezhskaya Pushcha (i.e., Belaya Vezha Forest) Accords null and void. To the revisionists, this was a Belovezhsky *putsch*. The implication was that the U.S.S.R. continued to legally exist, and, even more absurdly, that the Russian Federation itself was illegal. This produced an acute political crisis between the president and the Duma, but the proponents of the restoration of the U.S.S.R. effectively exposed their agenda as both dangerous and preposterous.

On the whole, Russian society has been adapting, albeit reluctantly, to the new situation. The pragmatism of the upper strata of society, which sometimes turns cynical, is keeping nostalgia in check.The basic need to survive, virtually on a daily basis, has blunted the heartfelt feeling of nostalgia for the U.S.S.R. on the part of the "masses."

Still, it would be wrong to ignore the unease that many elites and many ordinary people experience toward the new borders. This is not to suggest that Russian revisionism is historically inevitable, but rather to point out that internalizing the post-imperial condition will be a long process, complete with serious complications and even crises, for which one should be intellectually prepared. One thing that cushioned the blow in the Soviet case and that was singularly absent in the Yugoslav one was the creation of the Commonwealth of Independent States, first by the three Slav republics which had just disposed of the Soviet Union, and later embracing the entire post-Soviet territories, with the exception of the three Baltic States.

The Commonwealth of Independent States (CIS) is routinely blamed for things it was never designed to do, and is not recognized for its very real and truly tremendous achievements. Its historic role was that of a shock absorber, which it accomplished brilliantly; the promise of integration was nothing but a great illusion, which turned out to be a most useful instrument of separation.

There were serious reasons for the CIS's failure to act as a vehicle for post-Soviet integration:

- Elite resistance to any supranational organization, despite nostalgic popular longings in some countries;
- Prevailing outward economic and political orientation of all CIS states (toward the West, but also Romania, Turkey, Iran, etc.). Russia's reluctance to become a donor to the process of new integration, and its unattractiveness in the eyes of the other CIS states;
- Diverging levels of economic development, different political and legal regimes, different cultural backgrounds; and
- Vastly different security agendas of the participating states.

Thus, the loose association of Russia and its former borderlands could not become a vehicle for new integration, owing to the general lack of mutual interest, the paucity of resources, and the absence of political will. The post-Soviet Commonwealth became famous for producing, within its first eight years, over 800 agreements, most of which were never implemented. Many argued that it had become irrelevant.

At the same time, by keeping up the fiction of CIS "integration," the old-new elites were able to keep open channels of communication among themselves; they cushioned the blow that division dealt to millions of ordinary people, and won critically important time to proceed with state- and nation-building in the former republics. In 1991, it was not a given that they would succeed. Wars over borders were often predicted, with devastating consequences; nuclear proliferation was considered a real threat; and few observers doubted that some of the new states would not survive. A violent conflict between Ukraine and Russia or their disintegration was regarded as a distinct possibility.

Not one of these predictions became a reality. Immediately following the defeat of the August 1991 putsch, Boris Yeltsin sent Vice President Alexander Rutskoi to Kiev and Almaty to reassure the Ukrainian and Kazakh leaders that existing borders between the republics would not be called into question. More recently, the CIS, as a transition mechanism and a safety net combined, has worked well indeed. It did not evolve into a Russia-led power bloc complete with a military alliance, but it did much to prevent the former Soviet Union from following the path of former Yugoslavia.

To summarize, the main achievements of the CIS are as follows:

- The sovereignty of all Soviet republics was recognized within the existing Soviet administrative borders, some of which had no historical foundation. The much-feared Yugoslav scenario was, thus, averted;
- The unprecedented break-up of a nuclear superpower did not result in nuclear proliferation;
- The conventional forces and assets of the former Soviet Army were divided up, and the Soviet quotas under the 1990 Conventional Forces in Europe (CFE) treaty were reapportioned;
- The abbreviation itself (CIS) created a useful fiction of the continuation of the "common space" for ordinary citizens. Inter-state travel became more cumbersome, but for ten years it has remained virtually free, and no insurmountable barriers to migration were erected;[17]
- The elites in the newly independent states became satisfied and confident within their old-new but now "very own" fiefs; and
- CIS summitry served well as a vehicle for communication, especially while the diplomatic services in

most former republics were just being organized. As most leaders were former *nomenklatura* members, they enjoyed this new "Politburo of equals."

In short, the CIS, rather than being an instrument for imperial restoration, was really a tool for nation- and state-building. Of course, there was a price to be paid for the stability of borders between the new states, as most conflicts (Georgia, Moldova, the North Caucasus) occurred *within* those borders where all sorts of crevices and cleavages developed. But even more important are the conflicts that have not happened—between Russia and Ukraine over the Crimea, Russia and Kazakhstan over the northern provinces, or Uzbekistan and Kyrgyzstan over the Fergana Valley. Not a single separatist-ruled unit that unilaterally proclaimed its independence was recognized by any CIS state.

Over time, the CIS has become increasingly fragmented. A political alliance was achieved between Russia and Belarus; a Customs Union was agreed among Belarus, Kazakhstan, Kyrgyzstan, Russia, and Tajikistan; a security alliance united the same five countries plus Armenia. On the other hand, five other states (Georgia, Ukraine, Uzbekistan, Azerbaijan, and Moldova) joined GUUAM, which was dubbed an "anti-CIS" by the Moscow media, for it did not include Russia and enjoyed U.S. diplomatic support. Lastly, Turkmenistan pronounced itself neutral and did not enter any grouping.

Thus, within the CIS there are many kinds of borders to deal with. First of all, there are inter-state boundaries, to some still "internal." Second, there are "common borders of the Commonwealth," i.e., the old Soviet borders, occasionally referred to (especially in Moscow) as "external." Third, there are Customs Union[18] borders. And lastly, there are Russo-Belarussian Union borders. This confusion was illustrative of the nation- and state-building processes in the ex-Soviet space.

More disturbingly, for some Russian politicians, recognition of the borders was implicitly tied to political alignments. It was one thing, so the argument went, to recognize borders within the U.S.S.R. or CIS, and another between two *absolutely independent* states. The message was heeded in Chisinau, Tbilisi, and Baku, which were all threatened with secessionist movements drawing their support from political forces in Moscow. In 1993, these three states reluctantly joined the CIS. Moscow's triumph, however, was short-lived: once pseudo-integration of the post-Soviet space was complete, its hollowness was for all to see.

Russia's relations with the former borderlands apart, another major problem was potential border disputes involving CIS states and third countries, where Russia could be implicated. The most serious occasion was the rise of tensions between Armenia and Turkey at the height of the Karabakh conflict in 1992-1993. Russia not only professed general responsibility for the entire post-Soviet space, but assumed the special role of Armenia's principal security guarantor.

The most important thing, however, is that CIS boundaries are unfinished borders between the not yet fully fledged states. Their separating and uniting functions, though rarely in the balance, are equally important. Ambiguities can be useful for countries that at the same time need and detest their umbilical cords. Thus, for almost a decade, CIS agreements allowed visa-free travel within the entire twelve-country space. Although in view of the many conflicts, migration flows, and the like this brings with it as enormous security problems, the mere fact of relatively free movement makes many people put up with the Commonwealth. One can easily imagine the bureaucratic bottlenecks that visa requirements would have created if introduced immediately. The gradual dismantlement of the visa-free regime, begun in 1999 and greatly enhanced by Russia's decision, in mid-2000, to withdraw from the CIS-wide visa-free regime, comes at a time when separation has become a reality, and new states have gained a fair measure of acceptance by their populations.

Most of the plans for intra-CIS integration were only good for propaganda purposes. They ignored political realities and had a flimsy economic foundation at best. More realistic was the plan proposed in 1998 by the controversial Russian financier and then CIS executive secretary, Boris Berezovsky, to gradually upgrade the CIS from a free trade area to a customs union to a common economic space. Though also ambitious, it was not necessarily infeasible, over the medium- and long-term. By contrast, the European Union, especially in its present form, is a poor model for the CIS, because the EU is too tight.[19] Other looser models were proposed, such as NAFTA,[20] but even they are not feasible in the short term.

Why the Phoenix Won't Fly This Time

Despite the apparent similarities between the predicament of post-Soviet Russia and the previous periods of trouble, the present situation with borders and ethnicity is of a very different quality. This makes the application of the "phoenix theory" doubtful at best.

Previous losses of territory were normally a result of wars with clear victors and losers. In 1917-1920, Poland and the Baltic States received diplomatic recognition from Soviet Russia after the local revolutionary forces in their territory or the Red Army had been defeated. Finland was allowed out before the start of the civil war there, probably in anticipation of a future Red victory. With the sole exception of Bessarabia, everything else was covered by treaties and thus uncontested. By contrast, in the 1990s, separation came under peaceful conditions; it was supported by the bulk of the Russian elite and was ratified by parliaments and endorsed by popular referenda. While what was lost in a war could be recovered through armed force, the democratization of politics makes it virtually impossible to resort to such crude methods of *Realpolitik*, especially when the territorial changes had originally not been imposed on Russia, but actually supported and even initiated by it. Under the new conditions, in principle, independence can only be abolished by elite-driven and popularly supported integration. This was a hope widely shared in the early 1990s.[21] Ever since then, it has appeared increasingly less likely.

Ever since Ukraine and Belarus joined Russia, over 300 and 200 years ago respectively, never has the core of the historical ancient Russian state (Kievan Rus) been split. Before the official notion of supranational unity of the Soviet people, an earlier idea persisted of an "inseparable union" of the three branches of essentially the same nation, i.e., the Russians, the Ukrainians, and the Belarussians. This was the official theory in tsarist times. In the 1990s, this merger was undone. Zbigniew Brzezinski is right: without Ukraine, Russia is not an empire—especially if one looks at it from the west. Ukrainian independence makes it imperative that Russia find a new identity and a new international role, again above all vis-à-vis the West. It also affects Belarus, which, for all its friendliness toward and dependence on Russia, is unlikely to fully renounce its state sovereignty. As a result, a new geopolitical reality has been created, the new Eastern Europe, which has important implications for the continent as a whole.

Within its new borders, Russia is much more ethnically homogeneous than ever before in its modern history. Over 80 percent of its population are ethnic Russians, compared to just above 50 percent in the U.S.S.R. While it still has about 10 percent Muslims, the country, despite its apparent geographical marginalization in Europe, is culturally closer to the rest of the continent than the Soviet Union had ever been, even though its military presence and political preponderance extended to the Elbe. Despite the important difference between the Orthodox and the Catholic/Protestant communities, this divide is not as deep as the one between Communism and capitalism. Take, for example, Orthodox Greece and Roman Catholic Italy.

There has been no recent evidence of a "clash" between the two religiously defined civilizations. NATO already includes two new Slav member states, along with an old Orthodox ally. The enlargement of the European Union will eventually extend membership not only to more Slav and Orthodox countries, but also to former Soviet republics containing hundreds of thousands of ethnic Russian residents. Complexity brings with it many problems, but management of these problems in the first post-Cold War decade has been generally satisfactory. This gives Russia a chance to rethink its place in the world and progressively fit itself into a wider Europe.

The dismantlement of the Soviet Union immediately put the unity of the Russian Federation, a mini-U.S.S.R. itself, into question. Even though the Soviet model doesn't apply here, in one part of Russia, the North Caucasus, secessionism and ethnic conflict have become endemic features. Chechnya's de facto independence, declared in the fall of 1991—when the Soviet Union still existed—and confirmed by the outcome of the 1994-1996 war, presented Russia with a set of seemingly intractable border and security problems, many of which are still unresolved, despite the second military campaign of 1999/2000. The situation is complicated by the existence of other conflicts in the area, such as the ones between the Ossetians and the Ingush, the "twin" republics of Kabardino-Balkaria and Karachaevo-Cherkessia, or in Dagestan. For the foreseeable future, the Russian government will have to concentrate its resources on dealing with this serious challenge. Both the national security and foreign policy concepts adopted in 2000 stress the preservation of the country's territorial integrity as the prime policy goal.[22] The need to fight separatism at home logically makes the Russian leaders support the territorial integrity of the fellow CIS states.[23]

Except for the 3 million Russian émigrés in the wake of the 1917 Bolshevik Revolution and the ensuing civil war, a relatively small number of those who were residents of the Baltic States, Finland, and Poland and the displaced persons at the time of World War II, virtually all ethnic Russians lived inside the country's borders. After the break-up of the U.S.S.R., some 25 million ethnic Russians found themselves permanently outside of Russia. Unlike the post-revolutionary émigrés, however, these people do not normally identify themselves with Russia—they are becoming slowly integrated within the emerging political nations along Russia's periphery. Even in the Baltic states, the process is under way. The only major worry is Kazakhstan. This phenomenon is as important as the political separation of the Russian Federation, Ukraine, and Belarus.

Until virtually its last days, the Soviet Union was a walled-in society. The new Russian state, intent on becoming "integrated" with the outside world, has been rethinking the whole concept of borders, which in the meantime have become remarkably porous and transparent. This has not always been a welcome development, owing to the exponential rise in non-traditional challenges to national security, from drug trafficking to infectious diseases. Once securely insulated from the outside world, Russia is now open and vulnerable. This vulnerability may be reduced in the future as the country stabilizes and its government pursues a more coherent set of policies. Suppressing its new openness is technically as well as economically and politically infeasible.

Geopolitical Concerns

Contrary to some predictions, the Russian Federation did not break up. Having lost many historical borderlands, post-Soviet Russia is still in possession of a vast territory.[24] No longer "a sixth of the world bearing the short name of Rus," in the affectionate words of the poet Sergei Yesenin, it is down to something like one-eighth of the earth's surface. In Russian, this still rhymes well. To a distant observer who only looks at the map, Russia has just shed some weight at the margins, but has basically kept its own. Or has it?

There is no doubt that the bulk of the elite exhibits a strong sense of insecurity. Both imperial and Soviet borders were seen as "natural" and stable. The Russian current borders are believed to be neither. There has been an important change recently. Whereas in the early and mid-1990s the most vocal group were the "nostalgics," who, regarding the new borders as unsustainable, were advocating something like a Russia-plus (the Crimea, eastern Ukraine, Abkhazia, etc.), at the end of the decade, it was the bulk of the political class who became concerned over the territorial integrity of Russia.[25] The nationalist wing is arguing that Russian resources have become the principal object of a new division of the world. In the west, there is a picture of a new *Zwischeneuropa*, even less stable than in 1919-1939, with Germany poised to rise again. In the south, there is a shadow of Great Turan stretching from the Crimea to Chuvashia to Tuva and Yakutia. To a true nationalist, the "attitude to Russia's territorial integrity is the main political dividing line of the 1990s."[26]

Russia's internal borders, which are a real problem in the North Caucasus, where, crossing the line between North Ossetia and Ingushetia, for example, could be as deadly as crossing a minefield, remain a sleeping issue in other parts of Russia such as Tatarstan, Bashkortostan, as well as the Urals, Yakutia, and the Far East, because Putin's administrative reforms notwithstanding federal laws are not necessarily supreme everywhere in Russia, either in the sense of regional constitutions or in practice.

In the future, the unity of the federation may be compromised in a way different from the case in Chechnya. Territories, already more autonomous than they have ever been, are being pulled in different directions. At the end of Yeltsin's presidency, there was a clear prospect that, over time, the art of governing Russia could mean, first of all, the ability to manage those different orientations. Putin has stopped this trend for the time being, but his mechanical recentralization may not be enough. Thus, to a greater extent than elsewhere, borders in Russia have become an interface between foreign policy and domestic politics.

It has become clearer by now that there is no easy or quick resolution for many border or border-related issues. An attempt to resolve them quickly and thus bring about clarity can lead to civil wars in the neighboring states, de-generating into border wars. Thus, there must be no room for complacency. Border-related disputes between Russia and its neighbors can adversely affect Russia's relations with the United States and other Western and non-Western countries. It is alarming that the oil-rich Caspian-Caucasus region, which is becoming a prime focus of Russian-Western (especially Russian-American) rivalry, is virtually rent by disputes and wars over borders.

From a nationalist perspective, America is chiefly to blame. Russia's problems are presented as designed or at least encouraged by the United States. Zbigniew Brzezin-ski's book *The Grand Chessboard* was translated into Russian less than a year after its publication in the United States and was still a best seller a year later. Many would agree with the assessment that Brzezinski follows all current policy options to their logical conclusions. While what he proposes may not necessarily be the U.S. policy at the moment, it could well become such.[27] In other words, what Russians read provided clarity with respect to many aspects of U.S. policy toward Russia. This clarity is frightening enough: the CIA and other members of the intelligence community and various interest groups within the "U.S. oligarchy" and their alleged Russian agents in high places plan to solve the world's geopolitical problems at the expense of Russia, which they want dismembered. Russia would be split into a Muscovy lying east of the Urals, with Siberia and the Far East forming a loose confederacy. American allies and ri-vals alike—from Germany and Japan to Turkey and China, even Iran and India—would be awarded or appeased, as considered appropriate. In exchange for the acceptance of U.S. global leadership they would be offered control over parts of the Russian and former Soviet territory.[28] Along

Russia's western frontiers, a new *cordon sanitaire* or buffer zone stretching from the Black Sea to the Baltic will be erected with the purpose of safely isolating Russia from the rest of Europe.[29] In short, having deemed Russia to be an "unnecessary country," the United States was busy organizing a "world without Russia."[30]

This dark view of Western intentions vis-à-vis Russia is supported by the historical memory of Western invasions in the 17th-20th centuries, the intervention by the Entente powers, the fact that the U.S. law on "captive nations" (PL 86-90) conspicuously fails to mention the Russians as victims of Communism, etc. The conclusion is that the West is consciously and pragmatically dismantling Russia, which is too unwieldy as a whole.

The reality, however, was very different from these conclusions. Although the challenge to Russia's territorial integrity arose in the area that the United States government had designated of vital U.S. interest (which much angered the Kremlin at the time), the challenge itself had no American connection.

What Union with Belarus?

The tale of Russia's union with Belarus is emblematic of the problems that Russia experiences with post-Soviet integration. Those supporting the union include a loose coalition of Communists who portray this as a step toward the eventual reconstitution of the U.S.S.R.; nationalists, who look at Belarus as a bulwark stopping the advance of the West; *Realpolitikers* and multipolar world ideologues interested in preserving the balance of power; pragmatics from the oil and gas industry looking for cheap and reliable export routes; and, last but not least, the military and security community determined to place a buffer between the expanding NATO and the Russian western border, just west of Smolensk. Underlying the broad elite support for the union were the fears that if Russia would not embrace Belarus tightly, it would "inevitably" be absorbed by "another state or a group of states,"[31] such as Poland, Germany, the United States, an enlarged NATO, or the European Union, and would "almost certainly" become hostile to Russia.

Opponents of the union included: economic liberals concerned about the financial costs of Russia's "enlargement"; human rights activists appalled at President Alexander Lukashenko's authoritarian practices; and regional elites fearing the lowering of their own status within the new confederal construct.

It is the viability of this construct that is raising serious doubts. Great Russia advocates suggest a "German solution," under which the six East German *Länder* of the former German Democratic Republic acceded to the Federal Republic individually, under the Federal Republic of Germany's 1949 Basic Law. This would also remove the concerns of the Tatarstan leadership. A confederation, whose closest model is Yugoslavia composed of Serbia and Montenegro, is believed to be unwieldy and unstable, and capable of upsetting the precarious balance of center-periphery relations within the Russian Federation.

The Belarussians, however, take the opposite view. The elites there recognize their country's dependence on Russia, and their own failure at nation-building. Still, they want to keep the trappings of statehood to which they have grown accustomed in the last decade, and share among themselves the benefits from the Belarussian economy's privatization, which has not yet started in earnest. Thus, they literally prefer to keep their cake and eat it too.[32]

This situation promises a natural, but necessarily long process of building a special economic, political, and military relationship that can eventually lead to the creation of a common economic space, currency union, and close coordination of Minsk's foreign, security, and defense policies with those of Moscow. On the other hand, a full merger of the two states appears unlikely in the medium and even long term.

The proposed trilateral union of Russia, Belarus, and Yugoslavia, of course, has little to do with the post-Soviet integration. The brief surfacing of that idea in the spring of 1999 immediately revealed that even elite expectations, let alone the national interests of the would-be partners, were vastly different.[33] Why, then, this preoccupation with erecting and erasing borders? The democratic ouster of Slobodan Milosevic in the 2000 elections put this odd idea to rest.

What's in a Border?

Few Russians regard borders as simply administrative lines denoting limits to national jurisdiction, currency regimes, etc. The mental picture of the border is not a checkpoint on the highway. Rather, the traditional view persists of borders as prima facie military barriers whose key features are barbed wires and minefields and which must be defended at all cost, if need be.

The U.S.S.R. was a walled-in society. The Soviet border was a non-transparent barrier, setting the country apart from the outside world, an enormous filter regulating the flow of people and goods, but also ideas. The filter was imperfect, and allowed for some "alien" imports in selected areas, such as culture and the arts, especially since the start of Khrushchev's thaw, but the bulk of the population was safely protected by the Communist ideologues from "damaging" knowledge or first-hand international experience. For a typical Russian, from the early 1920s through the late 1980s, the world was divided in two from the very beginning: it included his "Soviet Motherland," a huge and internally uniform country, where he was born and which in most cases he never left, even temporarily, throughout his entire life, and the rest of the world, of which he had no direct experience. The Soviet border was, in a way, larger than life.[34]

The ultimate penalty for illegally crossing these borders was, of course, death, and the ideal version was the Berlin Wall. In this, like in some other things, East German Communists were more consistent than their Soviet colleagues.[35]

The Berlin Wall did not only mark the limits of the East German territory. It was the Soviet Union's own strategic border, too. When this border was threatened, Moscow intervened with force, as in Berlin, Budapest, or Prague. Had Poland been strategically "exposed," the U.S.S.R. would probably have intervened there directly in 1980, too. (But Poland, as Soviet textbooks liked to point out, had an "advantageous geographical situation: it only bordered on socialist states.")

Within the U.S.S.R., proximity to borders gave enhanced status. Thus, to qualify as a constituent republic, a territory had to have a stretch of the external Soviet border. For Tatarstan, situated deep inland, that meant a reduced status, irrespective of its significant industrial potential and the number of ethnic Tatars within the U.S.S.R., which exceeded that of Estonians, Moldovans, and others. In the same fashion, borderline military districts were always in the top category, and were called "special" in the 1930s.

The border as a four-inch-wide strip in the middle of the Glienicke Bridge between West Berlin and Potsdam is one extreme case. The notion of a border as a fairly wide strip of territory, a borderland, is another. The word *pogranichnik*, now meaning a border guard, originally meant a borderlander. Historically, borderlands prevailed in the south and the east, where borders were fuzzier. After the end of the U.S.S.R., history made a comeback in the North Caucasus and southern Russia, which have actually become one vast borderland.

Borders, identity, and ethnicity are difficult to separate. In the Soviet Union, nationality was ethnically based, while practically all administrative units bearing the name of some ethnic group—which thus were known as "titular"—were in fact multi-ethnic. In sharp contrast to the Soviet external border, the internal Soviet boundaries were extremely arbitrary and insignificant.[36]

Next to some 25 million Russians now living outside the federation, there are about 50 million other former Soviet citizens who live beyond the boundaries of their homelands. If borders between the new states do "harden," this may lead to the spread of a "divided nation syndrome." In a more benign environment, one should expect the emergence of substantial Russian minorities—"non-Russian Federation Russians"—in several countries bordering on Russia. Thus, the two fundamental questions "What is Russia?" and "Who is a Russian?" are, in fact, two sides of the same coin.[37]

Double Border Strategy

Early on, the Russian authorities made a fundamental decision. "Arbitrary" or not, the internal Soviet borders were to be recognized as the new international borders. Despite very strong pressure from the opposition, official Moscow never wavered on this issue, which helped ensure peace between Russia and the new states. The borders between Russia and its neighbors are more stable today than at any time since 1991. The problems with borders along Russia's western façade are less political and more technical in nature. The southern flank is the most problematic for now and for the foreseeable future. In the east, the main problems are still behind the horizon.

The Yeltsin administration was slow on the delimitation of boundaries with CIS states. It was not before April 1993 that Moscow formally gave those boundaries the status of international frontiers. The reluctance to institute a regime of "real borders" was clearly linked to the fear of creating or strengthening the "divided nations" syndrome.[38] At the same time, influential Russian quarters supported separatist movements in the CIS states in an effort to de-legitimize *all* new borders and make some form of imperial restoration possible, if not inevitable.

At the end of 1991, Moscow still controlled boundaries with a few countries in Europe and the Far East, but its long frontiers with the former Soviet republics—7,500 km with Kazakhstan alone—were little more than imaginary lines on the map. And the Russian Federation lacked the funds[39] to turn them into much more than that. Acting out of necessity, Moscow came up with a concept of "double borders," which advocated the use of former Soviet border infrastructure along the entire perimeter of the U.S.S.R. borders for the protection of the CIS as a whole. This, it was argued, would stabilize the situation and buy Russia time to build up its own borders.[40] In effect, ensuring Russian national interests and security on the CIS countries' external borders was made into a priority of Russia's border policy.[41]

Ostensibly pragmatic—who needs more fences when Western Europe has been pulling them down since 1945?— this concept also begged for a different and far less charitable interpretation as well. If Russia were to keep borders with CIS states open, while actually protecting those countries' borders with the outside world, that would appear very much like Moscow's staking out its zone of influence. To the advocates of a Russian version of the Monroe Doctrine, the Russian military presence, including border troops, would be instrumental in keeping the new states in Moscow's political and even economic orbit. The function of the CIS, then, was that of a *glacis*, with the individual countries seen as buffers—not unlike the function of the Warsaw Pact states. The 1996 Russian national security policy paper referred to the need to "reliably protect borders along the CIS perimeter and, where that is not possible, along Russian borders."[42]

The Russian government, however, was only partially successful. At an early CIS meeting in Minsk on December 30, 1991 it was decided to keep joint control over former Soviet borders. Ex-U.S.S.R. border troops became hastily reorganized under CIS auspices, with a joint (Russian) Commander-in-Chief. This arrangement, however, was extremely short-lived and never fully implemented. In March 1992, Ukraine and Moldova refused to subordinate their border guards to a CIS authority. Even Belarus expressed some reservations. In July 1992, the Joint Command was abolished, and a council of border service chiefs was established. In the same year, Russian border troops were compelled to leave Azerbaijan. Despite repeated attempts by Moscow to have this decision revoked, they were never allowed to return. On the whole, Ukraine and Azerbaijan are the least cooperative in Russian eyes. When in October 1992 an agreement was reached in Bishkek to cooperate to ensure stability along CIS "common borders," only Belarus, Armenia, Kazakhstan, Kyrgyzstan, and Tajikistan signed up. Bilateral agreements with each of these states, plus Georgia, which joined later, gave Russia the right to deploy its border troops along several sectors of the outer perimeter.[43]

At the high point, in the mid-1990s, Russia had some 25,000 border troops under its command in Georgia, Armenia, Tajikistan, and Kyrgyzstan. It is important to bear in mind that the vast majority of these troops were local people. Whereas in the Caucasus, Russian citizenship was required, which was often procured without much difficulty (for example, through fictitious marriages), in Central Asia most troops were local draftees. In Tajikistan, local draftees whose legal status was ill-defined constituted up to 95 percent of the Russian border troops.

There are interesting parallels in Russian history. When Russia was organizing its defenses against the Golden Horde along the Oka River in the second half of the 15th century, it recruited Tatars into the Russian armed service.[44] Interestingly, among the Defense Ministry forces in Tajikistan the situation was the reverse. The 201st Motorized Rifle Division was made up of 87 percent Russians, and all the Tajiks serving there had Russian citizenship. With other CIS countries there were agreements on information exchange, coordination of efforts to combat crime, illegal migration, smuggling, etc.

Although Moscow relied on indigenous border troops in Belarus, and the Russian presence was confined to a Federal Border Service (FBS) liaison mission in Minsk, it is with that country that Russia has been cooperating most closely.

Since 1997, there has been a joint border committee. Moscow has agreed to help equip Belarus's new 350 km long border with Lithuania and Latvia. The principal—and usual—problem is the lack of funds, leaving Moscow's promises largely unfulfilled. The result has been an undesired transparency of Belarus's borders with the Baltic States. The "Belarussian gap" is considered to be responsible for some 40 percent of all reported cases of smuggling—of non-ferrous metals, petroleum products, and timber from Russia and tobacco and alcoholic products from the Baltic States—and westward-bound illegal migrants, mainly from Asia.

Ukraine, which refused any integration of border controls with Russia, has nevertheless been careful not to offend its neighbor. During the 1999 crisis over Kosovo, Russia was able to receive permission for its Belgrade-bound humanitarian convoys. The convoys' problems only started in Hungary. Moscow was also able to secure Kiev's permission for its paratroopers to overfly Ukraine en route to Kosovo—again something that was only prevented by Romania and Bulgaria, both aspiring members of NATO, which refused.

Russia's cooperation with Georgia has been far more difficult. The more accessible part of the border is with Abkhazia, which Tbilisi does not control; farther south, Russian peacekeepers along the Inguri River separating Abkhazia from Georgia proper, are accused of being de facto border guards for the Abkhaz; further, there are sharp disagreements about the borderline in the mountains, and finally Georgia is the only foreign country that has a border with Chechnya (about 80 kilometers long). Despite the signing in 1994 of an agreement providing for the stationing of Russian border guards in Georgia, the bulk of that country's political elite always resented their presence. Georgian officials complain about the Russians' failure to provide them with the relevant information about the situation on the borders. In 1996, the Georgian parliament passed a resolution demanding replacement of 8,000 Russian border guards with Georgians by 2001. Eventually, Moscow had to give way. In September 1998, the Russian coast guard had to withdraw from both Poti and Sukhumi. In November 1998, Moscow agreed to withdraw its forces from the 900-kilometer long Georgian-Turkish border. The rest of the border guards left in 1999. Importantly, they left the autonomous republic of Ajaria, whose ruler Aslan Abashidze had come to rely on the presence of Russian border troops and other Russian military units in his territory as a means of protection from Tbilisi's attempts to dislodge him and reinstate the central government's authority in the area. While insisting on its right to protect its own borders, Georgia is receiving assistance from the United States and Turkey, which raises suspicions in Russia.

While Armenia offers a friendlier environment for Russian border troops, geopolitically it is becoming more of an island, and the Russian forces, including border troops, are becoming more valuable to the host country than to Moscow.

In 1999, Russian border guards withdrew from Kyrgyzstan and Turkmenistan.

In Tajikistan, since 1992 the borderline has been a frontline. Following a 1993 agreement between Moscow and the Central Asian capitals, the Russian border troops in the country, then numbering 5,000, were soon boosted to 18,000. The local component of that force rose from two-thirds in 1994 to 95 percent at the end of 1997.[45]

In the late 1990s, some 25,000 non-Russians were serving with the Russian border forces. Half of that number were Tajiks. In Kyrgyzstan, 90 percent of the contingent were locals, in Armenia and Georgia, 60-70 percent,[46] and in Ajaria, 80 percent.[47] These foreigners took a national oath, and made an "obligation" to the Russian side. On a somewhat reduced scale, this pattern still survives. While the Russian border command is responsible for the boundaries with the non-CIS countries, intra-CIS borders are monitored by local authorities.[48]

Since the end of 1997, the Russians started to look for an exit. The number of border troops was reduced to 14,500.[49] One reason for this was the relative political stabilization in Tajikistan following the 1997 peace agreement between the Dushanbe government and the opposition, which has since returned home to Afghanistan. Another reason was the lack of resources to maintain a large physical presence and continue subsidizing the Dushanbe government.

Russia has had a difficult time with burden-sharing. Georgia was not regularly paying its 40 percent share, though the Ajarian authorities have been helpful. Tajikistan ostensibly picks up roughly 50 percent of the locally incurred costs, but the country itself is being heavily subsidized by Moscow. On the whole, however, the Federal Border Service believes that Russia benefits from the arrangement.[50]

Groups of Russian border troops, still in place in Armenia and Tajikistan, are being scaled back. However, the original plan to phase them out completely by 2005 and limit the Russian presence to small operational and interaction groups has been put off. At the turn of the third millennium, Russia is increasingly looking south. It will gradually reallocate resources in favor of protecting its own borders, but it won't be able, or willing, to fully withdraw from the ex-Soviet border. A future version of the double border strategy may be implemented increasingly through cooperation with several CIS countries rather than through direct Russian control of their borders.[51] Creation of "borderline security zones" making up a "collective security system of the CIS" is considered to be a prime goal of intra-CIS cooperation. The "border community" of Russia and Belarus was to open the way to creating similar communities with Kazakhstan, Kyrgyzstan, and Tajikistan, although in the last two cases this is highly questionable. Tighter security controls within the Central Asian region to reduce drugs traffic and illegal migration is envisaged. There is little doubt that the Russian border troops will leave in due course; as for CIS cooperation, it is likely to be bilateral, patchy, and difficult.

An analogue of the joint border controls is the joint air defense system of the CIS, which is the one active and generally successful element of intra-commonwealth military cooperation.

Still, the double border strategy, for all its imperfections, has given Russia a partial break to start constructing its own border controls along the new national perimeter, which is now Moscow's priority,[52] while at the same time assisting the new states to create their own border troops. This came at a price, both in lives and money. The break, meanwhile, is coming to an end.

Ways and Means

In the U.S.S.R., the protection of borders was the responsibility of the KGB. The Soviet border, the proverbial Iron Curtain, was in reality a gigantic system of electric signals. When the KGB was broken up, border troops were organized under a separate committee, which between 1992 and

1993 was briefly part of the new Security Ministry. The present Federal Border Service (in Russian, FPS) was established under the presidential decree of December 30, 1993 as an independent agency whose director reported to the head of state. In the following year, a concept of border protection was approved, together with the fundamentals of the "border policy." In 1996, a new law on the state border of the Russian Federation was enacted. These moves provided a new legal, administrative, and material basis for border controls in the post-Soviet era.

The Federal Border Service rose in prominence among Russia's "power agencies" under the assertive leadership of General Andrei Nikolayev, its first director (July 1993-December 1997). He quickly understood that preserving the Soviet border culture was a mission impossible. While an army officer himself with strong links to the Russian General Staff, where he had served as a first deputy chief, Nikolayev, driven as much by personal ambitions as by his convictions, started steering the FPS away from its Soviet-era reliance on an essentially military structure.

When the Soviet Union broke up, Russia was faced with a wide and growing gap between the mounting problems along its borders and its dwindling capacity to deal with them. It did not help that the best assets—accounting for some two-fifths of the overall capabilities of the Federal Border Service—had to be left behind in the newly independent states.

General Nikolayev, having centralized all spending in his own hands, made soldiers' pay, food, and medical supplies his priorities. There was little money left for buying fuel or replacing old equipment, but Nikolayev became popular with his subordinates, who were regarded with envy by their colleagues in other branches of the military and security establishment. The FPS chief was actively lob-bying both the government and parliament to legally allo-cate a fixed percentage of the GDP (0.3 percent) for its needs. He did not succeed in reaching that goal, but the funding of the FPS was generally better, in relative terms, than that of the Defense Ministry forces.

The border troops' strength was reduced from about 200,000 to 143,000 uniformed personnel (of which 32,000-36,000 were volunteers serving under contracts and 18,000 were women) and some 12,000 civilians. Relatively better social protection and confident leadership have attracted many officers retiring from the armed forces. But this effect was rather short-lived. In 1997, the border troops stood at 97 percent of their assigned strength, with 92 percent officer and 100 percent enlisted men's positions filled. It used 95-100 ships and 80-90 aircraft (out of 300) daily to patrol the border.[53] The equipment, however, was often deficient or obsolete. Between 30 and 50 percent of the equipment, including radar, electric systems, and vehicles, have served out their life cycles. One-half of the electric signaling sys-tems and radar need immediate replacement.[54]

Border Service Reform

The centerpiece of the Border Service reform conceptual-ized under Nikolayev and approved by a presidential de-cree of December 8, 1997[55] is the progressive demilitarization of the agency and its transformation into a "special state service." The FPS guidelines to 2000 and beyond (to 2010) suggest a phased reduction of the border troops' strength and an increase of the non-military component, which should amount to roughly one-half of the total strength of the service, giving it a wholly new and friendlier image. The rough model is the German *Bundesgrenzschutz*, although in many practical ways the Russians have emulated the Finnish Border Guards. From 1998, the border troops started giving up their heavy weapons, such as infantry combat vehicles, artillery systems of caliber 100 mm or more, Mi-24 attack helicopters, and some ships, which were useless against the new challenges and a substantial burden on the budget. A more difficult task, however, will be to get funding for procuring specialized vehicles, light aircraft, speedboats, and other technical equipment.

The reform provides for the formation of a Maritime Guard and the creation of a system to protect Russian interests in the Exclusive Economic Zone and on the continental shelf.[56]

From 1998, border troops' districts are being converted into ten regional border administrations.[57] By 2001, the FPS was set to become a "special government agency." As in pre-revolutionary Russia, the core of the service will consist of a border guard and a coast guard, *not troops*. Although the FPS denied that these measures will "immediately" affect Russia's presence on the borders of Tajikistan and in the Transcaucasus, in the latter case this was becoming increasingly likely.

In 1996, a presidential decree opened the way to an "experiment" of recruiting local civilians, preferably reserve military officers, for the guarding of Russia's borders with CIS states and Mongolia.[58] In Kazakhstan, however, concerns were raised at the highest level about a possible creation within the FPS of armed Cossack units, which would mean a potential for troublemaking along the common border. Since 1997, recruitment of local civilians as part-time FBS employees to police Russian borders has been officially designated standard practice.

Another "experiment" is leasing checkpoints to commercial firms, as on the Russo-Chinese border.[59]

Although FPS reform is advertised as part of a general reform of the military establishment, the key bureaucratic reason for it is to prevent all attempts to integrate the FPS into the Defense Ministry structure. The new regional command structure has been devised to avoid border service headquarters' being absorbed within the military districts. By dropping the word "troops" from its title, the border guards hoped to escape from being integrated within the General Staff-run comprehensive military organization, vigorously promoted by the General Staff's chief, Anatoly Kvashnin.

The relations between the two were uneasy from the start. First, both agencies compete for the same limited pool of manpower, financial, and other resources. The FPS was more successful in public lobbying, which made the Defense Ministry naturally envious. Second, the Defense Ministry has been consistently trying since the tenure of General Grachev to bring the border troops under at least the operational and ideally also the administrative control of the General Staff. In the FPS view, on the contrary, it is the Border Service that should be Russia's only "gatekeeper."

The process of making the FPS a more civilian force appears to be a reversal of previous policies aimed at giving it a combat role supported by a mightier military arsenal (including tanks, self-propelled artillery, and helicopter gunships). The number of general officers within FPS rose to 195 in 1997 compared with 70 during the time at which border guards were part of the KGB.[60] Under the concept, the Defense Ministry will be responsible for guarding and protecting the border, as well as defending it.

Nikolayev wanted the FPS to be the sole gatekeeper, running a system that combined border, customs, immigration, and other controls. Bureaucratic wars followed. The 1997 National Security Concept, however, only talked about ensuring the "consolidation of efforts" of all government agencies and giving the FPS a "coordinating role."[61]

Nikolayev's unexpected dismissal in December 1997 left the agency temporarily leaderless and virtually defenseless against attempts at bureaucratic conquests. In January 1998 President Yeltsin placed the FPS under partial operational control of the Federal Security Service (FSB), the main domestic successor to the KGB. After his retirement, General Nikolayev criticized "persistent attempts" to return the border service to the tutelage of the counter-espionage agency.[62]

The reform concept treated borders as interfaces, rather than fortress walls. It contains provisions for facilitating border crossings, building more checkpoints, etc. But, along the perimeter of Russian borders, the FPS is confronted with very different challenges. Problems include: large-scale poaching in the Far East and the Caspian; smuggling along the borders with the Baltic States, Ukraine, and Georgia; weapons and drugs in Tajikistan and the Caucasus; and illegal migration in the Far East.

To deal with these problems, since 1994, the FPS has mounted several major operations to strengthen controls. One of these, code-named "Putina," had the purpose of keeping Russian fisheries safe from transgressors; another, "Zaslon," was meant to stop illegal exports of raw materials; a third, "Rubezh," was aimed at illegal migration. Only a small fraction of these border violations can be prevented.[63]

Development of international border cooperation has been the hallmark of General Nikolayev's directorship. His professed goal was the creation of a borderline security belt and security zones along Russia's borders. "Border diplomacy" has become a tool to reach that goal.

Since 1993, Russia has signed border cooperation agreements with Norway, Finland, Estonia, Latvia, Lithuania, and Poland. The Russian FPS is a member of the International Conference on Border Issues. Encouraged by professional cooperation with Finnish and Estonian colleagues, Nikolayev proposed in May 1997 the creation of a Baltic regional council of border service chiefs as part of the Baltic Sea States Cooperation Council. Compiling a common data bank, improving communication, and creating a unified command for joint operations have been suggested as specific areas of interaction. Since 1996, FPS operations such as "Rubezh" are being organized in cooperation with European neighbors, including Ukraine, Belarus, and the Baltic States. In 1997, Russian and Norwegian border and coast guards were engaged in joint training as part of the international Barents-97 exercise. Nikolayev, naively, went as far as to suggest that cross-border cooperation, in particular the creation of a security belt along the borders, could be a "real alternative to military blocs" such as NATO.[64]

Conclusion

The dismantlement of the U.S.S.R. raised the important issue of the Russian government's general attitude to the changes of borders outside of the former Soviet space. As its policies in the 1990s demonstrate, Moscow does not object to voluntary mergers (such as the reunification of Germany) and separations (as in the case of Czechoslovakia and Ethiopia/Eritrea), but it is very concerned in cases where separation is less than amicable. (In Europe, the most serious case was that of Croatia and Slovenia in 1991/1992.

Many in Russia still lay a heavy part of the blame for the conflicts in Yugoslavia on the action of the German government, which was the first to recognize Zagreb and Ljubljana, making the rest of the European Union follow suit.)

Faced with the problem of Chechnya, Russia has become an even stronger supporter of the territorial integrity of states, especially in the face of armed rebellions. It regards Taiwan, Tibet, and Xinjiang as integral parts of China, and has joined Beijing and the Central Asian states in an effort to fight Muslim separatism. By tradition, Moscow has been supportive of the Indian position on Kashmir, which Soviet and Russian maps consistently show as part of India, divided by a demarcation line. Politically, Russia condemns rebel incursions into the Indian-held territory: Moscow and New Delhi (and indeed Beijing) are faced not just with similar problems, but also a similar kind of enemy.

Muslim separatists worry Russia elsewhere. Moscow firmly states that even after the 1999 conflict in Kosovo it regards the province as part of Yugoslavia. It darkly warns the Western powers against encouraging Greater Albanian nationalism, fearing that it could undermine the stability of the neighboring states. However, Russia did not support Slobodan Milosevic's attempts to turn Yugoslavia into a unitary state, liquidating Montenegro's status as a constituent republic alongside Serbia. Equally, Moscow sided with the international community at the UN Security Council in pressing Jakarta to release East Timor, which it had occupied for 23 years. As a nominal co-sponsor of the Middle East peace process, Moscow favors any agreement that can be reached between the Israelis and the Palestinians (with the United States acting as a mediator).

Russian officials and experts agree that eventually Korea, like Germany and Vietnam, will be reunified, though they would very much prefer it if this proceeded along the German, not Vietnamese, model. They also believe that in the long run Taiwan should join the mainland, but would abhor a military conflict across the Taiwan Strait, which would probably involve the United States and could suck in others, including Russia itself. Thoughtful Russian analysts are already thinking about the implications of both of these momentous potential developments for the Russian Far East and Siberia.

Thus, Russia is in principle a status quo power, but it supports territorial changes on condition that these are resolved peacefully. The break-up of the U.S.S.R. marked the end of a long tradition of Russia's integrating neighboring territories and turning the new arrivals into parts of Russia itself. The end of the Soviet Union is final, and the links that will survive and—in some areas—develop between Russia and the former republics are unlikely to lead to the creation of a new federation. A loose political union would not be in the interests of Russia, and recentralization would far surpass Russia's capacity for absorption, and run contrary to the current processes in the former Eurasia. Hypothetically, Russia can enlarge itself, but in a modest way, to include Belarus (although there are substantial problems related to that). As to eastern Ukraine/the Crimea, or northern Kazakhstan, such "augmentation" can hardly be peaceful; it will only come as a result of new geopolitical catastrophes resulting from the failure of the two other biggest post-Soviet successor states.

NOTES

[1] Ivan Ilyin, *Osnovy borby za natzionalnuyu Rossiyu* (1938), Moscow, 1992, p. 62.

2   See, for example, Vitaly Tretyakov et al., "Vozroditsya li Soyuz?" Theses of the Council on Foreign and Defense Policy, *NG—Stsenarii*, May 23, 1996, and his more recent piece, "Rossiya: posledny pryzhok v budush-cheye," *Nezavisimaya gazeta*, February 24, 2000, p. 8.

3   Interestingly, Vladimir Putin repeated the phrase during the 2000 presidential campaign.

4   Hannes Adomeit, *Imperial Overstretch: Germany in Soviet Foreign Policy from Stalin to Gorbachev*, Nomos, Baden Baden, 1998.

5   Vitaly Tretyakov, "Razvalitsya li Rossiya?" *NG—Stsenarii*, No. 12, 1998, p. 2.

6   Anatol Lieven, *Chechnya: A Tombstone of Russian Power*, Yale University Press, New Haven, 1998.

7   To avoid further embarrassment, the authorities attempted to recast June 12 as "Russia Day" (1998), then "Sovereignty Declaration Day" (1999), and finally going back to "Russia Day" (2000).

8   This was no case of ineptly handling the situation, but an abrupt loss of interest. It was not until the start of the NATO enlargement debate in the fall of 1993 that the Russian political elite rediscovered an interest in Eastern, now Central, Europe—and again, typically, for strategic reasons.

9   Paul Kennedy provides an impressive list of those. See Paul Kennedy, *The Rise and Fall of Great Powers*, New York, Vintage Books, 1987, pp. 488-514. Yet, even Kennedy emphatically stated at the bottom of the list that Soviet deficiencies did not mean that the U.S.S.R. was close to collapse.

10 For an excellent analysis of the Soviet Union's secular decline, see Thomas Graham, "A World Without Russia?", a paper presented at the Jamestown Foundation Conference, Washington, D.C., June 9, 1999. Note also the Russian translation of this piece in *Nezavisimaya gazeta*, December 8, 1999.

11 In a very prescient comment dating back to the late 1920s, Georgy Fedotov, a major Russian émigré thinker, wrote that "under the cover of international Communism cadres of nationalists are being formed, determined to tear apart Russia's historical body." See Georgy Fedotov, "Budet li sushchestvovat Rossiya?" *Vestnik RSKD*, No. 1-2, 1929, quoted from *Novoye vremya*, No. 10, 1992, pp. 57-59. Stalin's subse-

quent purge of "bourgeois nationalists" only delayed, but did not stop this process.

[12] Even Gorbachev in his international best selling book, *Perestroika*, which appeared in 1988, failed to see the imminent threat of disintegration (see Russ. ed., pp. 118-122).

[13] The so-called Novo-Ogaryovo process, from the name of a government residence outside Moscow where the meetings were held in 1990-November 1991, between the Soviet president and heads of the republics.

[14] The signing of the treaty was scheduled for August 20, 1991. The conspirators struck on the 19th. In the days that followed, most Soviet republics declared their independence from the U.S.S.R. Russia and Ukraine issued their declarations on the 24th, Belarus on the 25th, Moldova on the 27th, Azerbaijan on the 30th, Kyrgyzstan and Uzbekistan on the 31st. The Baltic States, which de facto broke off from the U.S.S.R. on August 19, were formally recognized as independent on September 6, 1991.

[15] See Art. 5 of the *Agreement on the Formation of the Commonwealth of Independent States* of December 8, 1991.

[16] "Re-establishment by the Bolsheviks of the Russian empire under the name of the U.S.S.R. is a unique case in modern history, but this may not be a unique precedent for Russia 'picking up the pieces' of a 'disintegrated state,'" said a statement by an influential group, the Council on Foreign and Defense Policy. See "Vozroditsya li Soyuz?" in *NG—Stsenarii,* May 23, 1996, p. 4.

[17] It was only in June 1999 that Turkmenistan became the first state to introduce visa requirements for travelers from other CIS countries.

[18] Membership of the Customs Union includes Belarus, Kazakhstan, Kyrgyzstan, Russia, and Tajikistan.

[19] See Boris Berezovsky's interview with *Sodruzhestvo NG*, No. 10 (November), 1998, p. 1.

[20] This idea was suggested by Andrei Zagorsky, the Russian political analyst.

[21] Even the hard-nosed realists from the Council for Foreign and Defense Policy believed in 1992 that reintegration of most of the former U.S.S.R. was feasible. See "Strategia dlya Rossii," *Nezavisimaya gazeta*, August 19, 1992, p. 5.

22 See the *National Security Concept*, approved on January 5, 2000; the *Military Doctrine*, approved on April 21, 2000; and the *Foreign Policy Concept*, released on July 10, 2000.

23 This was especially evident during the Chechen war of 1994-1996 and again in the wake of the Dagestani fighting in 1999.

24 The Russian Federation remains the world's largest country by far. It covers 17.4 million sq. km of territory, plus 8.5 million sq. km of exclusive economic zone.

25 See, e.g., the statements made in 1999 by Prime Ministers Stepashin and Putin, former Prime Minister Primakov, and leading political strategists such as Sergei Karaganov.

26 Yury Golubchikov, "Russky shchit dlya velikikh civilizatsii," *Pravda-5*, January 4-9, 1998, p. 6. See also Vladimir Zhirinovsky's speech in the Duma on August 16, 1999, during the confirmation of Vladimir Putin as Russia's prime minister.

27 Alexei Pushkov, "Amerika—novaya sverkhderzhava Yevrazii," *Nezavisimaya gazeta*, November 14, 1997, p. 5.

28 Sergei Glaziev, "Russofobia," *Nezavisimaya gazeta*, November 11, 1997, p. 5. For a more recent reference, see ITAR-TASS commentary published in *Krasnaya Zvezda*, September 29, 2000, p. 3.

29 See Yury Godin, "Zapad vsyo aktivneye ispolzuyet Polshu," *Nezavisimaya gazeta*, June 5, 1999.

30 This is indeed the title of a most insightful piece by Thomas Graham, cited above.

31 Alexander Fadeyev, "Belarus kak soyuznik Rossii," in Konstantin Zatulin (ed.), *Na puti k vossoyedineniyu Belarusi i Rossii*, Institute of CIS Countries, Moscow, 1999, p. 76.

32 See President Lukashenko's clear statement in his 2000 annual message to the National Assembly: "I believe it necessary to dwell once again on the issue of the sovereignty of the Republic of Belarus within the Union state. . . . As President of my country I repeatedly said and will say it again: Belarus is and will remain independent and sovereign. Such is our course. This is the people's choice." Quoted from *Yevraziisky vestnik*, No. 1-2 (April-May, 2000) (www.e-journal.ru).

[33] For Slobodan Milosevic, the idea of a trilateral "union" was a clear propaganda ploy. It was never raised after the end of the 1999 air war.

[34] The typical Stalin-era phrase reflects an idea that has become deeply ingrained in the Soviet collective mind, which is: "Our frontiers are impregnable, they are clothed in steel and concrete." See *Rodina*, A Reader, Molodaya Gvardiya, Moscow, 1939, p. 22.

[35] The aerial dimenzion of the border was as important. The downing of the American U-2 spy plane over Sverdlovsk in 1960 was a major boost to the Soviet leadership's self-confidence. The resolve was still there in 1983, when a Soviet fighter shot down the Korean Air Lines Boeing 747 over Sakhalin Island. It was symptomatic, however, that only five years later a light Cessna plane piloted by a German youth could manage to fly across Russia and land in Moscow's Red Square, which resulted in the dismissal of the defense minister and an unprecedented fall in the military's prestige as an institution.

[36] This issue is explored in more detail in Chapter 6.

[37] These same questions were first discussed in a modern context by Alexander Solzhenitsyn, in his "Kak nam obustroit Rossiyu?" See *Literaturnaya gazeta*, September 18, 1990, pp. 3-6.

[38] Russian nationalists, such as Konstantin Zatulin and Dmitri Rogozin, on the contrary, argue that precisely that syndrome should be cultivated as a prime factor working for integration. See "Vozroditsya li Soyuz?" p. 5.

[39] Estimated to be around $1.5 billion over ten years. See Andrei Nikolayev (former director of the Federal Borders Service) writing in *Nezavisimaya gazeta*, December 26, 1997, p. 2.

[40] *Nezavisimaya gazeta*, December 17, 1992, p. 2.

[41] *Osnovy pogranichnoi politiki Rossiiskoi Federatsii* (Fundamentals of the Border Policy of the Russian Federation), as approved by the President of the Russian Federation on October 5, 1996.

[42] *Poslaniye po natzionalnoi bezopasnosti Prezidenta Rossiiskoi Federatsii Federalnomu Sobraniyu Rossiiskoi Federatsii*, June 25, 1996, Annex 10. Policy Toward the CIS.

[43] For Moscow, formally guarding foreign borders was not entirely new. In 1944-1945, the Red Army temporarily controlled the frontier between

Poland and Czechoslovakia, and in 1949-1952, Soviet forces patrolled the inter-German boundary.

[44] Pavel Milyukov, *Istoriya russkoi kultury*, Progress, Moscow, Vol. 1, Part 2, 1993, p. 460.

[45] Vitaly Strugovets, "Strategiya dvukh rubezhei," *Itogi*, December 9, 1997, p. 28.

[46] Andrei Nikolayev, *Na perelome: zapiski russkogo generala*, Sovetsky Pisatel, Moscow, 1998, p. 171.

[47] *Kommersant-Daily,* December 6, 1997, p. 2.

[48] See, for example, "Tam vdali, za khrebtom." (An interview with Lieutenant General Mikhail Naimilo, Commander of the Russian operational border group in Armenia), *Krasnaya zvezda*, May 27, 2000, p. 2.

[49] Andrei Korbut, "Gruppirovka pogranvoisk RF v Tadzhikistane sokrashchayetsya," *Nezavisimaya gazeta*, February 7, 1998.

[50] Anyone so naive as to hope that the presence of Russian border guards would make the host countries safe for Russian trade and investment was bitterly disappointed. Investments, of course, are in short supply in Russia itself; as to trade, Russia's share in Tajikistan's foreign trade dropped to 20 percent, roughly the same share as in Lithuania. The volume of Russo-Tajik commerce fell from $2.9 billion in 1991 to $215 million in 1996. See *Itogi*, December 9, 1997, p. 29.

[51] Andrei Nikolayev, "Sozdany osnovy spetsialnoi gosudarstvennoi sluzhby," *Nezavisimaya gazeta*, December 26, 1997, p. 2.

[52] FPS Director Konstantin Totsky, writing in *Krasnaya zvezda*, December 15, 1998, p. 2.

[53] *Itogi,* December 9, 1997, p.18.

[54] See Andrei Nikolayev's interview with *NVO*, November 19, 1997.

[55] Andrei Nikolayev, "Sozdany osnovy spetsialnoi gosudarstvennoi sluzhby," pp. 1 and 2.

[56] Yury Golotyk, "Na okhranu ekonomicheskoi zony Rossii zavtra mogut vyiti kreisery," *Russky telegraf*, November 26, 1997, p. 1.

57   Arctic, Northwestern, Kaliningrad, Western, North Caucasus, Southeastern, Baikal, Far Eastern, Pacific, and Northeastern, with headquarters in St. Petersburg, Smolensk, Voronezh, Stavropol, Chelyabinsk, Chita, Vladivostok, and Khabarovsk.

58   Nikolai Plotnikov, "Federalnaya Pogranichnaya Sluzhba provodit eksperiment," *Nezavisimaya gazeta,* July 11, 1997, p. 2.

59   Vladimir Chesnokov, "Zastava Rodinu zashchitit," *Noviye izvestia,* December 18, 1998, p. 7.

60   *Kommersant-Daily,* January 24, 1998, p. 1.

61   "Kontseptsiya natsionalnoi bezopasnosti," *Rossiiskaya gazeta,* December 25, 1997, p. III.

62   Andrei Nikolayev, *Na perelome*, p. 11.

63   In 1996, the FPS apprehended 3,000 people traveling on false papers, and detained 6,000 people who tried to violate borders. Border guards seized 3.5 tons of drugs, 430 guns, and 120,000 rounds of ammunition. See Colonel General Alexander Tymko, "Rubezhi otechestva—ponyatiye svyatoye," *NVO,* No. 20, June 7-13, 1997, p. 1.

64   Andrei Nikolayev, "Vzaimodeistviye na gosudarstvennykh rubezhakh," *NVO,* No. 34, September 12-18, 1997, p. 1.

Part Two

RUSSIA'S THREE FAÇADES

Russia's Three Façades

Geographically, Russia has three principal borders with the outside world connecting it to three very different macro-regions and three very different civilizations: the European West, the Islamic South, and the Asian/Pacific East. At the turn of the 21st century, European integration, Muslim revival, and the rise of Asia present very different, but direct challenges to Russia's emerging post-imperial identity. The way the Russian government decides to tackle these challenges will not only reflect, but also have an impact upon the nature of the Russian political regime.

The contraction of national territory did not lead to a reduction of Russia's problems with its neighbors. In fact, the opposite is true.[1] When the Soviet Union came apart, 13,500 kilometers of the borders of the Russian Federation—roughly four-fifths of the entire land boundary of Russia—were not fixed de jure. The new borders were neither delimited nor demarcated. This led to overt or latent border disputes. By one count, in December 1991, Russia had border problems with 10 out of its 16 neighbors. Conscious of Russia's weaknesses, Russians were afraid that, in the wake of the dismantlement of the Soviet Union, neighboring states would make claims on Russian territory, and that the borderlands, this time on the fringes of the Russian Federation, would be only too happy to secede from an impoverished and enfeebled Russia. Territorial issues with Finland and Germany over Karelia and Kaliningrad, respectively, were of particular concern in Moscow at that time. Those concerns have since been put to rest, but many problems remain. Not even Russia's Arctic frontier is problem-free. Thus, the goal of forming a "belt of good-neighborly relations along the perimeter of Russian borders," a task first formulated by Andrei Kozyrev in the early 1990s, is still very much on the agenda at the start of the new century.[2]

Border-related issues are as different as Russia's neighbors from the Baltic States to Tajikistan to Japan. It would be useful to group them according to the geographic regions: the Western façade; the Southern tier; and the Far East.

The problem on Russia's European borders is the emergence of new states; the advantage here is that this is proceeding within an integrated environment, a pan-European context, which provides some mechanisms for dealing with the problem.

For generations of Russians, Europe had long been a pole of attraction, and borders there had added significance, fixing the country's standing vis-à-vis other powers. This was especially so in the wake of World War II. The 1945 lines, marking Russia's longest reach into the heart of Europe, were considered to be among the Soviet Union's supreme achievements from the war. By the mid-1980s, the Soviet establishment had developed a conviction that these borders, sanctified by the 1975 Helsinki Final Act, were not only inviolable, but also immutable. When changes started under Mikhail Gorbachev, their significance was initially downplayed. East Germany's absorption by West Germany was taken to be an exception. No non-German territory was involved, the reunification had a clear popular mandate, ratified by international consent. Soon, however, the number of states in Europe has increased by more than a dozen, with armed conflicts erupting within some, not least in the former Soviet territory. The Helsinki principle thus became hotly debated.

The Kosovo and Chechnya crises raised two issues: the right of secession and the right of outsiders to intervene in what since the 1648 peace of Westphalia had come to be regarded as the internal affairs of sovereign nations. For Russia, Chechnya raises the all-important issue of its relations with the Muslim world both on Russia's periphery and within its borders. The alternative to broadening the Russian identity to fully integrate the Muslim component is turning Russia into a hotspot, if not a battlefield, in the conflict between Islamic revivalists and Russian nationalist protectors of Orthodoxy. The alternative to building a viable relationship with the Muslim world along its southern borders is the emergence of a conflict with a neighborhood that is becoming increasingly populous and better armed. This could take the form of Russia's assuming its "traditional" role of a shield of Western civilization against the dark forces of barbarism, extremism, and terrorism.

This argument, although popular, is fundamentally flawed. First, Russia is defending itself. Second, the notion that Russia is defending global values comes after the fact. Necessity is turned into a virtue. Third, when it is in its interest, the West occasionally cultivates Russia's enhanced self-image.

The terrorist attack against the United States, launched on September 11, 2001, radically changed the situation. Non-governmental actors have demonstrated the capacity to use violence on a scale previously thought to be the sole privilege of the states. In a globalized environment, the terrorists have also shown the ability to easily cross borders and operate networks that link countries and continents. A fight against terrorism is being waged on different levels and in various spheres. It has become clear, however, that much of the action will concentrate on the

Greater Middle East, and that Russia will be one of the key players.

In the mid-18th century, Mikhail Lomonosov, the leading Enlightenment figure and founder of Russia's first university, claimed that "Russia's might will be growing thanks to Siberia." At the turn of the 21st century, the fate of Siberia and the Russian Far East is likely to be Russia's most crucial geopolitical problem. There is a rapid disintegration of the entire infrastructure of the area, which was essentially more Soviet than virtually any other part of the U.S.S.R., owing to the heterogeneous population, which had come from across the Soviet Union; the dominance of the military industrial complex; the massive industrial projects; the gigantic scientific centers; the heritage of the Gulag; especially tight isolation from the outside world, including the immediate neighborhood; a relatively higher standard of living; and the prevalence of Soviet societal norms. Unless ways could be found to reintegrate the Asian portion of Russia within the Russian Federation, and simultaneously to integrate it into Asia-Pacific, Russia might well lose 13 million square kilometers (three quarters) of its territory east of the Urals, and the vast expanses and the natural riches of the territory might become an object of intense international competition.[3]

NOTES

[1]   The Russian Federation borders on 16 countries, and the total length of these boundaries is 60,930 km, compared with the Soviet Union's 61,000 km and the Russian Empire's 64,900 versts, or 69,300 km.

[2]   *The Foreign Policy Concept of the Russian Federation* (July 2000), Section I ("General Provisions").

[3]   See ibid.

CHAPTER III

The Western Façade

Russian leaders have traditionally regarded their country's position in Europe as critically important to Russia's overall international posture and its role in world affairs. It is in Europe that post-Soviet Russia's situation has undergone the most profound changes. It is also in Europe that Russia can now hope to seize the best opportunities available to it. In the west and the north, Russia borders on three sets of countries:

- the traditional Western nations;
- the new Western nations;
- the former Soviet states.

Vis-à-vis the traditional Western nations, it is not the borders per se that are of primary importance: boundaries with Norway, Finland, and the United States are generally unproblematic (though not without latent disputes and lingering suspicions); the biggest problems stem from the enlargement of the "territory" belonging to Western institutions, such as NATO and the European Union. This enlargement challenges Russia to reappraise its position in Europe.

With the countries of the "new West" (Poland and, by extension, other countries of Central and Southeastern Europe which border on the CIS states, i.e., Hungary, Romania, and Slovakia), territorial boundaries are nominally more important. They are changing their nature thanks to the finality of the Russian withdrawal from the region and the prospects of these countries' accession to NATO and the

EU. For the first time in 50 years, Central and Eastern Europe will belong to an alliance that excludes Russia. The three Baltic countries, Estonia, Latvia, and Lithuania, form a very special subgroup within that category because of their long history as part of the Russian Empire and the U.S.S.R.; the existence of a sizable Russian minority, especially in Estonia and Latvia; the still formally unresolved territorial disputes between Russian and those two countries; and the Kaliningrad enclave, wedged between Poland and Lithuania.

Lastly but most importantly, borders with the former Soviet states, Belarus and Ukraine—with Moldova more or less loosely associated with this group—raise the most difficult challenge flowing from the split of the Eastern Slav core of old Russia. Is the separation of Russia, Ukraine, and Belarus final, or merely an interlude, to be followed by new "reunification"? The pull of history is enormously powerful. At the same time, acceptance of the new realities is an admission fee for participating in a pan-European process where the Russian Federation could use its advantages to pursue emerging opportunities.

The Traditional West

In its northwest and the Arctic, Russia has:
- a latent issue of Karelia, part of which used to belong to Finland before 1940;
- a lingering dispute with Norway over a portion of the Arctic;
- a broadly similar dispute with the United States settled in a 1990 agreement, which remains controversial in Russia and has not been ratified by its parliament; and

- the problem of the continental shelf in the Arctic ocean.

Moreover, Russia faces the challenge of the territorial and functional expansion of Western institutions and the quality of the boundaries separating it from its Cold War adversaries.

When the U.S.S.R. collapsed, the only legally defined and properly demarcated borders the Russian Federation inherited were with Finland, Poland (in Kaliningrad), and the land border with Norway.

Finland, of course, was a largely self-governing part of the Russian Empire between 1809 and 1917, whose independence was recognized by Lenin's government in December 1917 and where the local Bolsheviks failed to prevail in the civil war of 1918. Since the dismantlement of the U.S.S.R., claims have been raised by various political forces in Finland to the part of Karelia which was annexed by the Soviet Union as a result of the Winter War of 1939-1940 started by Stalin, and confirmed by the treaty of peace of 1947, which ended the second Soviet-Finnish war (1941-1944) begun by the Finns in alliance with Germany to regain the lost province.

During the Cold War, Soviet-Finnish relations were based on the Treaty of Friendship, Cooperation, and Mutual Assistance signed in 1948, which barred Finland from joining any alliance with Germany and provided for Finnish-Soviet cooperation in case of external aggression. Thus, Finland was turned into a protective Soviet buffer vis-à-vis NATO. This arrangement, while meeting Moscow's security concerns, did not curtail Finland's internal freedom. Though the term "Finlandization" was often used in a derogatory way, this was the best possible arrangement given the circumstances of the Cold War. Too bad it was not expanded at the time to include Central and Eastern Europe. An attempt to introduce it there in the late 1980s came too late.

Having fashioned a more equitable but still friendly relationship with Moscow after the end of the U.S.S.R., Helsinki chose not to challenge the existing borders. Still, statements of individual politicians and activities of associations such as the Karelia Union and the focusing of nearly all Finnish aid to Russia on the border region have kept some Russian officials on alert. These suspicions have contributed to the rather sorry state of cross-border cooperation in this region. The major change along the Russo-Finnish border, however, is linked to Finland's accession in 1995 to the European Union.

In 1997, President Yeltsin went as far as to suggest "joint control" of the 1,300 km long Russian-Finnish border, the first frontier between Russia and an EU member state.[1] President Ahtisaari politely refused, and suggested raising the efficiency of border and customs controls instead. Finland's EU membership was not responsible for the decline of trade relations between the two countries, but it disappointed those who had hoped that this expansion of the union would immediately stimulate cross-border economic cooperation with Russia. Instead, the Finnish-Russian border has turned into a clear and dramatic dividing line between the Europe of the European Union and Russia. The question is whether this line will turn into a permanent watershed, which the Russians fear would permanently isolate them from a "Europe" that will have reached its eastern limit on the Russian border. The Finnish government's Northern Dimension initiative attempts to lay bridges to the east across the divide, linking the expanding European Union with the only country in the region unlikely to join the EU in the foreseeable future. This time, some

Russian officials are getting nervous about the possibility that northwest Russia could "defect" to the EU. So much for "Finlandization."

Norway presents Russia with a very different set of problems from Finland. Norway is not a member of the European Union, but during the Cold War it was one of only two NATO countries that had land borders with the U.S.S.R. In an attempt to keep tensions with the Soviet Union under control, Oslo assumed unilateral restrictions on allied military activity on its territory. A ban on permanent stationing of foreign military forces in Norway and on military exercises close to the Soviet border were in force throughout the period of confrontation. The buffer thus formed: (1) was unilateral; (2) was essentially a military confidence-building measure rather than a political commitment; and (3) existed only in peacetime. The end of the Cold War has made this self-restraint unnecessary, but Russia has been watching Western, especially U.S., military and intelligence-gathering activities in northern Norway and the Arctic with a wary eye.

The land boundary between the two countries is unproblematic. It was virtually uncontested ever since the times of Novgorod the Great.[2] In 1945, Soviet troops briefly invaded northern Norway to dislodge German occupation forces, but left promptly after the end of hostilities. The dismantlement of the Iron Curtain has led to massive cross-border exchanges in this region, remote by both countries' standards, but mass migration from Russia, much feared in the early 1990s, never took place.[3] Rather, a sense of a common belonging is emerging among the population of the Arctic region. Europe's Far North is slowly taking shape. The creation in 1992 of the Euro-Arctic Barents Council, which Russia co-founded, both reflected and promoted this.

By contrast, Moscow and Oslo have a long-standing dispute over a portion of the Barents Sea. The disputed area, between 155,000 and 180,000 square kilometers in area, is thought to contain large amounts of oil and gas. Some Russian estimates put it as high as 88 billion tons, comparable to Western Siberia's.[4] Negotiations on the border issue have been continuing since 1970. In 1978, unable to reach a final agreement, the two countries agreed to declare the contested borders a common "Gray Zone," and abide by certain rules.

Until the late 1990s, this issue had never aroused any emotions, and was routinely handled by diplomats. Problems were rare. In 1998, Russian fishermen, going after cod, ignored Norwegian restrictions en masse, which led to a brief diplomatic conflict. Since then, Russians have been increasingly concerned about Western (Norwegian, American, German) designs on their Arctic shelf. The Russian Security Council warned the government of the threat of Western economic expansion, coupled with military-political pressure "that could result in Russia being gradually eased out from the Arctic."[5]

Gone are the days when the U.S.S.R. was seeking to expand its presence in the Arctic Ocean. In 1920, Russia became one of the co-signatories of the Treaty on Spitzbergen (Svalbard), which was placed under Norwegian sovereignty, but where Russia retained the right to mine coal. During the Cold War, this foothold was of substantial strategic importance to the Soviet Union, but this role was lost with the end of confrontation, never to be replaced by any serious economic role.

In more general terms, Russia has a very special problem related to its Arctic sector established by the Soviet government's unilateral decision in 1926. This decision declared all the islands discovered within the portion of the Arctic ocean formed by the lines linking Russia's easternmost point on the Arctic coast and the westernmost one to the North Pole to belong to the U.S.S.R. The total area of Soviet polar possessions was 5.8 million square kilometers. The 1926 decision was never recognized by the Western countries and Japan, but neither was it challenged by anyone.

The issue is becoming more relevant now because of the vast fuel deposits expected to be located under the Arctic ice.[6] However, Moscow had to revise its stand on the sovereignty issue. In 1996, the Russian Federation joined the Law of the Sea Convention, which recognizes only a 200-mile-wide continental shelf as Russia's economic zone, with the rest of the sector, 1.7 million square kilometers, being made free for economic activity of all states.[7] All islands within the sector, of course, remain Russian, and their coastline adds to the shelf. This step was supported by a group of Russian governors who in 1999 introduced a bill on Russia's Arctic zone, which others, including Gazprom, contested trying to prove that the rest of the former Soviet sector is in fact a continuation of the Siberian continental shelf. The Russian media name the United States, Germany, and Norway as Russia's potential prime competitors in this area.

It took Moscow 12 years to negotiate an agreement with the United States on the sea border in the Bering Sea. The deal was signed in June 1990, and was ratified by the United States in the following year. The Soviet and later Russian parliaments refused to follow suit. The issue remains bitterly contested in Russia. Claiming that the agreement was a mistake (a "second Alaska sale"), for which then Foreign Minister Eduard Shevardnadze was responsible, Russian critics point out that 70 percent of the disputed area went to the United States, which has begun exploitation of the continental shelf, keeping Russian ships away from it.[8] In addition, there is some concern in Russia over the potential U.S. claims on the Wrangel Island off the coast of Chukotka.

Thus, the countries of the traditional West are Russia's direct neighbors in the very north of Europe and in the Arctic. These countries are stable, mature democracies, and are among the world's most prosperous nations. They also boast exemplary achievements in social justice, women's rights, environmental protection, and humanitarian assistance. The disputes among Norway, Finland, and Russia are perfectly manageable; moreover, the proximity to them—and through Finland, to the European Union—is a major external resource for Russia's domestic development. Finland's Northern Dimension initiative aims to help create a common space that would include Scandinavia and Russia. For its part, Russia has been slowly re-establishing links with its Nordic neighbors, but it is too far behind in development to actively engage them. Still, cross-border cooperation with the Nordic countries remains one of the most promising areas for Russia's "re-entry" into Europe.

The New West

The expansion of the European and Euro-Atlantic institutions, first of all, NATO and the European Union, is remaking the image of the "West." Former East European, now Central European countries, and the Baltic States, even as they are being Westernized, are adding new colors and qualities to the expanded Western community, which they are about to join.

Russia does not border on those countries directly, except for a relatively small sector in its Kaliningrad enclave that borders on Poland, but the westward march of the former Soviet satellites concerns Russia in several ways:

- it marks the finality of the Soviet withdrawal;
- it brings NATO and the EU to Russia's doorstep;
- it has a direct impact on Ukraine and Belarus, the two most important CIS countries to Russia, as well as Moldova.

Of all former Warsaw Pact countries Poland is the most important by far. Its population is 40 million, roughly 30 percent of Russia's own, and its GDP in 2000 was about one half of that of Russia. Poland is also strategically positioned on the main road linking Moscow to Berlin. It was in Poland that the fatal erosion of the "socialist community" began at the turn of the 1980s, led by the election of the Polish Pope and the rise of the Solidarity movement, and it was there that the first East European government headed by an anti-Communist politician was sworn in, in 1989.

After the fall of the Berlin Wall the Poles were concerned with keeping their borders intact in the face of Germany's reunification, and Warsaw quickly abjured historical claims to Ukraine's Lviv (Lwow), Lithuania's Vilnius (Wilno), and Belarus's Grodno, which were taken over by the Soviet Union as a result of the August 1939 deal between Molotov and Ribbentrop.

It was also because of the historical memories of being invaded, divided up, and ruled by Russia and Germany that the Poles were determined to become fully integrated within Western security and economic structures. After the Warsaw Pact was formally disbanded in early 1991, it took Warsaw only two years to apply for NATO membership. The Russians, who had come to regard the neutrality of their former allies as a protective buffer between their Western ex-adversaries-turned-partners and themselves, became deeply worried. They also believed they had been cheated by the West, whose leaders had given private and non-binding promises at the time of Germany's reunification that the NATO alliance would not move eastward. The dispute over NATO enlargement, which lasted from 1993 through 1999 when Poland, the Czech Republic, and Hungary were admitted into the alliance, was the defining episode in the post-Cold War security and political relationship between Russia and the West.

To the Russian military, Poland in NATO was above all an advantageous forward position vis-à-vis Russia. They feared Western nuclear and conventional deployments in that country and the extensive use of its infrastructure, which would enable NATO to strike anywhere west of the Volga River. When these concerns were alleviated in the Russia-NATO Founding Act of 1997, the breach of faith was already too wide to be fully repaired before the Kosovo crisis in 1999 sent the relationship to the lowest point after the end of the Cold War.

The Poles, however, can be relied upon to support Russia on one crucial point: its sovereignty over Kaliningrad.[9] In the Soviet-West German treaty of 1970 and again in the treaties governing German reunification twenty years later, Germany formally renounced any claims to any territories east of the Oder-Neisse line. Yet, there were lingering suspicions in Russia that once the former East Germany was fully reintegrated within a unified German state, it would be the turn of other territories lost in 1945 to be brought under the sway of Europe's most powerful country. The more Germany proceeded to liberate itself from the stigma of Nazi guilt, the argument went, the more "normal" it became, and the more likely it was to raise the territorial issue. The Russians were largely convinced of the sincerity of the current German leadership, but they feared those who would come after them. To some skeptics, NATO enlargement represented a step in that direction.[10]

In resisting this chain of events, however, the Russians believed they had allies in Poland. The reopening of the sovereignty issue would have automatically cast doubts over Poland's own boundaries. Two-thirds of the former Eastern Prussia was placed in 1945 under Polish administration. Exactly one third of the current Polish territory was German before World War II.[11] It may have been tempting for Poland in the early 1990s to seek full demilitarization of the enclave and its transformation into a fourth Baltic republic under EU protection, but realistically this could hardly have taken place smoothly; and once implemented, the new regime might not have proved sustainable.

It was Baltic independence that turned Kaliningrad into an exclave—the only case of non-contiguous land territory in modern Russian history.[12] Anyone traveling overland from mainland Russia to Kaliningrad would have to cross two borders. The most pressing problem was Russian military transit to and from Kaliningrad. Moscow was able to reach a compromise with Vilnius, which allowed an early Russian troop withdrawal from Lithuania itself, but this did not eliminate all concerns on either side. Moscow, worried that Vilnius may cut off the rail link to Kaliningrad, started to look for a possible alternative route. In order to avoid having to go through a Baltic country, deemed unfriendly almost by definition, in 1995-1996 the Russians floated a project of a rail and road connection linking Kaliningrad to Russia-loyal Belarus through Poland. Whoever thought this up was probably totally ignorant of the issue of the Danzig corridor, which became one of the principal points of tension between the two World Wars. The very idea of another "corridor," even the word itself, made the Poles allergic and suspicious. Moscow withdrew the suggestion, but Poland's decision to join NATO was thus vindicated.[13]

For their part, the Lithuanians are afraid that Russian forces in transit may pose security risks to them. They are determined to win an invitation to join NATO, even ahead of its two other Baltic cousins. When Lithuania becomes a member, Kaliningrad will be fully encapsulated inside the NATO territory. Analogies are already being drawn between its future fate and that of West Berlin during the Cold War. Of course, it would take a new Cold War for the analogy to stick.

In the case of Lithuania, the status of the boundary that separated it from Kaliningrad was not properly regulated within the U.S.S.R., which gave rise to two rival claims. Some Lithuanian national radicals demanded the annexation of Kaliningrad, which they called "Little Lithuania"; others voiced their preference for its becoming an independent statelet. This was countered by Russian nationalists in Moscow and Kaliningrad itself[14] who disputed Lithuania's rights over Klaipeda, the former Memel, which historically was part of the German East Prussia.[15] Unlike in the cases of Latvia and Estonia, however, the border issue never came to a head in Russia's relations with Lithuania. In October 1997, Lithuania became the first Baltic nation to have signed a treaty with Russia fixing the border de jure as well as de facto.[16] Lithuania had been singled out for reward before, with a Russian troop withdrawal, in 1993, a year earlier than the other two Baltic States. Moscow's special treatment of Lithuania had much to do with Vilnius's decision in 1991 to grant citizenship to all permanent residents of Lithuania. With less than 10 percent ethnic Russian population, compared with over 30 percent in the case of the two other Baltic States, the Lithuanians were prepared to be generous.

The very emergence of independent Estonia and Latvia, however, led to border claims by Tallinn and Riga. Whereas Moscow believed that it had generously granted independence, no strings attached, to the three former Soviet republics, the latter viewed this as a restoration of their independence unlawfully suspended by the Soviet Union—from 1940 through 1991—of which the Russian Federation claimed to be the successor. As both Estonia and Latvia lost parts of their pre-1940 territory to the Russian Republic while they were within the U.S.S.R., the border issue became emblematic of their attempts to "eliminate the consequences of Soviet occupation." Soviet-era decisions on territory transfer were nullified. This was logically linked to the overriding desire to recreate nations on the basis of pre-war citizenship.[17] In Tallinn's case, the additional problem was that the borderline had been fixed in the 1920 Treaty of Tartu, which also serves as a legal basis for Estonian independence. For the Russians, of course, there could have been no question of ceding the two overwhelmingly Russian-populated districts to Estonia (800 and 1,500 square kilometers in area, respectively) or Latvia (1,600 square kilometers).

The Baltic border claims initially conferred on their leaders an aura of romanticism at best, irresponsibility at worst. Ironically, however, these claims allowed Moscow, which did not have to worry about Estonian or Latvian "aggression," to declare that the two countries' policies were immature, obstinate, ethno-nationalistic in nature, and thus dangerous for peace and security in Europe. On the border issue, the Balts were diplomatically isolated, for no country would support their claim. In effect, the United States and the rest of Europe had to side with Russia on the issue. Unresolved border issues were also threatening to become obstacles on the way to Riga's and Tallinn's accession to Western institutions such as the European Union and NATO.

Russian nationalists even claimed that the Baltic States' unconstitutional secession from the U.S.S.R.—based on the decision by the U.S.S.R. State Council rather than on the relevant law—meant that they had forfeited their rights.[18] Ironically, in 1998 a few hundred Russian residents of Ivangorod, hard-pressed economically, ran a petition to join the sister city of Narva (also predominantly Russian-populated) in Estonia.

There was never any doubt about the outcome of the Russian-Baltic territorial disputes, of course. When the Russian government decided in 1992 to treat the existing boundaries with the Baltic States as full international borders, complete with border controls, and proceeded, in the absence of formal agreements, to demarcate the borders unilaterally, neither the Estonians nor the Latvians made any move to resist those attempts, which Moscow appreciated. However, when Latvia proceeded, in 1998, to demarcate its border unilaterally, Russia objected. Latvia and Estonia realized that they had no choice but to formally recognize Russia's sovereignty over the districts involved. Even if Russia had wanted to give the districts back, this would have only exacerbated the problems for Latvia and Estonia with their Russian minorities. Northeastern Estonia, for example, could have become a major ethnic Russian enclave.

As a result, from 1995 to 1996, both governments' positions became more flexible. Russia, however, showed little willingness to reach an early agreement on the border. Evidently, Moscow decided to use this as leverage in a double attempt to improve the legal status of ethnic Russians in Estonia and to put brakes on the Balts' integration into Western structures such as NATO. They warned that if Estonia and Latvia were to become members, their border problems with Russia would be "elevated to a higher level." This tactic, however, has been less than wholly successful, as the Baltic States were quick to present Moscow's attitude as obstructionist. It appeared then that, for both sides, the important thing was to make a political point; to insist on this point for much longer, however, could only be counter-productive. The Estonians and Latvians recognized this before the Russians. Moscow agreed to sign the Estonian border treaty only in March 1999. The Latvian one is still pending. For all the problems of borders, transit, and ethnicity, as well as the looming NATO enlargement, Moscow has officially proclaimed the Baltics the "most stable region" on its periphery.[19] Ironically, border issues are often more difficult and explosive in Russia's relations with its CIS partners. The main problem lies deeper.

The cumulative impact of all these different and interrelated processes is the end of the buffer zone, which many members of the Russian elites thought necessary for national security and for Russia's great power status, and the emergence of the new West. As a result, Russia is likely to come into direct contact with NATO and/or EU territory along the entire northwestern sector from the Kola Peninsula to Kaliningrad. Consequently, Russia's policy choices become starker, and the reasons for *both* integration and isolation become more compelling.

The *New* Eastern Europe

Russia, however, is not the only country in Europe unlikely to be integrated within the new West in the foreseeable future. Following the natural erosion of the post-Soviet space, a new Eastern Europe has emerged, whose members are grouped together not so much due to their participation in the CIS (which is not integrationist) but on the far firmer basis of the closeness of their economic situations, political systems, and societal processes. This new and only loosely organized region is made up of Ukraine, Belarus, Moldova, and European Russia. Since the three Eastern Slav republics of the former U.S.S.R. formed the nucleus of the traditional Russian Empire, the Russian Federation faces the most important identity problem in relating itself to Ukraine and Belarus.

Belarus, or Northwestern Territory?

The challenge Russia faces in its relations with Belarus is to go ahead with broad integration which is natural and beneficial for both countries, while still resisting the temptation of a full merger of the two states, which can only come in the form of Belarus's absorption by its eastern neighbor.

In purely strategic terms, Belarus is perhaps the most important country to Russia in Europe. It lies on the traditional main East-West axis for military invasions; it allows Russia direct access, through export pipelines, rail, and road links, to the core countries of Europe, NATO, and the European Union member-states; finally, it brings Russia in close proximity to its Kaliningrad exclave and hosts important Russian defense assets.

Traditionally viewed as an extension of Russia, Belarus had real problems establishing its own distinct identity. Upon independence, achieved automatically in 1991, which had virtually no precedent in history, the nationalist wing of the Belarussian elite attempted to reconstruct Belarussian sovereignty on the distant and vague memories of the Grand Duchy of Lithuania. On the face of it, their arguments appeared compelling,[20] but they logically demanded an anti-Russian sentiment to be converted to a popular myth, which was sorely lacking. The attempt to cast the 1514 defeat of the Moscow (i.e., Russian) troops by Lithuanian (i.e., Belarussian) forces at Orsha into a symbol of independence utterly failed.

Despite the many changes that the border between the Russian and the Belarussian republics has witnessed since the early 1920s, the existing boundary remains noncontroversial. This is primarily because, in Belarus, Russia is seen as the "Big Country," the main point of reference and the principal source of support; and in Russia, Belarus is deemed to be permanently friendly, unambitious, and deferential. If this had been different, for instance if the Belarussian Popular Front had come to power in Minsk, border problems would have possibly arisen. In the early 1990s, the Popular Front claimed the Russian regions of Pskov, Smolensk, and Bryansk as historically Belarussian. Meanwhile, the border, not yet properly delimited, is being de-demarcated: several of the few hastily installed border posts were dug out, with much fanfare, and in the presence of the two countries' leaders, in 1995. The Russian authorities had long been saying that they would like to restore the de facto "administrative" nature of borders with Belarus,[21] and by the turn of the century this was achieved.

It was this deficit of national identity that made the Belarussian nomenklatura lean on Moscow. A year before the arrival of Alexander Lukashenko, Prime Minister Kebich compromised Belarussian neutrality by joining the Collective Security Treaty and was negotiating accession to the ruble zone (1993). The populist Lukashenko, who nurtured ambitions reaching as high as the Moscow Kremlin, made a sustained effort to unify the two countries, often working against the more skeptical Russian leadership. Thus, a succession of treaties emerged that formed first a Russo-Belarussian Community (1996), then a Union (1997), and finally a Union State (1999). Yet, despite this paperwork a confederacy is still a long way off, and it is probably already too late for a merger. Unlikely as it appears, President Lukashenko, who created a neo-Soviet authoritarian regime in his republic, replaced national symbols with Soviet ones, and aspired to a union with Russia much more so than Moscow was ready to embrace Belarus, could be regarded as the true father of Belarussian independence. In his years in power, Belarus became so different from all its neighbors that it received for the first time a distinct image, if not an identity. And during this same period a critical momentum was built among the local elites in favor of continuing independent existence, while at the same time relying on Russia's support.

This was broadly supported by public opinion, which is in the process of a retarded self-identification. In the spring of 2000, over three quarters of the population identified themselves as Belarussian citizens. Just under one-half of those polled believed that Belarussians were a separate nation, as opposed to some 40 percent who thought that they were a branch of the three-part Russian (actually, Eastern Slav) nation. Nearly as many people favored a one-dimensional foreign policy orientation toward Russia and simultaneous orientation toward both Russia and the West, etc.[22]

Immediately, Russian-Belarussian integration will need to focus on creating a common economic space, coordinating foreign and defense policy, and harmonizing legislation. Although a common union territory, and hence a common external border, has been proclaimed, the two countries will retain their separate sovereignties.

Happily for Russia, Belarus for all its domestic problems does not have border disputes with any of its neighbors.[23] Still, one effect of NATO enlargement is that the West will necessarily have to pay more attention to Belarus, which now shares a border with an alliance member country. For Belarus, this means having to deal with the reality of NATO at its doorstep. Although here much will depend on the state of Russia's relations with the West. Minsk faces the choice of unquestionably playing the part of Russia's forward defense base, or looking for a distinct relationship with the Western alliance.[24]

So far, Russia has managed to keep Belarus within its orbit while avoiding paying the full cost of taking over the country. The Belarussian regime, however, poses problems to its partners, which can only be dealt with by means of a coherent strategy and close engagement. Under Yeltsin, both were clearly lacking.

Ukraine or "Little Russia"?

In contrast to Belarus, Ukraine is a totally different case. It was the Ukrainian referendum on independence on December 1, 1991 that finally sealed the fate of the Soviet Union. The main issue between Russia and Ukraine was the latter's independence from the former, not borders. For Ukrainians, independence means independence from Russia. It was thus natural, although unpleasant, to start constructing Ukrainian identity in opposition to Russia's. A Ukrainian, simply put, could be defined as a non-Muscovite. Thus, in principle, from the very beginning there was no territorial issue between Russia and Ukraine; the issue was rather Ukraine's existence within, or independent from, Russia. Acceptance of Ukrainian independence is essential for a Russia that has outlived the empire.

Thus, the territorial issues between Russia and Ukraine were raised, debated, and settled against the background of the divorce between the former Soviet Union's two largest republics. While in the 1990 Russian-Ukrainian Treaty, concluded when the U.S.S.R. still existed and neither contracting party was fully sovereign, both sides reaffirmed the borders existing between them at the time (those lines mattered little within a union state), territorial claims were raised immediately after Ukraine opted for full independence.

The claims laid by various Russian and Ukrainian marginal nationalist groups to large parts of the neighboring country's territory, whether eastern Ukraine and Novorossia or the Kuban and Don districts, respectively, were of little consequence. In a way, it is difficult to get a feel for the border between the two countries. The population of the border regions of both Ukraine and Russia is ethnically mixed and culturally and linguistically very close, even symbiotic, and ethnic nationalism is virtually non-existent. Moreover, local authorities on both sides of the border tend to work together rather than against each other.

The more serious issue was the Crimea and especially the city of Sevastopol. Influential quarters in Russia maintained that, with Ukraine now a foreign country, the previous border agreement was no longer valid. Later it was suggested that Russia's agreement to the borders was implicitly tied to Ukraine's full integration in the CIS and its "friendly attitude" to Russia. Officially, Moscow saw no urgent need for demarcating intra-CIS borders, while urging Ukraine to agree to joint protection of "external" CIS borders.

The Crimea, with its close to 70 percent Russian population, a distinctly Russian linguistic environment, and strong historical links to Russia, was given to Ukraine as recently as 1954 as a "present" to mark the tri-centennial of its accession to Russia. The Crimea, of course, has always occupied a very special place in the collective Russian mentality, and Sevastopol, a "city of Russian glory,"[25] is believed to be essentially Russian not only by the retired naval officers. Inside the Crimea, constituted in 1991 as a sovereign republic within Ukraine, political forces demanding full independence or accession to Russia were gaining the upper hand. Kiev's authority in the peninsula was becoming nominal. In this situation the Russian parliament officially raised the Crimea issue in the summer of 1993. The Russian government, which rejected any territorial claims to Ukraine, denounced the move, and the United Nations repudiated the parliament's demarche, which damaged Russia's reputation.

Seeking to win Ukraine's agreement to give up the Soviet nuclear arsenal in its territory, Russia consented to officially guarantee Ukraine's borders by virtue of the Tripartite Accords (Ukraine-Russia-the United States) of January 14, 1994 and the Budapest Declaration of December 5, 1994. The Russian government also refused to support the Crimean separatists. Still, Moscow was reluctant to sign a political treaty with Kiev, apparently hoping to wrestle some political concessions from its neighbor. In particular,

Russia tried to turn the whole city of Sevastopol into a sovereign naval base, akin to Guantanamo in Cuba or the two British bases in Cyprus.[26] While the government was dragging its feet on the border issue, various spokesmen for the national patriotic wing of the Russian political elite, most prominently Yury Luzhkov, the mayor of Moscow, were raising claims to Sevastopol and the Crimea. Still it is hard to believe, as suggested by some outside observers, that Russia was engaged in a "bad-good cop" game.[27]

The Russian government was slow to deal with the Ukrainian border issue for a number of reasons:

- Until about 1994, Moscow was not sure that Ukraine would survive as a state, and not break up (the Russian government analysts were not alone in the world in their skepticism);
- Russia's government was careful not to provoke a backlash among its population, which would have been useful for the Communist and nationalist opposition: after all, it was the Yeltsin administration that had taken the lead in dismantling the U.S.S.R.;
- The substantial costs of border delimitation and demarcation would be an added burden on the federal budget; and
- Keeping the issue suspended, Moscow thought it could use its eventual concession as a bargaining chip.

The ambiguity of Russia's approach stimulated suspicions in Ukraine about Moscow's ultimate goals. By keeping alive the "Russian threat," Moscow's recalcitrance helped solidify Ukrainian independence and internal cohesion in the first crucial years after gaining independence. A potential conflict between Galicia and Eastern Ukraine was prevented in part by Moscow's crude divisive tactic. The change in the Russian attitude came in late 1994-1995 and was linked to the first war in Chechnya. Confronted with Chechen separatism, Moscow's official position changed in favor of the central governments in Georgia, Moldova, and Ukraine. Still, it was only in August 1996 that Ukrainian and Russian negotiators agreed to establish a subcommittee on state borders. But even then the Duma deputies continued to raise the issue of Sevastopol. The Federation Council, the upper chamber of the Russian legislature, appealed to Ukraine as late as April 1997, to study the question of a condominium for Sevastopol. The condominium would create an inseparable link between Ukraine and Russia. Unsurprisingly, these ideas were categorically rejected. Only a few observers pointed out[28] that the Crimea in Russian hands would dramatically increase Kiev's leverage vis-à-vis Moscow. The peninsula lifelines—water and electricity supply, rail and road transportation links—all lead to Ukraine, not Russia.

1997, however, saw at last a momentous break-through between Russia and Ukraine. Defying many of his advisers and associates, President Yeltsin went to Kiev to sign a Treaty on Cooperation and Partnership on May 31, 1997, which finally recognized Russia's borders with Ukraine. The treaty affirms the "immutability of existing borders." As an additional step to bar the possibility of a border dispute by proxy, in 1997 Ukraine also secured its border with Russia's ally Belarus. The agreement on the Black Sea Fleet authorizes the leasing to Russia of Crimean facilities rather than territory. In exchange, the Russian Black Sea Fleet gained the right to be present in the Crimea for the following 20 years.[29] These accords did not enjoy the full support of Russian elites. The Duma finally endorsed the treaty only in December 1998, and the Federation Council in February 1999. Thus, it took the Russian political class as a whole seven years to internalize Ukraine's independence and the loss of the Crimea and Sevastopol.

The breakthrough meant primarily exiting from the danger zone of potential conflict and confrontation, not the start of an era of close cooperation. In the second half of the 1990s, Russo-Ukrainian differences have become chronic, making the relationship unpromising, although not particularly dangerous. Rather than continuing on a collision course, Ukraine and Russia have been drifting apart.[30]

Although resolved for the moment as a Russian-Ukrainian issue, with the Russian public following the government in accepting the peninsula's status as part of Ukraine, the Crimea has the potential of re-emerging as a seat of conflict, involving the third major ethnic group, the Crimean Tatars who, unlike both Slav nations, are indigenous to the area. The Crimean khanate, under Turkey's protection, was overrun by the Russian Empire in 1783, and the Crimean Tatar autonomous republic, which was established in 1920, was suppressed in 1944.

Since the late 1980s, the Tatars have been returning to the Crimea, mainly from Uzbekistan, numbering now anywhere between 250,000 and 500,000. More accurate figures are not available, for the status of many of these people is not fixed. Many are still citizens of Uzbekistan. Their lack of political rights and widespread unemployment makes them easy converts to militant Islam. Fears are expressed in Russia that the new situation favors Turkey by destroying the historical Russian-Turkish Treaty framework[31] and thus removing obstacles to restoring Turkey's involvement in the Crimea in the future, when the local Tatars grow more powerful and become more assertive.

A footnote to the Crimea issue is the status of the Sea of Azov, which is rather small (38,000 square kilometers) in area and until 1991 a Soviet internal body of water. Moscow's concern is that delimitation of the basin between Russia and Ukraine would leave the sea open for third-country ships. Some Russians raise the specter of NATO navies sneaking in and threatening the Russian heartland with cruise missiles. Instead, they propose joint use of the sea as internal waters, preventing internationalization of the Kerch Strait, which is the only outlet from Azov to the Black Sea. According to this view, Azov should not be allowed to repeat the fate of the Caspian, where Russia suffered a major setback, having to agree to a division of the seabed.[32]

The negotiations will take much time. Initially, Russia insisted on preventing the internationalization of the Sea of Azov. Later, it preferred a bilateral agreement modeled on the Soviet-Iranian treaty on the Caspian, or a multilateral one, similar to the Montreux convention regulating the regime of the Black Sea Straits.[33] Meanwhile, mutual complaints will be traded, but a serious border conflict off Kerch remains unlikely.

In the medium term, ethno-political issues in the Crimea, geopolitical concerns over NATO enlargement, domestic instability in Ukraine, and the revival of great-power politics in Russia can, in declining order of probability, threaten the current balance in Russo-Ukrainian relations. The border issue as such is not a major problem,[34] but it could become a symptom of the bilateral and even regional political dynamic.

Ukraine's problem is not so much Russian neo-imperialism as the country's marginalization because of the elites' inability to go ahead with reforming the economy, state, and society. The initial political choice ("Ukraine is not part of Russia"), essentially negative, was comparatively easy to make and, surprisingly to many, also to carry out. The positive choice ("Ukraine is part of Europe") was even easier to make, but is extremely difficult to realize. Right now, Ukraine is caught between the two: it is no longer part of Russia, but not yet—and this is a long yet—part of organized Europe. Ironically, at the end of the first post-Soviet decade, Ukraine has appeared perhaps the most "Soviet" of the former republics of the Union.

Still, the re-emergence of the Eastern Slav trio as a coherent political and economic whole is not to be expected. For both Moscow and Kiev (an eventually for Minsk too), the major pole of attraction will be the European Union. Even though they recognize that there is not a chance they will be admitted to the European Union in the foreseeable future, they (Moscow, Kiev, and Minsk) will not team up. Integration of the poor and destitute is rare; rivalry is far more probable. Finally, once independence is proclaimed, it is difficult to go back on it. Nothing illustrates this better than the example of Moldova, one of the smallest and least ethnically distinct countries to have emerged from the break-up of the U.S.S.R.

Moldova: An Outpost Too Far

Russia has no border with Moldova, wedged between Ukraine and Romania, but it has been closely involved in its domestic conflict, which tore the country apart roughly along the Dniester River in 1991-1992. Russian troops, which first allowed themselves to be drawn into the confrontation and then used force to stop the hostilities, are still deployed in Transdniestria, which has been acting as an independent state since the break-up of the U.S.S.R. Russia has also been the principal third-party mediator in the conflict and the main peacekeeper. Thus, the territorial unity of Moldova depends to a large extent on Moscow's position.

From the outset, there were two schools of thought in the Russian establishment. One, largely pro-Western, believed in the finality of post-Soviet territorial arrangements, and preferred to deal with the recognized governments, treating separatists as rebels. The other one, bent on the re-establishment of the U.S.S.R., attempted to use the cases of separatism as instruments of pressure vis-à-vis the newly independent states. The first school was located mainly in the presidential and some government structures (above all the Foreign Ministry); the other one prevailed in the parliament and had influential allies in the power ministries, above all the military. In this particular case, there were fears initially that an independent Moldova will not be a viable state, and will soon be absorbed by Romania.

This neat division continued until late 1994, when the Russian government launched its ill-fated first attempt to crush Chechen separatism. The need to fight the rebels on its own territory diminished the political and material support that Russia was giving to other separatist statelets. Moscow reaffirmed its recognition of CIS countries' territorial integrity, and intensified its mediating efforts. Yet, no about-face occurred. Russia could not overlook the geopolitical value of the unrecognized entities, which allowed it to use their existence, and Russia's mediation services, to make the NIS more pliant. In view of the scarcity of other resources available to the Russian government, geopolitical resources were the most reliable ones.

Russia's interests are geopolitical (keeping Moldova within its orbit, through its participation in CIS and bilateral economic and political agreements, and preventing its merger with Romania); geostrategic (maintaining a military presence in the area and preventing Moldovan membership in NATO); and humanitarian (ensuring fair treatment of the local Russians, but in fact preserving the special identity of Transdniestria). Ideally, the Russian government would welcome a Moldova that is sovereign (no integration within a Greater Romania),[35] federated (with Transdniestria having a special status, and a special relationship with Russia), neutral (but with a Russian military base in its territory), and gravitating toward the Russian Federation. Communist and nationalist factions within Russia, however, consider the self-proclaimed Dniester Republic as Russia's strategic bridgehead, aimed at both the Balkans and Ukraine. These forces are even prepared to treat the conflict along the Dniester River as a Russian-Moldovan problem. The unrecognized government in Tiraspol has come to rely on support from influential Russian quarters.

In the future, NATO enlargement toward Southeastern Europe, Romania in particular, could play a significant role in shaping Russian policies. Under certain circumstances, Moscow may become interested in having a buffer wedged between second-wave candidate Romania and third-wave hopeful Ukraine.

Conclusion

Overall, Russia's European frontier appears the most stable and peaceful. Peace and stability are highest where Russia borders on Norway and Finland. The Baltic states may eventually join this category, but the hard legacy of recent history and the difficulties that ethnic Russian populations have had in becoming naturalized there has increased tensions with Russia.

With Belarus, Russia faces the challenge of integration, which has already proved to be difficult. The difficulties of separation will continue to have an impact on border-related problems between Russia and Ukraine, potentially the most dangerous in the former Soviet Union. In Moldova, stitching the country together will be a long-term process, with Russia playing a role, and insisting that its interests be respected.

The defining factor in the European security landscape is NATO enlargement. Russia's failure to prevent its first wave and the likelihood of successive waves make the prospect of dividing lines in Europe real. Some of the borders, for example between Belarus and Poland, could assume those functions. Thus, the extent, pace, and quality of enlargement will be of key importance.

NOTES

[1] This pioneering role succeeds Finland's previous role as the closest Western country to the U.S.S.R., a Soviet "window on the West," and a neutral venue for various contacts between Cold War adversaries.

[2] The direct contact between Norway and Russia was restored in 1947 when Finland lost its narrow corridor to the Arctic (with the town of Petsamo, now Pechenga, in the Murmansk Region).

[3] Immigration restrictions imposed by Oslo were one reason; most Russians, however, did not want to emigrate permanently.

[4] Pyotr Vlasov, "Mir v Barentsevom more," *Expert*, No. 40, October 25, 1999, pp. 16-17.

[5] The Security Council document, as quoted in the above article.

[6] According to the Russian Minister for Natural Resources, these may reach 88 billion tons of nominal fuel (*Kommersant,* May 12, 1999, p. 7).

[7] Ibid. This sector may be endowed with 15-20 million tons of fuel.

[8] See Andrei Nikolayev, *Na perelome: zapiski russkogo generala,* Sovetsky Pi-satel, Moscow, 1998, p. 111.

[9] Kaliningrad, until 1946 Königsberg, and the region (15,000 sq. km) were placed under Soviet administration in 1945 by the Potsdam agreement until the peace treaty with Germany. The treaty was never signed, and the German peace settlement had to follow a long and tortuous route before it was finalized in 1990.

[10] Andrei Nikolayev, op. cit., p. 87.

[11] Exactly one-third of Poland's territory, or 104,000 sq. km, was part of Germany in 1937.

[12] Kievan Rus had something like this in Tmutarakan, a small principality that between the 10th and 12th centuries controlled both sides of the Kerch Strait, linking the Sea of Azov to the Black Sea.

[13] Some credit for Russia dropping the word *corridor* from official commu-nications with the EU should go to a senior Finnish diplomat who in 1999 immediately drew the attention of the Russian Foreign Ministry to the connotations involved.

[14] Including, in the latter case, Kaliningrad's Governor Leonid Gorbenko.

[15] Lithuania also found itself in the somewhat unusual position of a country that actually gained territory through the actions of the Soviet Union. The Vilnius region, occupied by Poland since 1920, was returned to Lithuania when the Red Army marched into Poland in September 1939. Once Ger-many was defeated, the Soviet authorities also returned Klaipeda (Memel), German-held until 1923 and from 1939 through 1945, to Lithuania. When Lithuania was trying to break away from the U.S.S.R. in 1988-1991, local pro-union circles and Moscow were not shy to point out to these facts in a vain attempt to deter the pro-independence movement. The arguments suggesting the "non-finality" of Lithuania's territory were later used by Russian nationalists such as Sergei Baburin. See "Spor vokrug Klaipedy," *Nezavisimaya gazeta,* November 22, 1997, p. 6.

[16] The Lithuanian treaty is still not ratified by the Russian parliament.

[17] The actual borders with Estonia and Latvia followed the lines drawn in 1944, which left parts of the first Estonian and Latvian republics: Ivang-orod, Pechory/Petseri, and Pytalovo/Abrene with Russia.

[18] Sergei Baburin, *Territoriya gosudarctva: Pravovye i geopoliticheskie prolemi*, Moscow, MGU, 1997.

[19] For instance, during President Yeltsin's state visit to Stockholm, in December 1997.

[20] In the 14th and 15th centuries, the Grand Duchy, which at that time included Belarus, central Ukraine with Kiev, and the principalities along the western edge of the current Russian Federation, as well as Lithuania itself, was overwhelmingly Eastern Slav in ethnic composition, Orthodox Christianity was its religion and the old Belarussian dialect was its official language. Except for the ruling dynasty, which was Orthodox but Lithuanian, the bulk of the nobility were Slavs.

[21] *Belaya kniga rossiiskikh spetssluzhb*, Obozrevatel, Moscow, 1995, p. 214.

[22] Leonid F. Zaiko, *Belarus na puti v tretiye tysyachaletiye*, Skakun, Minsk, 2000.

[23] In the early 1990s, potential trouble spots involving Belarus included Grodno, the center of the country's Catholic minority (a very conservative estimate of officially 10 percent) and the Vilnius district in neighboring Lithuania.

[24] In fact, President Lukashenko pursues both options simultaneously. In his 2000 annual message to the National Assambly he called for "normal relations" with the North Atlantic Alliance, and in anticipation of Putin's visit to Minsk in April 2000 he called for the creation of a 300,000-strong joint Russo-Belarussian force to deter NATO.

[25] It is famous for the staunch defense it offered in the Crimean War of 1853-1856 and during the Second World War in 1941-1942.

[26] A long-term lease of the naval base was also believed to be able to soothe the public sentiment in Russia. See Yevgeny Primakov, *Gody v bolshoi politike*, Sovershenno Sekretno, Moscow, 1999, p. 395.

[27] James Sherr, "Russia-Ukraine Rapprochement? The Black Sea Fleet Accords," *Survival*, Vol. 39, No. 3, Autumn 1997, pp. 33-50.

[28] Such as Alexei Miller, "Ukraina kak natsionaliziruyushcheyesya gosudarstvo," *Pro et Contra*, Spring 1997, p. 95.

[29] Alexei Arbatov calls this an example of "intimacy" existing in Russo-Ukrainian politico-military relations, and cites U.S. agreements with

Britain and other countries (Alexei Arbatov, *Bezopasnost: rossiisky vybor,* EPI Center, Moscow, 1999, pp. 144-145). A more appropriate parallel could be drawn with Britain and France maintaining their military presence in their former colonies.

[30] In 1995, Ukraine ceased to be Russia's main trading partner, sliding by 1998 to fourth place, right behind Belarus. In this period, the trade volume was halved from $14 billion to $7 billion, while Ukrainian gas debt to Russia, and Kiev's inability to pay, has become the principal economic issue between the two countries.

[31] In particular, the 1791 Yasi Treaty, which recognized Russia's sovereignty over the Crimea and the 1774 Treaty of Kucuk-Kainarji, in which Turkey granted the Crimea full independence.

[32] Alexei Alexandrov, "Ten Kaspiya nad Azovskim morem," *Nezavisimaya gazeta,* January 17, 1998, p. 3.

[33] See, for example, *Biznes v Rossii*, supplement to *Rossiiskaya gazeta*, April 29, 2000, p. 1.

[34] At the end of 1999, Russian experts ranked it the third most serious problem, after NATO enlargement and the Russian language issue.

[35] The Romanian-Moldovan treaty, which took seven years, from 1993 to 2000, to negotiate, stresses Moldova's independence and national identity, while recognizing the commonality of the language, culture, and civilization. Neither side wants unification: Moldovan elites prefer independence to subordination to Bucharest, and Romania is set on the prospect of EU and NATO membership. Unity, both sides agree, can only be achieved within a united Europe, which won't come soon.

CHAPTER 4

The Southern Tier

On its southern borders, from the Caucasus to the Caspian to Kazakhstan, Russia confronts a set of problems very different from those that the new Eastern Europe faces. The states formed there, following the break-up of the U.S.S.R., were even less homogeneous than those to the west of Russia. Moreover, there was virtually no experience of running a modern state to rely upon. Instead of the European Union, whose proximity was the principal moderating influence in CEE, the most powerful factor in the south was Islam. The importance of that factor has been growing ever since the Iranian revolution of the late 1970s. Long gone were the days when Russia could dream of gaining access to the warm seas. The unsuccessful intervention in Afghanistan in 1979-1989 was the last and unsuccessful attempt to project Russian power southward—whatever the actual reasons for the intervention itself. The tide has turned since then, and Russia has had to retrench farther and farther north. Russia's problems in Chechnya and, more broadly, in the North Caucasus are emblematic of the far more important and fundamental issue of establishing Russian identity in relation to Muslim peoples both inside and outside Russia's borders. The uneasy fact that international terrorism has been able to exploit the many problems of contemporary Islamic society adds extreme poignancy to this problem. In a different way from what is happening along the country's

European boundaries, the processes along the Orthodox Christian/Islamic interface will profoundly affect Russian nation- and state-building.

From the Black Sea to the Altai Mountains, Russia has no borders inherited from the Soviet past. All its boundaries are very new; many are considered arbitrary; and all are still uncertain. Russia's immediate neighbors, Georgia, Azerbaijan, and Kazakhstan, are weak and occasionally failing states that are threatened with real or potential domestic turmoil and fragmentation. In several cases—Abkhazia, Karabakh, Ossetia—domestic strife has resulted in civil wars and armed conflicts that threatened to spill over into other countries, including Russia, which is fighting secessionism in Chechnya. By the same token, the war in Chechnya threatens to spread to Georgia. As in all wars of secession, it was the rebels who, at least initially, gained the upper hand over the forces of the central government, creating the phenomenon of unrecognized but very real statehood. Moscow, which gave de facto support to the Abkhaz, Karabakh Armenians, and South Ossetians, receives little cooperation from Georgia and Azerbaijan in its own effort to put down the Chechen resistance.

In the west, the 15 million ethnic Russians permanently living in Estonia, Latvia, and eastern and southern Ukraine, including the Crimea, are a salient presence. In the south the problem of some 6 million Russians in northern Kazakhstan and 5 million more in Uzbekistan, Kyrgyzstan, Turkmenistan, and Tajikistan is compounded by the issue of the identity of Muslims living inside the Russian Federation, mainly in the North Caucasus and along the Volga, from Kazan to Astrakhan, the two medieval khanates that were overrun by Moscow in the 1550s. Several ethnic groups uncomfortably straddle the new borders, creating the reality of divided nations. All these issues come against the background of intense international commercial and political competition centered on the oil-rich Caspian basin, which has clear strategic overtones. Thus, old-style geopolitics is meeting novel geo-economics, and the meeting is rather tumultuous.

In the present chapter, we will first deal with the Caucasus, moving from north to south (i.e., from the current Russian border outward), and then with Central Asia, again going in the same direction.

The North Caucasus

In the Caucasus, Russia has to deal with a layer cake of territories: the traditional far abroad (Turkey and Iran), the post-Soviet near abroad (Armenia, Azerbaijan, and Georgia), and what some European analysts call the *inner abroad*. It is the inner abroad, which includes Chechnya and a string of republics stretching from the Caspian to the Black Sea, that poses the most concern. A Russian author even suggests that "the North Caucasus has become to the Russian Federation what the Baltic republics were for the U.S.S.R. or what Poland had been for the Russian Empire," namely, an inherently alien and permanently subversive element.[1] Whatever happens to the North Caucasus has implications for Tatarstan and Bashkortostan, which consider themselves to be only associate members of the Russian Federation.

How real is this danger to Russia's territorial integrity? The North Caucasus is a relatively small area of fairly limited economic value (except for the Caspian oil transit routes) and populated by ethnic groups that both imperial and Soviet authorities have traditionally found very difficult to control. There is little cultural affinity between the Russians and the Caucasian mountaineers. They are as distant from each other in terms of ethnicity and religion as most Europeans are from the peoples of the Middle East. The dismantlement of the U.S.S.R. divided some close relatives and lumped together several strangers. As Vitaly Tretyakov, the founder of the influential *Nezavisimaya gazeta*, has said (before the second Chechen war), "it is a strange Russia that includes Chechnya but excludes the Crimea."

To others, it is no less clear that Moscow must try to hold on to the North Caucasus no matter what, for letting it go would provoke a domino effect across the country, leading to Russia's collapse as a state.[2] Traditionalists who usually see reality in stark black and white terms argue that the only alternative to Russia's southern expansion is continuous retrenchment farther and farther to the north.[3]

Chechnya

Chechnya stands out as the most important factor by far, not only in the North Caucasus, but also across the entire southern periphery of Russia. Through its treatment of Chechnya, the Russian Federation actually defines itself.[4]

Chechnya unilaterally proclaimed its independence in the fall of 1991, when the Soviet Union still formally existed and the Russian Federation was not yet a de facto sovereign country. The government of the Russian Republic, which two months previously had encouraged the nationalist leader Dzhokhar Dudayev to carry out a *coup d'état* that toppled a pro-Soviet administration, made a feeble and failed attempt to crush the UDI. In the three years that followed, Moscow tolerated lawlessness in Chechnya, its rapid criminalization and de facto independence. Chechnya's contacts with the outside world were beyond the federation's control; yet its administrative boundaries with the neighboring Russian regions remained fully transparent. This made Chechnya a prime source of contraband of all kinds.

The first Chechen war (1994-1996) was adventurously started in an attempt to crush the Chechen independence movement that Moscow itself had been fostering and ended in disaster for Russia, which was forced to concede military defeat.[5] Under the Khasavyurt Accord negotiated by General Alexander Lebed, Russia reluctantly agreed to postpone consideration of Chechnya's final status, which had to be determined within a five-year period, extending to December 31, 2001.[6]

This deadline should have moved the Russian government to define its goals in the region, work out a policy to reach those goals, and map out an appropriate strategy. Given its financial levers, the economic incentives of its market, and Chechnya's need for rehabilitation, it could have achieved an acceptable solution. If the government had opted to bring Chechnya into the Russian economic, political, and security fold as an associate member of the Russian Federation, it could have supported moderate leaders such as Aslan Maskhadov, isolated the radicals, and provided the necessary material incentives for it to remain part of the federation. If the federation had concluded that the best option for Russia would be an independent Chechen state, it could have adopted a policy aimed at helping Chechnya toward independence, while negotiating economic, security, and other arrangements with it. Had the Chechens proved to be independent-minded, but too intransigent as partners, Russia could have imposed an economic, financial, and transport blockade, cordoning it off from the outside world, as a means of softening Grozny's position. But following the Khasavyurt Accord, nothing was done.

General Lebed's ouster as secretary of the Security Council and the unpopularity of the Khasavyurt Accord, which some critics compared to the 1918 Treaty of Brest-Litovsk (only this time the German giant was replaced by the Chechen dwarf), left Russian policy toward Chechnya an orphan. Ivan Rybkin, the new secretary, was a political lightweight, and although Moscow accepted the results of the Chechen presidential elections and signed another agreement with Grozny in May 1997, no policy emerged. Meanwhile, Chechnya was sliding into anarchy and chaos. The resulting drift was in fact preparing the way for a new confrontation.

A number of Russian government officials believed that the failure of Chechen state-building would almost naturally lead the republic back into the fold. From their perspective, bolstering the moderates was against Russian interests, for this would guarantee Chechen independence and weaken Russia's position in the entire region. Runaway radicalism and the resulting chaos, on the other hand, would serve Russia's goal by preventing Chechnya from consolidating itself and allowing Moscow to win in the second round. Russia was, thus, reluctant to use its economic leverage to bolster the Maskhadov government, which felt increasing pressure from Chechnya's warlords. In October 1998, Moscow stopped pumping oil along the Baku-Novorossiisk pipeline via Chechnya.

True, most members of the Russian political and military elite saw Chechnya all along as the prime source of tension, a haven for terrorism, and a geopolitical threat.[7] Chechen expansion, they felt, was aimed at creating a Grozny-dominated Islamic "mountainous confederacy" from the Caspian to the Black Sea and effectively easing Russia out from both. Dagestan was believed to be the first target of this expansion.[8] Moscow's passivity with regard to Chechnya in 1996-1999 turned this into a self-fulfilling prophecy.

Immediately following the ignominious defeat of 1996, there was no question of taking further military action against the separatists. Most Russian leaders and the majority of public opinion discussed the various ways of isolating the rebellious republic, by means of "closing" its border.

Chechnya, however, was still officially a subject of the federation, its refusal to act as one notwithstanding. Using this legal fiction, Grozny could legally establish relations with Russia's regions, such as Tatarstan and Dagestan, and its high-level representatives, including President Aslan Maskhadov, could travel abroad—departing from Georgia, Azerbaijan, and Turkey to the United States. A more serious case was linked to a road across the mountain passes that linked Chechnya to Georgia and thus provided Grozny with its only free overland access to the outside world. Moscow, however, was initially constrained in its criticism by the fact that a road agreement had been concluded between local Chechen and Georgian communities.

This legal situation had implications for the 774 km long boundary between Chechnya and the adjacent Russian regions. Under Russian law, the "Chechen border" remained an internal administrative line, to be patrolled by police, not protected by border guards. Organized crime took full advantage of these transparent administrative boundaries. Cross-border raids into the neighboring provinces of Russia became commonplace.[9] Kidnappings for ransom became one of the principal sources of income for the warlords.[10] Slavery made an ugly comeback. The perpetrators of these crimes were never caught or brought to justice. Chechnya, to them, was a safe haven. Russia's problems were both legal and resource-related. Using the border troops to close an internal boundary was not legal, and the regular armed forces, interior troops, and police units were not effective. They were also inadequate. The Operational Federal Task Force, numbering in 1997-1998 about 20,000, was unable to protect even its own units from Chechen commando raids.[11]

The openness of Chechnya's borders made it a safe haven for political extremists who raised the banner of Wahhabism and for plain criminals. Both used the lawless republic as a base for their activities in the North Caucasus region.

Since Khasavyurt, the Russian government had not grown more inclined to grant Chechnya independence. Although keeping Chechnya within Russia appeared next to impossible, turning the administrative line into an international border was fraught with many problems.[12] Moscow's prime concern was the implications of the Chechen precedent for the rest of Russia. There was a constant fear that the Russian Federation could follow the Soviet model of disintegration. "Expelling" the Chechens from the federation also raised a difficult constitutional issue. It couldn't be done by the president and/or parliament alone. One would have had to go to the nation. The Russian Constitution, however, prohibits holding referenda on the issue of cession of territory. Even if those hurdles were overcome, one would have to deal with territorial issues. The Cossacks resolutely oppose ceding two historically non-Chechen districts on the left (i.e., northern) bank of the Terek River that were added to the Chechen-Ingush Republic when it was formed in 1957; for Grozny to have agreed to that, it would have demanded as compensation the Chechen-populated districts in Dagestan, and most likely access to the Caspian Sea. Even if the issues of status and territory were to be resolved, the borderline between Russia and Chechnya would likely become a permanent frontline.[13]

In an attempt to square the circle, the federal authorities came up with various versions of a new status for Chechnya—more elevated than any other region of Russia, but definitely less than full sovereignty. Political parties, including Yabloko[14] and Zhirinovsky's LDPR, drafted their own bills. They all tended to explore the legal territory between Tatarstan and Belarus (within a union with Russia). Grozny, of course, would have none of that. They kept the option of joining the CIS, but only as an independent state. Even the moderate President Maskhadov was not prepared to give up to Russia in peacetime what was gained on the battlefield. The result was a stalemate.

Attempts to isolate Chechnya were largely unsuccessful. In December 1993, a year before the first war started, the Russian law-enforcement agencies insisted on "closing the Chechen border," totally ignoring Ingushetia and Dagestan as factors and strangely oblivious of the paucity of their own resources. It was too facile to claim that since Dagestan, Ingushetia, and North Ossetia had "made their choice" to stay within the Russian Federation, Chechnya could be placed in a *cordon sanitaire*. For one thing, Chechnya shared a common 80 km long border with Georgia, which was practically off limits to the Russian forces until December 1999. Most importantly, however, in the Russian-Chechen situation non-military threats such as organized crime, drugs, and arms trafficking prevail. Even a more massive presence of Russian troops would not yield results. In fact, the opposite has proven to be true. The troop presence in the area (which Chechens said was emblematic of

"Russia's occupation of the Caucasus") had both served as an excuse for commando raids on Russian forces, as in Buinaksk in December 1997, and continued to function as a reliable and cheap source of weapons/ammunition supply to the Chechens.

The local authorities, while wanting military protection, were mindful of the underside of the military presence. While the Stavropol authorities were asking the Interior Ministry to deploy a regiment close to the Chechen border to prevent the "annexation" of the adjacent strip of land, they opposed any widening of the security zone, fearing a de facto annexation of their lands by federal forces—like those of the Lezghin people!

The federal authorities' inability to protect Chechnya's immediate neighbors made some of those neighbors turn to self-defense. In early 1998, Dagestan planned to raise a 1,000-man strong special militia regiment for border protection. For its part, Ingushetia, ever suspicious of the federal forces, started putting together a native Ingush division controlled by the republic itself.

Surrounding and cordoning off the Chechens did not bring them to submission. Russia helped create a critical mass, which later exploded. Cornered and having nothing much to lose, the Chechens became more, rather than less, of a problem for Russia. By the late 1990s, Russians awakened to the prospect of Chechnya's turning into a radical Islamist territory, a haven for international terrorists, and an incitement for the rest of the North Caucasus to shake off Russian rule. The local conflict over Chechnya threatened to become a regional one, with a clear possibility that it could turn international. In August and September 1999, the Russian forces found it hard to beat off a Chechen invasion of Dagestan. They would not have succeeded had it not been for the unwillingness of the Dagestanis themselves (above all the Avars) to submit to Chechen domination.

The Russian government initially took a cautious approach to the scope of its "anti-terrorist operation" in Chechnya. At the beginning it spoke about a sanitary zone around Chechnya, then about a security zone inside the republic, and later about creating a liberated area north of the Terek River. The latter formula suggested a de facto partition of Chechnya whose Russian-administered northern third should have become a showcase for the benefits of staying within the Russian Federation. Eventually, its power of attraction was to have undermined Chechen separatism. Meanwhile, the Russian military advance went so well that the government dropped its cautious stand and decided on the total eradication of the armed rebellion and re-incorporation of Chechnya into Russia. The Khasavyurt Accord was declared overtaken by events, and the principle of the territorial integrity of the Russian Federation was reasserted.

Military victory, claimed by Russia in April 2000, however, does not equal a political solution. In the absence of such a solution, military control over the territory can only be tenuous and limited to the major towns and main roads in daytime. Russian military losses continue to mount.[15] Military occupation under a hand-picked civilian or a Russian governor-general demands loyalty, but it does not inspire it. It could last a long time without solving Russia's problems with Chechnya. War atrocities breed hatred. Eventually, the Russians will either have to agree to give Chechnya a very high degree of autonomy that is only available in a confederacy (which are not very durable arrangements), at the price of making the federation even more asymmetrical, or start helping the Chechens build a modern state of their own that would not be a threat to its neighbors. Any eventual solution must meet Chechnya's fundamental interest in self-government and access to economic opportunity, and Russia's basic interest in national and regional security.

The tragedy of Chechnya (and of Russia) lies in the Chechens' continuing inability to organize themselves politically for peacetime reconstruction and nation-building. A prerequisite for any lasting political solution should be the formation of a credible Chechen authority, based on a power-sharing system, that commands the support of the population of the republic, the refugees, and the diaspora. This authority would develop a new constitution for Chechnya and negotiate its final status with Moscow. Simple in principle, this plan is extremely difficult in execution. Yet, it is the only one that offers even a remote chance of solution to Russia's worst running sore.

The Rest of the North Caucasus

The Russian military campaign in Chechnya in 1999-2000 has averted the danger of disintegration of the federal authority in the North Caucasus. Yet, even after military victory has been claimed, many border-related problems still remain in the region.

In Dagestan, there are three sets of border-related issues: the external border with Azerbaijan that divides the Lezghin people; the border with Chechnya; and the internal boundaries among the three dozen ethnic groups that make up the republic.

In July 1992 the Dagestani parliament, openly defying Moscow, ruled against establishing a border regime with Azerbaijan that would severely constrain contacts among the Lezghins. At that time, the federal government chose not to confront the republican authorities. In any case, Russia had few resources to implement border controls. The border hardened progressively as a result of the Russian forces' pullout from Azerbaijan in 1993 and the Chechen wars, the first of which began a year later.

Dagestan suffered much from that first Chechen war and the lawlessness that reigned in Chechnya thereafter, but in 1999, for the first time, it was close to being drawn itself into another war. The loss of Dagestan, besides creating a regional generator of tension dominated by Chechen radicals, would have meant that Russia would lose two-thirds of its remaining Caspian coastline and the continental shelf; a potential territorial dispute with Kalmykia over the Nogai steppes; a possible Muslim separatist revival in Astrakhan; and a critical loss of Moscow's influence across the entire region south of the Volga-Don line.[16]

The changing power balance among the various ethnic groups in Dagestan was also opening the door to domestic conflict with the prospect of the republic's disintegration into small warring enclaves. Between 1996 and 1999, three villages in the Kodor Valley functioned as a de facto mini-state under a Wahhabi leadership.[17]

Throughout the first post-Soviet decade, Chechnya remained the only Russian territory with clear separatist aspirations. The example of the two wars must have reduced any attraction for going the way of Chechnya in the region. Yet, internal boundaries remain an issue virtually everywhere in the Northern Caucasus. North Ossetia and Ingushetia fought a brief conflict over territory in 1992. Political leaders in Adygeya claim much of the Russian Black Sea coast all the way to Abkhazia. There are suspicions that they may not only be after territory, but independence as well.[18] The twin republics of Kabardino-Balkaria and Karachaevo-Cherkessia had been edging toward divorce, which Moscow was able to forestall at the last moment. But it has not been able to reconcile the parties. A moratorium on the 1991 ill-conceived law on territorial rehabilitation is still in place. Unfreezing it would open a Pandora's box. There can be no solution based on the exclusiveness of an ethnic group's control over a given territory. The main problem is that the Russian government does not have a coherent policy or even a region-wide approach to the political issues in the North Caucasus. The most the federation has been able to achieve is to keep an armed truce between North Ossetia and Ingushetia, and largely let the local leaders manage the situation elsewhere as they see fit. These leaders, however, are not in full control of the situation, including the flow of money, contraband, and weapons.

Lying just north of the mountains, up to the Rostov-Astrakhan line, southern Russia has become a vast and vulnerable borderland. The Cossacks, both descendants of the real ones and pretenders, have been lobbying Moscow to grant them a status and supply them with weapons. Arming the Cossacks and recognizing their traditional role as border keepers are unlikely to solve any serious practical problems. Rather, this would immediately create many more new ones. The presence of large but ill-disciplined militias, largely unresponsive to Moscow, is one of them. Provoking an explosion of official, semi-official, and unofficial local armed formations in the non-(ethnic) Russian republics is another. Then all the borders in the North Caucasus, not just one, would be turned into battle lines.

Under the Putin administration, the emphasis has been on strengthening the power of the state bodies. Following the 2000 administrative reform, southern Russia was de facto placed under the authority of a presidential representative whose headquarters is located in Rostov. In the figure of Viktor Kazantsev, a former commander of the North Caucasus military district and a veteran of the second Chechen war, the region received its first post-tsarist governor general.

The South Caucasus

Russia's border problems within the "second layer" of the cake stem from the unfinished business of border delimitation, the divided nations phenomenon, and the reality of conflicts from Abkhazia to South Ossetia to Chechnya. By the start of the 21st century, these borders had not yet been formalized. Only 70 percent of Russia's borderline with Azerbaijan had been agreed on, and a mere 40 percent with Georgia.[19]

Georgia and Azerbaijan

Within the U.S.S.R., Russia's borders with Georgia, running mostly through very rugged terrain, were defined only rather generally. During the brief presidency of Zviad Gamsakhurdia (1991-1992), maps were published in Georgia showing a stretch of the Russian Black Sea coast, including Sochi, as part of historical Georgia. Officially, however, no territorial claims were raised, as Georgia struggled to exercise control within its Soviet-era borders. Thus, there are only small issues that remain between Russia and Georgia directly. They will be referred to later. The big issues confronted the two countries indirectly, but in a very serious way. They relate to Abkhazia and South Ossetia, the two independent-minded regions inside Georgia, and Chechnya. Similarly, there is no direct territorial dispute between Russia and Azerbaijan, but the Lezghin issue (like the Ossetians, a divided people), and the conflicts in Karabakh and Chechnya weigh heavily on the bilateral relationship.

Russia shares a border with Georgia's breakaway republic of Abkhazia. In 1992-1993 this greatly facilitated Russia's direct military involvement in the conflict there. Ever since, the border has provided Russia with a channel for exercising influence in Abkhazia and—indirectly—on Georgia by such means as altering the border regime, applying or easing sanctions, etc. On issues pertaining to the functioning of the border, Russia routinely deals with the Abkhazian authorities. The Russian peacekeeping forces on the ceasefire line between the Abkhazian and the Georgian forces are sometimes referred to in Tbilisi as "border guards for Abkhazia."

The Russian military, acting with or without the formal approval of the Russian government, helped the Abkhazian separatists defeat the Georgian forces in 1992 and 1993. Ever since, Moscow attempted to use the Abkhazia issue to bring pressure to bear on Tbilisi, while rejecting nationalist calls for admitting Abkhazia into the Russian Federation. The Russians, again led by the military establishment, also helped the Karabakh Armenians to consolidate their control over the area. In both cases, however, Moscow failed to convert these tactical military successes into lasting strategic ones. Tolerating separatism in a neighboring country and fighting it only 200 to 400 kilometers away on one's own territory essentially undermined the credibility of Moscow's position in both Tbilisi and Baku.

Eventually, Moscow must realize that the unresolved Abkhazian conflict is not only undermining its credibility as a mediator between Tbilisi and Sukhumi, but encourages separatism in the North Caucasus and further spoils the relationship between Georgia and Russia.[20]

On South Ossetia, the federal authorities in Moscow and the government of North Ossetia took a moderate position. Despite the 1992 referendum in the south that called for reunification of the two Ossetias, this option was never seriously considered, despite the abject poverty of the territory and its significant Georgian minority which, unlike in Abkhazia, was not expelled on a grand scale. A battalion-strong Russian force is stationed in South Ossetia, nominally as peacekeepers, and Moscow evidently hopes that any future agreement on the area's status will preserve its influence there—either directly or through North Ossetia. However, this influence does not extend very much to Tbilisi.

The Georgian-Ossetian conflict resolution, aided by Russia, has been as slow as the Abkhazian one. Even if an acceptable arrangement is finally worked out, it is hard to believe that the Ossetians on both sides of the border will treat each other as foreigners. The South's relationship with Georgia proper can be tenuous at best. Russia can hardly ignore this. For Moscow, the Ossetians, occupying a central position in the Caucasus, have traditionally been the most loyal ethnic group in the entire mountain region, which gave Vladikavkaz, the North's capital, unique leverage with Moscow.

The Lezghins, another divided people who unlike the Ossetians lack any form of territorial autonomy in either Russia or Azerbaijan, resent the underside of Russian-Azeri border controls with their inevitable bureaucratic abuse, bribes, and constant humiliation. The rising ethnic tensions within Dagestan, where the Russian Lezghins live, and the domestic problems in Azerbaijan provide fertile ground for

Lezghin ethnic nationalism, which views the border along the Samur River, which seasonally changes its bed, as a clear and present irritant. Moscow's plan, supported by Makhachkala (Dagestan's capital), to create a standard five kilometer-wide border zone, which would include many of the most fertile lands that the Lezghins possess, have provoked the Lezghin nationalist organization, Sadval, to demand a full demilitarization of the border. Others called for recruiting border guards mainly from among the local conscripts.[21]

The smaller issues between Russia and its neighbors in the Caucasus concern the actual passing of the borderline in strategically important areas such as mountain passes. One such issue surfaced in the Daryal Valley in 1997 during a customs conflict over the smuggling of alcohol into Russia. When Russia unilaterally moved a checkpoint inside what the Georgians regarded as their own territory, Georgians led a "peace march" on the Russian post. The Kremlin chose to back down, which prompted FPS Director Andrei Nikolayev to resign.

More serious disputes relate to the Chechen war. The emergence, in 1991, of Chechnya as a defiant anti-Moscow factor has complicated the situation on Russia's borders with both Georgia and Azerbaijan. The two countries served as corridors for the land-locked Chechnya. During the 1994-1996 war, Moscow attempted to cut off those supply lines by closing borders. In a most unusual arrangement, the Russians won Georgia's consent in 1995 to deploy Russian border guards along the Georgian side of the Chechen sector of the border. Russian attempts to isolate Chechnya from the south were never fully successful. Russia's closure of its border with Azerbaijan in 1995-1996 angered the Azeris, whose overland trade is mainly with Russia, but it did not prevent the Chechens from receiving war materiel. In fact, the common Georgian-Chechen border and the geographical proximity of Chechnya to Azerbaijan in a situation where, as in Dagestan, Russia's borders are notoriously porous, have facilitated Chechnya's entry into the world of regional politics in the Caucasus. Direct Chechen-Georgian and semi-direct Chechen-Azeri connections increased between the two wars, greatly angering Russia.

In 1999, Georgia charged that Russian aircraft were violating its airspace and bombing its territory. Russia accused Georgia of tolerating the Chechen military presence on its territory. Tbilisi rejected Moscow's proposal for a joint patrol of the Chechen stretch of the border. The possibility of Russian forces hitting the alleged Chechen military camps in Georgia or pursuing the rebels across the border raised the specter of a direct conflict between the two countries, possibly leading to a confrontation between the West and Russia. The OSCE mission in Georgia had to begin monitoring the "Chechen sector" of the Russian-Georgian border. The situation is compounded by the existence of a Chechen community in Georgia's Pankisi Gorge, which is only nominally controlled by Tbilisi, and the activities of Georgian free-lance paramilitaries inside Abkhazia, where they have been holding the Kotori Valley. Although the worst (i.e., a Russian incursion into Georgia) has so far been avoided, as long as the conflict in Chechnya drags on, and the situation in Abkhazia at an impasse, the danger of their spillover into Georgia remains. This was illustrated by the rise in tensions that coincided with the U.S. strikes against the Taliban in October 2001.

Finally, by virtue of the 1921 Russian-Turkish Treaty, signed in Moscow, Russia remains a guarantor not only of the border between Turkey, on the one hand, and Georgia, Armenia, and Azerbaijan, on the other, but also of the status of the autonomous republics of Ajaria (part of Georgia) and Nakhichevan (part of Azerbaijan). Geopolitically minded Russians stress the importance of the Megrin corridor (in Armenia) separating Nakhichevan from the main territory of Azerbaijan, which prevents Turkey from having a direct land link to Azerbaijan and, thus, to the Caspian Sea. Moscow saw with a wary eye the resurfacing of the old idea of a territorial exchange between Armenia and Azerbaijan (with the Karabakh and Lachin corridor joining Armenia, and Zangezur going to Azerbaijan, giving it direct land access to Nakhichevan and Turkey)[22] even though it had few supporters on the ground.

The Caspian

With respect to the Caspian, the issue has been the economic zones for the sea's exploration, rather than borders. From the start, Russia has been invoking the 1921 and 1940 treaties with Iran in an attempt to control much of the oil resources. Precisely that goal runs against the interests of the littoral states, who hope to extract the maximum from the Caspian oil reserves and want to escape restoration of Moscow's dominance in the region. That dominance, however, seemed increasingly improbable. Russia's main opponent on the issue of the sea's status was Azerbaijan, supported by Western oil companies and Turkey. Kazakhstan disputed Moscow's claim to an oil field in the northern Caspian. Russia's relations with Turkmenistan soured over Moscow's inconsistency in a dispute between Ashgabat and Baku. Most significantly, Russian oil companies, led by LUKoil, preferred gaining a stake in the oil deals without much regard for the Russian Foreign Ministry's official position. This apparently left Russia with a choice: withdraw its legal claim that the

Caspian is a unique water reservoir not covered by the Law of the Sea Convention or try to use its formidable capabilities for denying to others the benefits of the use of the sea's resources. In the latter case, however, Russia was as vulnerable to an increase in tension in the region as anyone. In fact, Moscow opted for a formula that would divide the seabed, but not the water or the surface of the sea. This formula was used in the Russian-Kazakh and Russian-Azeri agreement on the Caspian. As to the Russian oil companies, with the advent of the Putin presidency, they were told to follow the official government policy line.

Central Asia

In 1924-1925, Stalin almost single-handedly carved out Soviet republics from the territory of Russian Turkestan and drew their borders, deciding what should belong to whom, pragmatically applying the principle of divide and rule.[23] Old khanates such as Bukhara and Khiva and Russian-ruled oblasts alike were suppressed, and the new socialist nations of Uzbekistan, Turkmenistan, Tajikistan, Kyrgyzstan, and Kazakhstan were created from scratch. Most of these new republics lay very far from the core Russian lands, with the exception of Kazakhstan. Thus, as far as Russia is concerned, the principal issues in Central Asia relate to the border between the Russian Federation and Kazakhstan, the longest international border anywhere in the world; less directly, Russia might be involved in the latent border disputes among Central Asian states and between those states and other Asian countries, such as Afghanistan and China.

The principal problem that Russia confronts in the region, however, is not the borders, but rather the lack of barriers protecting it from the sources of instability farther to the south. The newly independent states are weak and fragile. Afghanistan-based insurgent formations, several hundred men strong, cross their porous borders at will. To attack Uzbekistan in 1999 and 2000, they traveled across Tajikistan and Kyrgyzstan. The Kyrgyz and Uzbek armies made the enemy retreat only after weeks of fighting. The small Russian force in Tajikistan controls only a portion of Afghanistan's northern border. From Osh to Orenburg to Omsk, there are virtually no obstacles that cannot be avoided. This applies equally to drugs, refugees, and terrorists.

Kazakhstan

The frictions over oil rights in the Caspian are not the most dangerous border problem between Russia and Kazakhstan. Historically, there was no border, only the outer limit of Russia's advance. While some Kazakh hordes joined Russia voluntarily, others had to be conquered.[24] The first Soviet republic of Kazakhstan, initially an autonomous region inside Soviet Russia, was proclaimed in 1920 in Orenburg, which became its (expatriate) capital. Its status was upgraded to that of a constituent republic in 1936. At that time a number of Russian-founded and -populated towns, such as Uralsk, Aktyubinsk, Petropavlovsk, Semipalatinsk, Ust-Kamenogorsk, and Akmolinsk[25] were placed outside of the Russian Federation. This probably constituted an attempt to promote "Soviet internationalism" as a means of political control and to speed up Kazakhstan's modernization. The growth of Kazakhstan's heavy industry from the 1940s made it necessary to send more industrial workers there, again mainly from Russia's industrial centers. In the 1950s and 1960s, the northern Kazakh steppes, called the Virgin Lands, witnessed a major centrally organized influx of settlers, mainly from Russia and Ukraine, whose task was to radically expand Soviet grain production. As a result, the north of the republic, which the Kazakhs regard as their historical land, had become heavily russified.

Many Russians would probably agree with Solzhenitsyn that modern Kazakhstan is composed of southern Siberia, the southern Urals, central Kazakh deserts developed by Russian settlers, and a belt of southern regions, only the latter of which can be called indigenous Kazakh.[26] The Kazakhs, for their part, fear that the Russians covet the northern part of the country and the Chinese the southeastern part, which leaves them only the deserts in between. There are 6 million Slavs, mainly Russians, who constitute up to 40 percent of the country's population. Still, there is no serious irredentism for now either in Russia or among the ethnic Russian population in Northern Kazakhstan.

From Russia's perspective, Kazakhstan is the most important country in the region, politically, economically, and strategically. There is no need (and no money in the foreseeable future) to fully "equip" the 7,400 kilometer long Russian-Kazakh border, cutting through as it does mainly Russian-populated areas. Rather, Kazakhstan's own borders—whether with China or (especially now) the Central Asian states—are of great importance for Russian security. Moscow would be right to coordinate its regional policies with Astana and offer whatever assistance necessary.

If Kazakhstan, however, fails to become a genuinely Eurasian state, where Kazakhs and Slavs are fully integrated, the northern provinces of Kazakhstan, populated largely by ethnic Russians, may wish to secede. That the Kazakh government sees the danger and is not prepared to tolerate secession is demonstrated by President Nazarbayev's decision to move the capital from Almaty to Astana, situated in the middle of the "northern territories." This move was accompanied by the less spectacular, but even more important, migration of ethnic Kazakhs from the countryside to the urban areas, where Russian dominance is, thus, being diluted. So far, inter-ethnic relations have been generally calm, but future conflicts can certainly not be ruled out. In the worst-case scenario, this could lead to a civil war in Kazakhstan, with cross-border involvement from Russia, where the Cossack organizations may play a major role as *agents provocateurs*.

Intra-Central Asian Issues

The borders between the five states that compose Central Asia are no less recent than the one between Russia and Kazakhstan. These borders are neither properly delimited nor, for the most part, demarcated. Often they cut through areas populated by the same ethnic group. Samarkand and Bukhara, ancient centers of Tajik culture, are in Uzbekistan, and many ethnic Tajiks who live there are officially registered as Uzbeks. On the other hand, one-quarter of the population of Tajikistan are Uzbeks. In both cases, the inhabitants think and act along local and ethnic lines, and do not yet share a national identity.

A salient example of how tensions can arise from the gross mismatch between political and ethnic boundaries can be found in the Fergana Valley, where Uzbek, Kyrgyz, and Tajik territories converge. That this area may become a tinderbox was demonstrated in the inter-ethnic clashes at Osh in 1990. In the decade that followed, many Uzbeks are known to have settled just across the border in Kyrgyzstan. There are also several Uzbek enclaves inside Kyrgyzstan. Altogether, there are 58 small cases of border disputes between Tashkent and Bishkek. Nevertheless, Uzbek military and security forces routinely cross the border in hot pursuit of Islamist opposition groups trying to seek refuge in the neighboring country. This was tolerated by the Kyrgyz, who were only outraged by Tashkent's subsequent decision to lay mines along the poorly defined borders.

A more serious potential dispute is between Uzbekistan and Tajikistan over the latter's northern Khujand province, where ethnic Uzbeks are a sizeable minority and the local Tajiks, who in the Soviet period formed the bulk of the governing elite of their republic, are in permanent opposition to the southern clans that now rule the country. So far, Tashkent has resisted the temptation to take over the province, but this remains a latent issue—as is the issue of Bukhara and Samarkand, the ancient centers of Tajik culture placed within Uzbekistan.

As in the Caucasus, it is reasonable to support the inviolability of the existing borders in order to avoid a region-wide conflagration. The leaders of all Central Asian states understand this and display solidarity on the border issue. The region, however, is entering a period of high political and social turbulence, and the continuation of the decade-long restraint cannot be taken for granted.

Through its haphazard political and military involvement in the region, Russia may find itself implicated in the events on those ill-defined borders, even against its will. Its principal allies in Central Asia, Tajikistan and Uzbekistan, much as their governments are concerned about the Taliban, continue to plot against each other, supporting rebels across the border.

It is the Tajik-Afghan border, however, that causes the most concern in Moscow. Afghanistan, Tajikistan, and Uzbekistan are all involved in the continuing instability on both sides of that border.

Tajikistan and Afghanistan

Early on, Russia pledged to protect the Central Asian states' borders with non-CIS states. Many in Russia, including then Defense Minister Pavel Grachev in 1992 and then Security Council Secretary Alexander Lebed in 1996, regarded the Tajik-Afghan border as the first in a series of dominoes: should it be allowed to collapse, other Central Asian states would be "lost" either to the Islamists or the Taliban, and Russia's strategic borders would be pushed back to Astrakhan or even the middle reaches of the Volga.

The issue here is not territorial disputes, but political control over Tajikistan, and especially its southern border. In 1993, Tajikistan became a test case for the credibility of the entire Russian policy in Central Asia. At that time, General Nikolayev made a famous gesture by saying that Russia would "never withdraw" its forces from the Tajik-Afghan border, which had become Russia's "strategic cross."[27] The Russians realized that the source of their problem was the 1979 invasion of Afghanistan compounded by the decision to withdraw support from the Najibulla regime in the spring of 1992: in both cases they eliminated their own protective buffer.[28] Now it is Tajikistan that has been assigned the role of a buffer state. Withdrawing from there, some argue, would constitute an "even greater blunder" than the Afghan fiasco.[29]

Andrei Nikolayev later confessed that during his tenure at the Federal Border Service he had two constant major problems: finding money for his agency and defending the border in Tajikistan.[30] For several years, that was a true line of defense. In 1995-1996, the Russians formed a "security zone" along the Afghan side of the border, a strip of land 15 to 20 kilometers deep, which was subjected to artillery bombardment whenever the border guards received intelligence reports that the Tajik opposition "bandits" were getting ready to cross the border.

Actually, the border troops had equal reason to fear attack from the rear. Despite the 1997 peace agreement jointly brokered by Moscow, Tehran, and the United Nations, Tajikistan continues to be a battleground for various regionally based clans. Russia will never have enough resources to control the area, and Russian national interests will never require that it do so. In fact, Moscow has been used by the competing forces in Tajikistan and Uzbekistan for their own interests. Under these circumstances, controlling the border is meaningless, unless one considers the problem of drug trafficking. Fighting that problem, however, demands an entirely different strategy, using other means.

By the mid-1990s, Russia became one of the world's major transit corridors of drug trafficking. Most narcotics arrive from Afghanistan[31] and South Asia via Tajikistan and Kyrgyzstan, and are exported to Western Europe by way of the Baltic countries and East Central Europe.[32] Russia itself has become a major drug-consuming nation.[33]

Russian border guards in Tajikistan stem the flow of drugs, but are unable to stop it altogether.[34] Osh in neighboring Kyrgyzstan, where in 1999 Russian border guards were replaced by locals allegedly under pressure from drug dealers, is one of the major hubs of drug trafficking in all of Central Asia.[35] Central Asian states are too weak, their bureaucracies are too corrupt, and their border controls, if they exist, are too inefficient to deal with the problem.

Russia's resources are limited, and its officials are certainly not immune to corruption.[36] Russian authorities have made constant appeals to the West, the ultimate destination of much of the drug exports, for an understanding of the role Russia plays in Tajikistan. These appeals, however, apparently lack credibility. The Russians, it is felt, are in Tajikistan to prop up a pro-Moscow government, and everything else is simply a spin-off.

Meanwhile, the problem of managing an ethnic Uzbek/Tajik exodus from Afghanistan, should the Taliban overrun the last strongholds of the northern alliance, remains as serious as ever. Such an exodus has the potential of destabilizing Uzbekistan, the region's linchpin, and threatening Kazakhstan, with all the attendant consequences for Russia. It is the realization that they share common interests that has pushed Tashkent and Moscow closer together.[37]

The situation in the region took a dramatic change in the wake of the start of the U.S. anti-terrorist operation in Afghanistan in the fall of 2001. Common interests have again prevailed over the old suspicions. Russia and the Central Asian states supported the U.S., the latter offering their air space and air bases to American forces. Moscow's decision to sanction U.S. troop stationing in the former Soviet territory, even if it represents a case of making a virtue out of necessity, is an important development signaling more realism in the Russian security policy. In the previous 10 years, the idea of U.S./NATO troop deployments anywhere in the CIS had been regarded as absolutely intolerable.

China and Central Asia

For the moment, old territorial disputes between China and the U.S.S.R. which led in 1969 and 1973 to armed incidents on the current Kazakh border have been settled. In 1996, Russia, Kazakhstan, Kyrgyzstan, and Tajikistan signed a border treaty with China, confirming the existing borderline—with relatively minor adjustments—and agreed on a set of confidence-building measures and military force reductions in the border area. Rather than disband after the signing of the treaty, the parties reconstituted themselves as the Shanghai Five, an institutionalized summitry arrangement. The deterioration of the internal security situation in Central Asia in 1999 made the group coordinate its efforts to put down "international terrorism."

Currently, China's main concern in the area is the stability of Xinjiang, where Muslim Turkic-speaking Uigur separatists have been active. This concern is felt even more acutely after Islamic terrorists had struck in New York and Washington. Having joined in the international condemnation of terrorism, Beijing demands cooperation from Kazakhstan and Kyrgyzstan where the Uigur activists once tried to establish themselves. The Central Asian governments have been cooperative, but they are vulnerable and generally weak. For the foreseeable future, China favors Russia's maintaining a presence and a measure of influence in the region. In the longer term, however, it probably hopes to displace Moscow gradually as the dominant outside power in Central Asia.

China became officially involved with Central Asian security with the creation, in 1996, of a Shanghai Five group which initially included countries that fixed their border problems with China following the disappearance of the U.S.S.R. A loose club at the beginning, the group evolved into a regional security panel assuming in 2001 the name of the Shanghai Cooperation Organization. The SCO not only gives China a say in Central Asian security issues, such as the fight against terrorism, it makes Beijing a co-guarantor of regional security alongside with Moscow.

The Central Asian states are careful to court China, but many there are afraid that a stronger China will demand territorial concessions from them. In Kazakhstan, there are fears that China plans to annex the fertile and water-rich southeastern region up to Lake Balkhash and the Irtysh River. For Russia, such an incursion into a neighboring country, although improbable in the medium-term, would be an unfriendly act that would require some response.

Now and for the foreseeable future, China and Russia will be united in their opposition to separatism, which is a latent problem among the Uigur minority in Xinjiang. Over time, however, the growing might of China may start to display Russia as the leading regional power in Central Asia.

* * *

Russia's southern tier has become its most vulnerable region. Along its southern border, Russia confronts weak states and unconsolidated societies that are generally at far less advanced stages of modernization. Some of the distant neighbors, such as Afghanistan, refuse to modernize altogether, and present a major challenge to their neighbors and others, including Russia. The southern border is not one of potential integration, as in the West, but rather a civilizational divide. The situation is complicated by the existence of numerous Muslim enclaves inside Russia and the presence of millions of ethnic Russians in Kazakhstan. There is no acceptable alternative to fighting Islamic terrorism. At the same time, cultural and humanitarian dialogue across that divide is a must, and the development of economic links, including new communications along both East-West and North-South axes, is one of the few instruments available to encourage modernization and help resolve or manage the various conflicts. Despite the strikes against the terrorists, Islam itself is on the rise, and will become a more potent political force in the regions that used to form part of the Russian Empire and the U.S.S.R. Russia will have to enter into a dialogue with it to work out a modus vivendi with which it can live. The prospects for positive dynamic change are diminished, however, by the rivalry among Russia, America, the EU countries, Turkey, Iran, and China for the control of and access to Caspian oil reserves. This rivalry has subdued somewhat in the wake of September 11, 2001, but its roots have not been eradicated. Ironically, it is precisely in this region of the former Great Game that Russian-Western cooperation is most needed, and, as demonstrated in the fall of 2001, most feasible.

NOTES

[1]   Yuri Golubchikov, "Gorny Altai na puti v XXI vek," *NG-regiony*, No. 4, 2000, p. 7.

[2]   Prof. Vladimir Degoyev (University of North Ossetia), "Regionalniye ugrozy globalnomu poryadku," *Nezavisimaya gazeta*, October 16, 1997, p. 5.

[3]   Alexander Dugin, *Osnovy geopolitiki. Geopoliticheskoye budushcheye Rossii*, Arktogeya, Moscow, 1997, p. 343.

[4]   There is also a much broader view of the importance of the Chechnya issue. According to the historian Natalia Narochnitskaya, what is at stake is the result of a 200 year long geopolitical effort of Russia, its presence in the Black Sea region, the military balance in the Mediterranean, the future of the Crimea, Armenia and Georgia, and of the eastern Christian world as a whole. See Narochnitskaya, "Politika Rossii na poroge tretyego tysyacheletiya," in *Vneshnyaya politika i bezopasnost sovremennoi Rossii*, Vol. 1, Book 1, p. 260.

[5]   Almost 4,000 Russian soldiers were killed and 18,000 wounded. Overall, between 80,000 and 100,000 people, mostly civilians, were killed.

6   Lebed, it must be said, had first attempted a military solution by ordering the army to break the Nazran Agreement negotiated in June 1996. The Russian forces, however, were unable to prevail and suffered heavy losses. From the Russian point of view, the Khasavyurt Accord was much worse than the Nazran Agreement: all Russian troops had to leave, the Chechens would "demilitarize" rather than disarm, and international law was enshrined as the basis for the Moscow-Grozny relationship.

7   See a characteristic article by Sergei Markov, "Piratskaya respublika Ichkeriya," published by *Izvestia* in the fall of 1997.

8   Grigori Kertman, "Neterpeniye, ili tantsy s volkami," Fond Obshchestvennoye Mnenie, *Vremya-MN*, June 8, 1998.

9   According to Russian official figures, about 200 armed attacks on the Russian forces were reported between 1996 and 1998 (*NVO*, No. 38, 1998, p. 7).

10   The most senior person held in captivity was Vladimir Vlasov, the Russian president's permanent envoy in Chechnya, who spent six months in captivity in 1998. The most widely reported atrocity was the beheading of four Western communications specialists in 1998. It is reported that kidnappers received up to $20 million in ransom money in 1998. See Charlotta Gall, "Chechens Weigh Choice Between East and West," *Financial Times*, December 12-13, 1998, p. 2.

11   When Salman Raduyev, the notorious Chechen commander, appeared in 1997 on the Chechen-Dagestani boundary, the Russian police were faced with a dilemma: let him through and make a mockery of the law, or arrest him and risk provoking a crisis in relations with Chechnya.

12   In the words of Alexei Arbatov, granting Chechnya independence would have outweighed the benefits of the Khasavyurt Accord. See Alexei Arbatov, *Bezopasnost: rossiisky vybor,* EPIcenter, Moscow, 1999, p. 79.

13   Alexei Arbatov, "Granitsa—eto lyudi, a ne prosto cherta na karte," *NVO*, No. 37, 1998.

14   Alexei Arbatov, *Bezopasnost: rossiisky vybor*, p. 80.

15   In the two years of the second Chechen war (1999-2001), the Russian military lost over 3,500 people, compared with 4,300 in the first war (1994-1996) and about 14,000 in Afghanistan (1979-1989).

[16] Elmar Guseinov, "Pokusheniye na Dagestan—ugroza bezopasnosti Rossii," *Izvestia,* December 26, 1997, p. 1.

[17] See *Izvestia*, December 26, 1997, p. 2.

[18] Andrei Nikolayev, *Na perelome: zapiski russkogo generala,* Sovetsky Pisatel, Moscow, 1998, p. 229.

[19] Colonel General Alexei Shcherbakov, "Kavkazskaya lavina," *NVO*, No. 38, October 9-15, 1998, p. 7.

[20] The fragility of the status quo between Georgia and Abkhazia and the link between the Abkhaz and Chechen problems were demonstrated yet again by the flare-up of tensions in the region in the fall of 2001.

[21] *Nezavisimaya gazeta*, October 24, and November 15, 1997.

[22] This is often referred to as the "Goble Plan." Paul Goble, a U.S. diplomat and broadcaster, did much to spread this idea.

[23] Felix Chuyev, *Sto sorok besed s Molotovym*, Terra, Moscow, 1991, p. 279.

[24] M. K. Kozybayev (editor-in-chief) et al., *Istoriya Kazakhstana s drevneishikh vremyon do nashikh dnei*. *Ocherk*, Almaty, 1993, p. 185.

[25] Now Astana, capital of Kazakhstan.

[26] Alexander Solzhenitsyn, "Kak nam obustroit Rossiyu," *Literaturnaya gazeta,* September 18, 1990, p. 3.

[27] Andrei Nikolayev, op. cit., pp. 95, 153.

[28] From the 1880s through 1917, Afghanistan was a buffer between the Russian and British Empires; in the 1920s, the Soviet Union again rediscovered the utility of the Afghan buffer. In 1978, the Soviet leadership was genuinely surprised by the pro-Marxist coup in Kabul, which it decided to support, against the U.S.S.R.'s best interests.

[29] Ilya Kedrov, "Afgansky sindrom," *NVO,* No. 9, 1998, p. 2.

[30] Andrei Nikolayev, op. cit., p. 158.

[31] Afghanistan produces 70 tons of heroin annually, worth $46 billion. See Andrei Nikolayev, op. cit., p. 171.

[32] From 1992 through 1997, the FBS seized 6.4 tons of drugs, over three-quarters of which were seized on the Tajik-Afghan border. Farther along

the way, the prices rise dramatically: 1 kg of raw opium costs $100 in Khorog (Badakhshan), $1,500 in Osh (Fergana Valley), up to $3,000 in Bishkek, between $8,000 and $10,000 in Moscow, and up to $15,000 in Western Europe. See Andrei Nikolayev, op. cit., p. 163.

[33] According to the Russian Interior Ministry, one-third of Russian students use drugs. See Nikolai Plotnikov, writing in *NVO*, July 11, 1997. This, however, seems to be too high a proportion.

[34] Russian border guard officers routinely complain that drug couriers from Afghanistan, whom they intercept and hand over to Tajik law-enforcement agencies, are then promptly released and return to their business.

[35] See Yury Razgulyayev, "Dyra na granitse," *Pravda*, January 28, 1998, p. 2.

[36] There were persistent allegations that individual Russian border guards and other military officers were directly implicated in smuggling drugs up north, using military transport aircraft.

[37] In September 1999, at the start of the second Chechen war, security-conscious Vladimir Putin paid his first official visit abroad as prime minister to Uzbekistan.

CHAPTER 5

The Far Eastern Backyard

The Far East is unique among Russia's regions in that it experienced virtually no border changes in the 1990s. Ever since the break-up of the Soviet Union, the situation along Russia's borders in the region has been generally stable, and even improving. Yet, it is there and in Siberia that Russia's geopolitical destiny is likely to be tested, and maybe even decided in the next century.

One reason for that is the state of the region itself. For nearly four centuries, both the imperial and Soviet governments exploited Siberia's fabulous resources, treating it as a colony. The pattern of development included the creation of military outposts and a fur trade, followed by colonization by peasants and government resettlement policies. In the 20th century, the Far East and Siberia were the most "Soviet" regions of the country, as far as its economy (defense industry and extraction of raw materials), social structure, and way of life were concerned.[1] This was also the land of the Gulag.

In the post-Soviet decade, continued economic degradation and depopulation of the Far Eastern provinces and the severing of many contacts between them and the rest of Russia threatened to produce a situation in which that outlying territory would be progressively alienated from European Russia, or simply Russia, as it is called east of the Urals. Russia's failure as a functioning state would have dramatic international implications.[2]

In principle, the economic reorientation of the Far Eastern provinces away from European Russia, thousands of miles away, toward the neighboring Asia-Pacific makes much sense. The way this has happened, however, has produced economic dislocation and misery.

A major external factor is the rise of China. Even as links between the Russian Far East and European Russia grow more tenuous, the economic pull of China is likely to continue to affect the province. Eventually, this will translate into the rise of China's political influence not merely over, but also inside, Russia. Within just one decade (the 1990s), the balance of power between the two countries has dramatically shifted in China's favor. Chinese immigration into Russia will probably grow, altering the ethnic composition of the region's population. In these conditions, the border issue, officially settled by Moscow and Beijing in 1991, may well be revisited.

Next, there is still an unresolved territorial issue between Russia and Japan that continues to be the principal obstacle to a formal peace treaty and the general improvement of bilateral relations. Japan is highly unlikely to drop its claim on the Kuril and Sakhalin islands, and a territorial adjustment, even if it were to occur, would be a long and painful process.

Finally, it should be kept in mind that in contrast to Europe, where some states have disintegrated as a result of domestic implosion but where otherwise few classical territorial issues remain, East Asia counts many such disputes, involving nearly all countries in the region, including China, Japan, Korea, Vietnam, the Philippines, and others.

The State of the Russian Far East

The severe economic and social crisis in the Russian Far East, the region's rapid depopulation, and the loosening of its ties with European Russia have raised the specter of regional separatism, stimulated by the vague and somewhat ambiguous experience of the Far Eastern Republic that existed east of Lake Baikal from 1920 through 1922.[3] Another cause for immediate concern was Yakutia (Sakha), a vast republic in eastern Siberia endowed with rich natural resources. Both can generate concerns. However, the regional authorities chose to become uncontrollable rather than independent. Even as they strove to create autonomous fiefdoms, the governors of the nine regions making up the Russian Far East continued to compete among themselves for Moscow's subsidies, and the Yakutian authorities were satisfied with a highly favorable deal that the federal government offered them. The only real case of attempted separatism was Tuva.

As to supposedly foreign-inspired irredentism, its potential can only be imagined in Buryatia, a republic whose indigenous population was closely related to the Mongols.[4] Although Mongolia claims 2,300 sq. km of Tuvinian territory and 120 sq. km of Buryatia's,[5] these claims are not creating serious problems for now. The specter of pan-Mongolism, historically seen in Russia as a vehicle for Japan's policy aimed at weakening both Russia and China, however, was very short-lived.[6] A far more complicated issue involved China. The Chinese contingency plans, some Russians suspect, include "participation" in the governing of Primorye should it declare independence from Russia.[7]

The Sino-Russian Border

Russia's current relations with China are marked by a radical improvement in political relations, large-scale Russian arms and technology transfers, and at the same time, just beneath the surface, growing unease in Russia concerning the future of these relations. In 1990, China and the U.S.S.R. were deemed equal in terms of their GDP; in 1999, the Russian leaders had to admit that China was leading Russia by a factor of five.[8] A leading Moscow academic calls China "the most formidable geopolitical rival it has ever had on the Eurasian continent since the Tatar-Mongol invasion."[9] To the scholars who live in the Russian Far East,[10] the territorial issue forms "the core" of Russia's China problem.

The border between Russia and China, 4,259 km long,[11] has traditionally been among the most important strategic frontiers in the world. The border between the two countries has existed for more than 300 years, in the course of which it moved significantly to accommodate Russia's expansion toward the Pacific. Actually, the areas that Russia wrestled from China were never part of China proper, but tributary territories with a non-Han population. The two treaties of Aigun (1858) and Beijing (1860) which formed the original legal basis for the current boundaries between the two countries fixed the power balance between the rising empire of the tsars, who aspired to regional hegemony, and the declining Chinese empire, which was about to lose its former predominance.

The large-scale Russian penetration of Manchuria in the late 19th century placed the border deep inside the Russian zone of influence. It was the rise of Japan, Russia's principal Asian rival, that made the Russians fortify the Chinese border for the first time. The Japanese occupation of

Manchuria in 1931 prompted the U.S.S.R. to assume control over all the islands on the Amur and Ussuri rivers, effectively—and unilaterally—pushing the border to the Chinese bank. Since Japan's defeat in World War II this move to strengthen the border has not been rescinded.

The border issue, ignored by Moscow and Beijing during their ten-year alliance in the 1950s, came to a head as a consequence of their split. Mao Zedong and other Chinese leaders publicly denounced the 1858 and 1860 treaties as "unequal," and referred to about 1.5 million square kilometers of Soviet territory as "annexed Chinese land." Diplomatically, however, China never officially made such claims, but rather demanded that Moscow recognize the existence of the territorial dispute. In the border talks that opened in 1964, Beijing only asked Moscow to consider some 20 relatively small territorial adjustments. The U.S.S.R., which now saw the People's Republic as a potential adversary, refused to give up its full control of the border rivers. It was over one of the small and insignificant border islands on the Ussuri in which Chinese and Soviet forces clashed in March 1969, raising the prospect of a war between the two major powers on the Asian continent.[12]

The end of the Sino-Soviet cold war led to the conclusion in May 1991 of an agreement on the eastern section of the border. Moscow decided to act in accordance with international law, which rules that river boundaries follow the deep water channel. This agreement was ratified by the Russian parliament in February 1992.[13] This was followed up in September 1994 by an agreement finalizing the western section, and later by other accords providing for the border area's partial demilitarization and a set of confidence building measures. After that, a 21 km long stretch of the common border remains disputed. Russia insists that two strategically positioned islands in the vicinity of Khabarovsk and another one on the Argun River[14] should be recognized as Russian, and China strongly resists this.[15] Interestingly, despite the steady expansion of political relations and strategic dialogue as well as Russian arms and technology sales to China, Beijing is standing firm on this sticky issue.

The border agreement was complemented in 1996 and 1997 by two agreements on confidence-building measures and the mutual reduction of armed forces in the border area. These put constraints on the military activity of both sides in the vicinity of the border and introduced ceilings on the number of heavy weapons and personnel that the parties to the agreement could deploy in the 100 kilometer-wide zone along the border. Alongside with Russia and China, the agreements were signed by Kazakhstan, Kyrgyzstan, and Tajikistan. In July 2001, Russia and China, on Beijing's initiative, signed a 20-year friendship treaty which confirms the present borderline.

The Sino-Russian accord on the border resulted from both sides' willingness to end their 30 year long confrontation and normalize and expand relations. Moscow's negotiators also realized that time was not necessarily working to Russia's advantage, and leaving the territorial issue open in the future was not in their country's best interest.[16] In 1991, Russia was still considered a superpower, and the fear of the threat from the north was still widespread among China's leaders.

Russia had to give more land, although not very much, and its government faced some criticism from the nationalist forces in the Duma and opposition from regional authorities. Some governors, led by Primorye Region's Yevgeny Nazdratenko, were clearly eager to ride the wave of patriotic populism. Many Russians living in the vicinity of the border were understandably unhappy about the government's ceding land that they had used for generations for various agricultural needs. It was also alleged that thanks to Russian concessions China would be able to build a deep-water port or even a naval base on the Tuman River, which would give it access to the Sea of Japan despite the well-known shallowness of the river and the fact that the final 17 km long stretch of the river is jointly controlled by Russia and North Korea.

The question that more insightful Russians ask is whether the delimitation/demarcation agreement fixing the current borderline amounts to a full-fledged border treaty?[17] The concern is that the border agreements will simply freeze the situation until China feels strong enough to present its full demands to Russia. The specter of border claims amounting to the 1.5 million square kilometers, which would include Vladivostok, Khabarovsk, and most of Russia's infrastructure east of Lake Baikal, has not disappeared entirely.[18] The slow but steady march of China, which re-absorbed Hong Kong in 1997 and Macau in 1999, and is focusing more and more on the Taiwan issue—all under the rubric of doing away with the vestiges of European imperialist domination—raises for some Russians the question of *when, not whether* the Russian Far East will have its turn.

Of course, unlike Hong Kong, Macau, or Taiwan the Russian Far East is overwhelmingly Russian in ethnic terms. There is virtually nothing there that would remind one of China.[19] Yet, the Chinese presence in the area is slowly but steadily growing. For the moment, there are few permanent settlers, a tiny number of mixed marriages, and little property owned by the Chinese—all traditional points of concern to the local Russians. More importantly, however, the Chinese are more competitive, whether in commerce or in agricultural production. They have vastly larger financial resources. The local Russians are becoming increasingly defensive. In the future, the Chinese may make their weight felt not so much politically or militarily, but increasingly by economic means.

In 1897, the population of the Russian Empire stood at 129 million, accounting for 8 percent of the world's total. The U.S.S.R. was the third most populous country in the world, after China and India. Today, the Russian Federation, with 145 million, or 2.5 percent of the global figure, ranks 6th or 7th, with Pakistan. It can be compared to Japan (125 million), and, in the European part of the country, to Germany (81 million). Moreover, its population is declining. In the last decade of the 20th century, it dropped from 148 million to just over 145 million. Between 1992 and 1997, Russia's population dropped by 4.2 million people. Had it not been for the influx of migrants from the new independent states, the decrease would have been much sharper.[20] The Russian Statistics Committee has projected continuing population decline, to 138 million by 2015. Some forecasts even predict that Russia's population will be halved in the course of the 21st century. In his first state of the nation report to both houses of parliament, President Putin quoted data which indicate that Russia's net annual loss of population was 750,000 and increasing, and that by 2015 it will have lost 22 million people, a seventh of its current population.[21] The decline of the ethnic Russian population is greater than the population decrease as a whole.

Russia is one of the least densely populated countries in the world (9 people per 1 square kilometer as compared with 337 in Japan, 230 in Germany, 118 in China, and 27 in the United States). Nowhere is this depopulation felt more acutely than in the Russian Far East. Russian Harbin (the chief city of Manchuria, founded by the Russians as recently as 100 years ago) and the Russian community in Shanghai (which was the largest foreign group in China's biggest city in the 1920s and 1930s) are all but forgotten. If anything, the specter of a Chinese Khabarovsk, Vladivostok, or Irkutsk appears more real to many Russians. Consider the following table:

	Russian Far East (southern regions)	North-East China
Population, million	5.0	104
Population density, per sq. km	3.8	132
Population growth, 000	–40	1,000
Regional GDP growth	–8%	13%
Industrial/agricultural growth	–12/–15	14/8

Source: Petr Baklanov. "Geograficheskie, sotsialno-ekonomicheskie i geopoliticheskie faktory kitayskoi migratsii na rossiyskii Dalnii Vostok." In: *Perspektivy Dalnevostochnogo regiona: kitayskii faktor*. Moscow: Carnegie Center, 1999, p. 37.

China's economic and demographic expansion is feared by both the local authorities and national border guard services.[22] There are no reliable figures about the number of Chinese already in Russia, but there are unsubstantiated rumors that suggest they number in the millions.[23] There are suspicions that the penetration into Russia by the Chinese is part of Beijing's grand design to alter the ethnic situation in the Russian Far East and turn it into an appendage of China, or even annex it altogether.[24] Meanwhile the reality is different: most Chinese come to Russia in search of economic opportunities, and many use Russia only as a temporary way station en route to Europe.

In one decade, the number of Chinese in Russia has increased at least 20 fold, albeit from a very low base of 11,000 in 1989. Chinese communities have emerged in a number of Russian cities. To the extent that Russia's domestic situation will ameliorate, the number of Chinese immigrants will grow. Within China, the number of unemployed and partially employed people exceeds by far the whole population of Russia.[25] Some Russian experts predict that by the mid-21st century the Chinese will become the second largest ethnic group in Russia, after the Russians themselves.[26]

Chinese food imports, which in 1991-1992 ensured the physical survival of Russian Far Easterners, remain highly competitive vis-à-vis Russian agricultural produce. The influx of cheap Chinese consumer goods has helped stabilize the social situation in the region.

One obvious alternative could be the Koreans, both from the former U.S.S.R. (hundreds of thousands of them were resettled in Central Asia, mainly in Uzbekistan, in the 1930s), and from North Korea. North Korean lumberjacks have long worked in secluded camps in the Primorye Region. In 1992, Russia stopped issuing long-term contracts to Koreans. Many Russians still fear them as much, if not more, than the Chinese,[27] and for the same reason: they suspect that a massive influx of immigrants will be followed by the demand for autonomy and end in the annexation of the region by a future united and powerful Korea.

In January 2000, Russia and South Korea signed an agreement leasing 7,000 hectares of land that is currently lying waste in Primorye to Korean rice farmers. There are suggestions that the two Koreas are quietly competing with

China for access to the Russian Far East. In this context, the Russian authorities are urged to play the Koreans off against the Chinese.[28] The year 2000 witnessed a turning point in Moscow's relations with Pyongyang. A new treaty was signed in February, and in July President Putin made the first ever visit by a Russian head of state to North Korea.

Asian migration into Russia is a very serious challenge. A totally new way of thinking is required to come to grips with it. Isolation and strengthening the immigration regime are not good solutions. The border is long and porous, and corruption is endemic. More important, in order to hold its own in the Far East, Russia will need more not fewer immigrants. One obvious alternative to Chinese migration could be immigration of ethnic Russians from the CIS and the Baltic States. This would follow both the pattern of post-World War II migration of Germans from Central and Eastern Europe and the practice of colonial withdrawal (for example, of the French from Algeria and the Portuguese from Angola and Mozambique, etc.).

A new policy à la Stolypin (an interior minister and premier under Nicholas II, Pyotr Stolypin introduced and executed a large-scale program that encouraged voluntary resettlement of Russian and Ukrainian peasants) is impossible because of the population shortage in European Russia and lack of incentives to move to the Amur and the Pacific. The hopes of attracting Russians from ex-Soviet republics are fading. Russia will have to look to Asian (mainly Korean and Chinese) labor.

This remedy resembles a double-edged sword. Domestic political implications aside, there are real civilizational problems that make the Russians and the Chinese poorly equipped at this point for close interaction. The Chinese assimilate very slowly and incompletely. The cultural divide between them and the Russians is very deep. The experience of interaction at the grassroots level is at best mixed. Neither side (especially on the part of the Russians) aspires to a more intimate relationship. Only very few Chinese would wish to live in Russia permanently.

Russia will need to adopt a set of forward-looking and courageous policies that would be a clear break with the past. These policies should be designed to identify Russia's need for labor, develop hiring criteria, and welcome, accommodate, and naturalize Asian aliens. The Russians would be right to avoid over-representation of any single ethnic group of migrants. They should reach out to the Vietnamese, Indians, and others in Asia-Pacific if they want to ensure that Asiatization of the Russian Far East does not turn into Sinicization. Russian officials could benefit from a close study of U.S., Canadian, and Australian experience in this field.

Russia will need to adopt criteria for admission, establish a resident alien status, institute naturalization procedures, and develop programs of teaching foreigners Russian culture and language, etc. It will need to work hard to ensure that newly arrived residents are included in society, ensuring their loyalty to the host country. Russia will also need to think through the issue of political participation.

The result of controlled cross-border migration would be neither an American-style melting pot nor a salad of multiculturalism. It could come closer to the Russian imperial and current French model, in which naturalized aliens are accepted as "Russians" with citizenship defined in non-ethnic terms. What should be avoided by all means is a revival of the Soviet model of territorial autonomy for ethnic groups and dual citizenship leading to split loyalties.

A strong China poses great challenges for Russia; if China were to enter a major political and economic crisis, however, the implications for the Russian Far East could be catastrophic. It takes only 4 to 5 million migrants to alter the existing ethnic balance on the territory stretching from Lake Baikal to the Bering Strait.

Here, as elsewhere in Eurasia, the centuries-old trend has been reversed, and the balance between East Asia's two largest continental countries has been decisively altered. China is now the more powerful and dynamic of the two. The Russian-Chinese border can be compared to a thin membrane between two areas of very different "demographic pressure." This promises more rather than less tension between the two countries in the medium- and especially longer-term.[29] Thus, the Russian-Chinese border problem, settled for the time being, is not solved. When it reappears, it could become one of the most important geopolitical issues of the 21st century. If by that time the issue of the three islands is not settled, this may give the Chinese a good chance to argue that the entire territorial settlement must be revised.

Southern Kurils or Northern Territories?

The disputed territory between Russia and Japan is relatively small—some 4,500 square kilometers, but the economic zone around the four islands is rather extensive, about 196,000 square kilometers. Tokyo claims as its own the southernmost islands in the chain—Iturup (Etorofu), Kunashir (Kunashiri), Shikotan, and the Habomai islets,[30] which it lost in 1945 as a result of the war. Japan officially maintains that what it calls the Northern Territories are not part of the Kuril islands, which it renounced under the 1951 San Francisco Peace Treaty. Unfortunately for Moscow, Stalin decided to abstain from signing the San Francisco document, thus creating added confusion.

The issue has been frozen for decades, and has prevented the conclusion of a peace treaty between the two countries and, more generally, the full normalization of their relations. Numerous plans have been suggested for solving the territorial issue,[31] but no breakthrough was achieved in the decade following the end of the Cold War and the dismantlement of the U.S.S.R.

President Mikhail Gorbachev was the last leader who, virtually single-handedly, could have rid the bilateral relationship of the burden of the territorial problem, but his window of opportunity was too narrow. The best moment for that was lost by Khrushchev in 1960 when in protest against the renewal of the U.S.-Japan Security Treaty, he withdrew the Soviet promise, made in the 1956 Moscow Declaration, to hand over two of the four islands.[32] Later the Soviet leaders believed their country to be too strong even to admit the existence of a territorial dispute, and Gorbachev, whom the Japanese had regarded with skepticism far too long, had little time to accomplish the feat. Boris Yeltsin, who succeeded him, considered several options, all of which were highly theoretical.

Since 1992, the island issue has since become an article of faith for Russian national patriots who vehemently oppose a "sellout" to Tokyo.[33] In the 1993 Tokyo declaration, Yeltsin pledged to work to resolve the territorial issue on the basis of legality and fairness, which implies an eventual change of the status quo. Since then, little progress has been made. The ill-advised surprise decision made by President Yeltsin and Prime Minister Hashimoto at Krasnoyarsk in November 1997 to complete the peace treaty by 2000, predictably, was not implemented.

Any peace treaty would require a resolution of the territorial issue, which involves compromises. Neither side, however, is ready yet for compromise. The Japanese public overwhelmingly supports the return of the Northern Territories, and the Russian public is generally reluctant to give up the Southern Kurils.

Russia's stated interests are largely of a geopolitical nature. Giving up the islands would be the first case of actually ceding *Russian* territory—i.e., territory lying within the borders of the former Soviet Russian Republic—to a foreign power. By extension, it is feared, this action would also bring into question the legality of other territorial arrangements made by the World War II victors, including above all the status of Kaliningrad.[34] This argument is far-fetched. There is no direct link between the two issues, and it is simply impossible to imagine that Germany would make official claims on Kaliningrad if Russia were to concede the disputed islands to Japan. Doing so, to start with, would undermine the very legal foundation of Germany's current position in Europe.[35]

Geostrategically, and this is the argument stressed by the defense establishment and the security community as a whole, the four islands close the bottleneck of the Sea of Okhotsk, virtually making it a Russian lake, considered safe for a ballistic submarine bastion, despite a short Japanese coastline. The islands have even been elevated to the role of a strategic outpost, a "key to the North Pacific." Ceding this key, it is claimed, would undermine Russia's entire posture in the region. These arguments are less than compelling. Russia is phasing out its SSBN force in the Far East. The likelihood of an armed conflict with the United States and Japan is extremely low. In the hypothetical case of such a conflict, Russia would not be able to use the islands to invade Hokkaido, and would be unable itself to defend them.

More important are the psychological reasons. Russian ownership of the islands has genuinely become an article of faith for both the elite and many ordinary Russians. There can be no comparison with the Soviet acceptance of the re-unification of Germany—for in that case no non-German territory was affected—or with the troop withdrawal from the Central European states, or even the recognition of the independence of the former Soviet republics. Kaliningrad, not the Crimea, is the closest analogy to the Southern Kurils. From the mid-1990s on there was also a feeling that Russia's global retreat was over, and that any further unilateral concessions to other countries would be unacceptable.

The Russians also treat the Japanese differently from the Germans. Since World War II, when the Soviet Union occupied Eastern Germany and then created a loyal Communist state out of it, the Russians over a half century have come to know the Germans well and gradually learned to trust them. The legacy of the Soviet-German war has not been erased, but the past has ceased to be an obstacle to bilateral relations. Germany, of course, has abjured all claims to the territory that belonged to the Reich in 1937, including the former East Prussia.

In its relations with Japan, the spirit of the two wars, 1904-1905 and 1945, lives on. The second one is regarded as the redemption for the ignominious defeat in the first war. Ironically, the Russians could be generous to the Germans, even though in 1941 Germany was the attacker. There is no generosity and little sympathy toward the Japanese, although it was the U.S.S.R. that attacked them in 1945. Nations that suddenly have grown weak can't be generous. It is also difficult for them to see the benefits of the win-win situations. In 1989, the political elite of the

U.S.S.R. still perceived itself as being strong and powerful, and the public had high expectations from a radical improvement of relations with the West: democratization, improvement of living conditions, joining the community of civilized nations, etc. A decade later, the popular and elite sentiment in Russia is substantially different.

It is also important to understand the difference between the Kuril question and the territorial adjustments along the Sino-Russian border. The May 1991 agreement between Moscow and Beijing was negotiated in a different era when the Russian public and the various interest groups within it had no means of actually influencing government policies. The process of democratization has changed that, as evidenced by later problems with the implementation of the 1991 accord.

A concession on Russia's part would not automatically bring it benefits. Investments, popularly believed to be the price Japan will pay for the islands, would probably not be forthcoming for clear economic reasons. The tables have been turned since the late 1950s: Japan is now too strong, and Russia too weak, for a solution. There is too little domestic pressure on both countries' governments to act on the basis of some compromise.[36] At the end of 1998, Russia rejected a Hong Kong-type solution offered by Japan, which would require a Russian recognition of Japanese sovereignty over the four islands, but would postpone their actual return to Japanese rule. In its turn, the Russian proposal of joint economic use of the islands, while shelving the sovereignty issue, was not acceptable to Japan. Thus, the political will for a workable solution is, at present, lacking. Russia even balks at reiterating the Soviet Union's 1956 offer of transferring two smaller islands.

Neither side, however, is profiting from the current impasse. Eventually, the basis for a compromise can emerge, albeit in the distant future. A change in the Russian and Japanese domestic environments will be the crucial factor.[37] For the governments to instruct their diplomats to move toward a solution, they must be pressured by their publics and major vested interests.

For Russia to give, it must win back a measure of self-confidence. A weak and disorganized Russia will not back down, whereas a stronger and more coherent one may consider a trade-off. This happier Russia would be less guided by traditional territorial geopolitics and, most important, would be able to absorb whatever economic benefits that would accompany a political settlement. For domestic political as well as constitutional reasons, the issue can also be rephrased. Instead of solving a territorial dispute, the two countries could agree on the delimitation of an internationally recognized border between them.[38]

In order to win back some self-confidence, Russians should introduce more legality and transparency into economic and social systems, thus creating the basis for a long-awaited economic boom in the Far East and making it at least marginally attractive to Japanese investors. Some compelling external reasons for compromise include the continuing rise of China, a possible Korean reunification, or the prospect, however unlikely at the moment, of partial U.S. disengagement from the region. A combination of domestic factors and the changing international environment could produce the incentives that are currently lacking for both sides to move forward.

It is possible to imagine the Russian Federation giving Japan the islands the Soviet Union promised in 1956 as the territorial settlement under a peace treaty and agreeing to negotiate the status of the two bigger islands, Iturup and Kunashir.[39] The Russians would be more willing to countenance the loss of territory in return for a finite border settlement (which would also give them a legal title to Southern Sakhalin) and the wider opportunities for investment, trade, technology transfers, etc. After all, even the Russian philosopher Ivan Ilyin considered that "it is not the territory that is sacred and inviolable, for Russia voluntarily ceded Alaska and nobody saw that as shameful, but the territory which is necessary for the flowering of Russian national spiritual culture."[40] This latter territory is the Russian Far East and Siberia.

As to the Japanese, they increasingly recognize that their overriding interest in the north is a friendly, democratic, and stable Russia, which also offers certain economic opportunities and provides some political reassurance. Thus, Tokyo could become progressively more willing to settle for less than its long-standing claim.

With both Japan and Russia becoming more pragmatic, it may be possible to act incrementally, downplaying in the Russian case the sovereignty issue and concentrating instead on the advantages of interaction. In Japan's case, this means actually taking a long view and assuming responsibilities that would allow it to become, with respect to Russia, a *new* "Germany of the East." If this happens, it will finally signal the end of a century of conflict and confrontation in Russo-Japanese relations.

* * *

Russia is a European, not an Asian country, but for the last four hundred years it has also been a country in Asia. It is precisely this eastern dimension that makes it Russia rather than Muscovy. Even as the Russians stress their European vocation, they must redouble their efforts to develop the three-quarters of their territory lying east of the Urals while ultimately resolving the outstanding border issues with its powerful and increasingly important neighbors. This is an inversion of Russia's historical task: instead of outward expansion, no longer possible or sensible, the country needs to concentrate on the development of the largest piece of real estate in the world.

NOTES

[1] Sergei Karaganov (ed.), *Strategiya dlya Rossii: Povestka dnya dlya Prezidenta-2000*, Vagrius, Moscow, 2000, p. 267.

[2] Thomas Graham believes it would "give China unimpeded access to the riches of that region or spark a destabilizing contest for them among China, Japan, South Korea, and the United States." See Thomas Graham, "A World Without Russia." A paper presented at the Jamestown Foundation Conference, Washington, D.C., June 9, 1999. See also Russian translation of this piece in *Nezavisimaya gazeta*, December 8, 1999.

[3] This state, which briefly existed in the final stages of Russia's Civil War, was a creation of Moscow's Bolsheviks, who used its nominal sovereignty to avoid a direct clash with Japan. When this geopolitical buffer outlived its usefulness, it was abolished and fully absorbed into Soviet Russia.

[4] See Sergei Baburin, "Problemy gosudarstvennykh granits Rossii na postsovetskom prostranstve," *Vlast*, No. 12, 1998, p. 44. When the republic was first established in 1923, it was named Buryat-Mongolia. In the 1930s, the Buryat intelligentsia and Buddhist religion were subjected to large-scale repression. The renaming came in 1958, officially, in order to reflect more accurately the ethnicity of the title group. However, a more probable reason was to shore up diplomatically the Mongolian People's Republic, a Soviet ally. At the time, Mongolia proper (or Outer Mongolia, as it was known) was flanked by Buryat-Mongolia in the north and the Chinese autonomous district of Inner Mongolia in the southeast. As relations between the U.S.S.R. and China were becoming increasingly

strained, Moscow sought to fend off potential Chinese designs on its ally by dropping its own hypothetical claims to Outer Mongolia. In the end, this Soviet policy paid off: in 1961, Mongolia was admitted into the United Nations, and its independence was for the first time universally confirmed. Characteristically, this was closely preceded by a similar move in the Soviet northwest, where the Karelo-Finnish constituent republic was converted into the Karelian Autonomous Republic, with a change of name and a loss of status, in 1956.

[5]   See Georgy F. Kunadze, "Border Problems Between Russia and Its Neighbors: Stable for Now, but Stubborn in the Long Run," in Gilbert Rozman, Mikhail G. Nosov, and Koji Watanabe (Eds.), *Russia and East Asia: The 21st Century Security Environment*, East-West Institute, Armonk, N.Y., M.E. Sharpe, London, 1999, p. 134.

[6]   An invective against this attempt to undermine the territorial integrity of Russia and China can be found in Sergei Berezin, "Professor iz Tokio reanimiruyet idei panmongolizma," *NG—Regiony,* No. 4, 2000, p. 6.

[7]   See Alexei Chichkin, "I kolonisty mogut byt soyuznikami," *Nezavisimaya gazeta*, February 1, 2000, p. 4.

[8]   Vladimir Putin, "Rossiya na rubezhe tysyacheletii," *Nezavisimaya gazeta,* December 30, 1999, p. 4.

[9]   Alexei D. Bogaturov. "Pluralisticheskaya mnogopolyarnost i interesy Rossii," *Svobodnaya mysl,* 1996, No. 2, pp. 25-36. Quoted from *Vneshnyaya politika i bezopasnost sovremennoi Rossii,* A Reader, Vol. 1, Book 1, Moscow Science Foundation, Moscow, 1999, p. 92.

[10]   See, for instance, V. Larin, *Kitai i Dalny Vostok Rossii*, Vladivostok, 1998, p. 6.

[11]   Of which the eastern section is 4,204 km long, and the western one just 55 km. The two sections are separated by the territory of Mongolia.

[12]   Previous Sino-Russian border conflicts include the siege of the Russian fort of Albazin by the Chinese troops in 1689; in 1929, Chinese troops clashed in Manchuria with the Soviet forces protecting the Russian-owned China Eastern Railway. In 1938 and 1939, there were two small border wars between the U.S.S.R. and Japan in the area, on Lake Khasan (Primorye) and on the Khalkhin Gol River (Mongolia). In 1945, the Soviet Union invaded Manchuria and defeated the Japanese Kwantung army deployed there.

13 For a good collection of different Russian attitudes toward this agreement, see *Rossiisko-kitaiskaya granitsa: dokumenty, argumenty, fakty*, NG Publishers, Moscow, 1997.

14 Bolshoi Ussuriisky and Tarabarov, and Bolshoi, respectively.

15 In the future, this unresolved problem may become exacerbated as the Kazakevicheva Channel, the southern arm of the Amur river where the actual borderline passes, becomes shallower and can cease to exist, which will give added weight to the Chinese demand that the border be fixed further to the north, making Khabarovsk, the center of the entire Russian Far East, a border city.

16 See, for example, Ambassador Genrikh Kireyev, writing in *Nezavisimaya gazeta,* January 31, 1997.

17 Vladimir Larin, *Kitai i Dalni Vostok Rossii,* Institut istorii, arheologii i etnogrphii norodov Dalnevogo Voctoka DVO RAN, Vladivostok, 1998, p. 189.

18 Zbigniew Brzezinski's geopolitical vision of a Greater China as a global power also includes the whole of Central Asia minus Turkmenistan, extending China's strategic boundary almost to Astrakhan and Volgograd. See Zbigniew Brzezinski, *The Grand Chessboard: American Primacy and Its Geostrategic Imperatives,* Basic Books, New York, 1997, p. 167.

19 Henry Kissinger, who during his short trip to Vladivostok in November 1974 had been struck that "physically it resembled a central European city plunked down at the edge of Asia" (Henry Kissinger, *Years of Renewal,* p. 287), mentioned in his conversation with Chou Enlai a few days later that Vladivostok had always been Russian. In response, Chou tersely reminded him, "In the past, the inhabitants were mainly Chinese" (ibid., p. 870).

20 *Naseleniye Rossii 1998*, Sixth annual demographic report, edited by A.G. Vishnevsky, Institute of Economic Forecasts, Russian Academy of Sciences, Moscow, 1999, p. 7.

21 *Annual Message of the President of the Russian Federation to the Federal Assembly of the Russian Federation*, July 8, 2000.

22 See Colonel General Konstantin Totsky (director of the Federal Border Service, or FBS), "Avtoritet gosudarstvennoi granitsy," *Krasnaya zvezda*, December 15, 1998, pp. 1, 2.

[23] A senior official of the Federal Border Guard Service claimed that from January 1999 through June 2000, more than 1 million Chinese entered Russia illegally (see Kevin O'Flynn, "Chinese Migration Alarms Border Patrol," *The Moscow Times,* July 1, 2000, p. 3). Most authors put the number of Chinese in Russia between a few hundred thousand and 2 to 2.5 million. Some unsubstantiated reports refer to 5 million, and call this "demographic expansion." See Vilya Gelbras, "Predvaritelniye itogi izucheniya problem kitaiskoi migratsii v Moskve, Vladivostoke i Ussuriiske (rezultaty anketnykh oprosov)," in *Perspektivy dalnevostochnogo regiona: kitaisky faktor,* Carnegie Center, Moscow, 1999, p. 9.

[24] The fear is not unique to the Far East: in Gorny Altai, which borders on Kazakhstan, Mongolia, and China, there are apprehensions that building a road linking Xinjiang to the Trans-Siberian railway and a parallel gas pipeline would stimulate massive Chinese migration to the region. See Sergei Golubchikov, "Gorny Altai na puti v XXI vek," *NG—Regiony,* No. 4, 2000, p. 6.

[25] In 1989, there were 11,000 Chinese in the U.S.S.R.

[26] Zhanna Zaionchkovskaya, "Russky vopros," *Migratsia,* No. 1, 1996.

[27] Colonel General Boris Gromov, former Duma member and now governor of the Moscow Region, spoke with apprehension about plans to resettle 100,000 Koreans to the Far East and projections of the Chinese diaspora exceeding 3 million by 2002-2003. See Boris Gromov, "Obshchechelovecheskiye tsennosti i sobstvenniye interesy," *Nezavisimaya gazeta,* October 2, 1998, p. 8.

[28] Interestingly, the farmers will come from both South and North Korea and Uzbekistan. See Alexei Chichkin, "I kolonisty mogut byt soyuznikami," *Nezavisimaya gazeta,* February 1, 2000, p. 4.

[29] Alexei G. Arbatov calls China "the only power in the world that can pose a long-term direct military threat to Russia's security." See Alexei G. Arbatov, *Bezopasnost: Rossiiskii vybor,* EPIcenter, Moscow, 1999, p. 281.

[30] Stalin's blunder of refusing to participate in the 1951 San Francisco Peace Treaty with Japan has also left the Soviet Union, and hence Russia, without a formal title to Southern Sakhalin and the Northern Kuril Islands, to which Japan, in any case, has no claims.

[31] A unique trilateral study prepared by Graham Allison, Hiroshi Kimura, and Konstantin Sarkisov listed no fewer than 66 ways of solving the problem. See *Beyond the Cold War to the Trilateral Cooperation in the Asia-Pacific Region,* Strengthening the Democratic Institutions Project, Cambridge, Mass., 1992. The issue was also tackled at the three Portsmouth seminars (also trilateral), held in 1994, 1995, and 2000.

[32] It is a moot question, however, whether the United States would have allowed a normalization of the Japanese-Soviet relationship. John Foster Dulles is known to have strongly resisted this.

[33] Alexander Solzhenitsyn was one of the few figures who was courageous enough to call this campaign "pseudo-patriotic." In his view, Russia's humiliation in 1904-1905 was lifted by its victory over Japan in 1945. See Alexander Solzhenitsyn, *Rossiya v obvale,* Russky Put, Moscow, 1998, pp. 45-46.

[34] See Dmitri Gornostayev, "Novy sezon dlya Rossii i Yaponii," *Nezavisimaya gazeta,* January 22, 1998.

[35] Lithuanian border claims to the region or Finland's to part of Karelia and Pechenga are likewise unlikely to be raised officially, and if they were, would be far less serious.

[36] Alexei Arbatov, "Kurilskoye 'lezviye' rossiisko-yaponskikh otnoshenii," *Nezavisimaya gazeta,* November 28, 1998, p. 3.

[37] For an excellent analysis of the Kuril issue and discussion of the options for the future, see Alexei Arbatov, *Bezopasnost Rossii,* pp. 287-300.

[38] Interestingly, the 2000 Russian Foreign Policy Concept refers to the "search for a mutually acceptable solution to the fixation of an internationally recognized border between the two countries" (*The Foreign Policy Concept of the Russian Federation,* Section IV).

[39] See, for instance, Georgy F. Kunadze,"Border Problems Between Russia and its Neighbors," in *Russia and East Asia: The 21st Century Security Environment,* G. Rozman, M. Nosov, K. Watanabe (Eds.), East-West Inst., M.E. Sharpe, New York, 1999. p. 145.

[40] Ivan Ilyin, *Put k ochevidnosti,* Exmo-Press, Moscow, 1998, p. 219.

Part Three

INTEGRATION

Integration

The problems of domestic territorial organization of Russia and its integration into the wider world are intimately linked with the nature of the Russian political regime and the policies of the Russian government. The country's authoritarian regimes, not to mention totalitarian ones, have been incompatible with federalism. Thus, the Soviet Union, a federation in name, quickly turned into a de facto unitary state. By the same token, the U.S.S.R. had to carry out policies of economic autarky and foreign policy isolationism.

Gorbachev's *perestroika* logically undermined both notions. It raised the issue of the nature of the Soviet federation, and set in motion the process of creating a better union. It did away with the Cold War in Moscow's relations with the West and China, which necessitated the Soviet military and political withdrawal from Central and Eastern Europe and Afghanistan, and included the Soviet agreement to the reunification of Germany. It also made Soviet borders porous from the inside, relaxing the movement of people and ideas across them.

While the liberal Communist Gorbachev was trying to reconfigure the Soviet Union along confederal lines and to fit it into a more cooperative global arrangement (by means of a "common European house" and a "Vancouver to Vladivostok" security system), the leading Soviet dissident, Andrei Sakharov, was conceptualizing the worldwide convergence of communism and capitalism, and proposed in his famous "Constitution" the remaking of the U.S.S.R.

as a "Union of Soviet Republics of Europe and Asia," with 40 to 50 members. Both were idealists whose ideas, whatever their merits, could not have been implemented.

The Yeltsin regime started as ultra-liberal, opening up to the West and aspiring to full integration with it, dissolving the Soviet Union and letting all the republics go unconditionally, and practicing laissez-faire in Moscow's relations with the Russian regions. Soon, however, it became more and more chaotic and occasionally defensive. Under Yeltsin, Russia fought two wars in Chechnya, while allowing the regions to turn into feudal fiefs; it mishandled NATO enlargement and the Balkan conflicts, which produced a permanent strain on Russian-Western relations; it sought refuge in multipolarity only to realize that Russia was far too small a pole to benefit from that game. Finally, it made a mess of the CIS and constructed a strange semi-detached "union state" of Russia and Belarus.

Putin's recentralization agenda was first reflected in his drive to reduce the powers of regional leaders, including by means of the newly created federal districts. Putin gave the military carte blanche on Chechnya. In Russia's relations with the Newly Independent States, specific security issues ("fighting international terrorism") and economic problems (such as Ukrainian gas payments) have come to the fore. Integration is on the back burner. Putin's widely publicized pragmatic approach to the regions, however, contains a few major chinks that could be his undoing. Should the recentralization effort seek to eliminate the regions as important power centers within Russia, should the guerilla war in Chechnya continue indefinitely, and should Russian "counter-terrorists" become bogged down on the borders of Afghanistan and the Central Asian states in the area, the prospects for economic modernization, the formation of a civil society, and democratization in Russia will be very bleak.

CHAPTER 6

Domestic Boundaries and the Russian Question

Historically, the Russian Empire developed as a continuous area. Two implications follow from that. On the one hand, with the exception of the Grand Duchy of Finland and the Kingdom of Poland, there was no clear and permanent division between the metropolitan area and the colonies, as in the British and French empires. The geographic contiguity and the policy of assimilation that followed annexation were chiefly responsible for that. Newly acquired territories were initially given special status, which later was progressively diluted and in most cases (Finland being the only exception) was formally abolished long before 1917.[1] Protectorates, retaining formal sovereignty, were rather rare in the history of the Russian Empire.[2] On the other hand, territorial centralization and the absence of autonomous power centers at regional or municipal levels were among the key pillars of the authoritarian and totalitarian political regimes in Russia. Thus, the territorial organization of Russian power is intimately linked both with the Russian national identity and the nature of Russia's political regime. Logically, when the Soviet Communist regime disintegrated, Russia became caught between separatist and recentralization tendencies. Democratic devolution is proving exceedingly difficult.

This chapter discusses the potential for regional separatism and territorial conflicts inside Russia. The National

Security Concept approved in January 2000 lays stress on the primacy of domestic dangers to Russia's security. It names "ethno-egoism, ethnocentrism, and chauvinism" among the principal factors undermining the common economic, political, and cultural space of the Russian Federation.[3] Separatism, as vividly shown in Chechnya, is a clear and present danger, but the poor governance of a country stretching across 11 time zones and composed of 89 regions is in the long run an even more serious one.

One of President Putin's first major moves was to strengthen the "vertical power structure" by reducing the powers of the regional heads and practically placing them under the authority of presidential representatives, each responsible for a federal district (seven altogether) made up of about a dozen regions.[4] This "federal reform," which greatly enhances the personal power of the president, is frankly aimed at recentralization. Its full implementation would ideally make Russia a unitary state. Such an outcome, however, is not a foregone conclusion, especially given that such a unitary state is not adequately suited to dealing with Russia's internal and external environment. The federal government has, at best, only modest means of mobilizing the regions. At the regional and federal levels, Russia remains a country where all players are rather weak. There can be shifts in the balance of power either toward or away from the regions, but probably no landslides. However, one thing is clear: the territorial organization of the Russian state will both reflect and shape the country's political regime. Soviet-era unitarism was succeeded by Yeltsin's laissez-faire regionalism which was actually federalism by default. For Russia to advance toward post-modernity, it will need to finally live up to its official title of a federation. This chapter will not discuss the problems of Russian federalism per se[5] but will focus more narrowly on the issues of the country's territorial unity. With the Chechen problem and the general situation in the North Caucasus generally dealt with in Chapter 4, the following discussion will focus on the six remaining federal districts.

Historical Evolution

As the Collection of Lands proceeded, old Russian principalities were progressively being absorbed into the Great Russian State, and the feudal boundaries withered away. Local political identities were destroyed: the local princely families and the boyars were resettled in Moscow where they finally became part of the Russian elite, and their former place was taken by the Kremlin-appointed military governors. In a symbolic move against the ancient freedoms of Novgorod, in 1478 Ivan III took away to Moscow the bell that used to call the Novgoroders to their popular assembly. A rare example of a Russian feudal constitution had ceased to exist. By the mid-16th century, all references to the former principalities had disappeared. Territories were grouped together according to Moscow's administrative, military, and economic needs.

Thus, from the time of Ivan the Terrible, Muscovy's main characteristic was its tight centralization. The empire founded by Peter the Great continued to operate in an even more unified fashion. Peter initially divided the country into eight governorates. Newly acquired territories in the Caucasus, Bessarabia, and Central Asia were becoming fully absorbed after a transition period of 15 to 30 years. The general trend was toward unification and Russification. Poland, in 1815 a "kingdom within Russia," with its own constitution, 50 years later became merely a collection of governorates in a loose group called the "Vistula territory" (*Privislyansky Krai*), mainly for statistical purposes. Finland, while still a Grand Duchy, was going in the same direction under Alexander III. Still, it managed to preserve most of its freedoms through 1917, protected by an administrative border that separated it from the rest of the empire, which made it relatively safe for Lenin, then charged with high treason by the Provisional Government, to go into hiding there in the summer of 1917.

The Soviet Union started in December 1922 as a treaty-based federation. However, its first Constitution, adopted in 1924, and especially the "Stalinist" basic law of 1936, clearly revealed an emphasis on the centralization of state power. Even more importantly, all real power in the country belonged to the Communist Party apparatus, which used the state as a front.

In the Soviet period, inter-republican borders were drawn rather arbitrarily, based on the needs of governing the country *as a whole* and treated as little more than administrative lines, but the nationalities issue was initially very prominent. When the U.S.S.R. was being formed, all of Central Asia was part of the Russian Republic. From 1924 through 1936, five separate republics were built there. The Transcaucasian Federal Republic, another founding member of the Union, was dismembered to create three individual entities. The Karelo-Finnish Republic was suddenly founded in 1940, and quietly abolished 16 years later. These constituent republics were declared sovereign entities, but their sovereignty was not real, and their proclaimed right of secession was all but impossible to exercise.

At the next levels of the hierarchy of "national-territorial entities," the autonomous republics and regions (oblasts) were even less stable. Abkhazia, initially on par with Georgia, was later "assigned" to it; Karabakh was granted to Azerbaijan, and the Crimea was given to Ukraine as a "present" from Russia to mark the tricentennial of the "reunification." Between Russia, Belarus, and Ukraine, whole oblasts were switched from one "sovereign Soviet socialist state" to another.

Some autonomous republics have fared far worse. Under Stalin, the Crimean Tatar Autonomy was abolished, alongside with the Republic of the Volga Germans and the Checheno-Ingush Autonomy. Only the latter was later restored. Boundaries between the autonomous units were routinely adjusted, but seldom finalized and made into law. When the U.S.S.R. collapsed, this became a burning issue.

Sources of Regionalization

Anti-Bolshevik White Russian forces in the civil war fought under the slogan of "United and Indivisible Russia." For most among them, even Polish independence was non-negotiable. The Bolsheviks, who in their search for allies against the imperial Russian state proclaimed the right of nations to self-determination, including secession, eventually created an elaborate state structure that was federal/confederal on the surface,[6] but was essentially strictly unified. The important but often underestimated difference between the U.S.S.R. and the Russian Empire was that all ethnic groups and the constituent republics within the Soviet state formally enjoyed equal rights. In reality, this was of course pure fiction. The national homelands, which were being created from 1920, had all the trappings of autonomy, but no actual powers to act independently from the central authorities, even on the most trivial issues. Their administrative limits were drawn, and redrawn by the central government. No opposition was tolerated. A number of "bourgeois nationalists" were sent to prison or executed,[7] and in several cases the Communist authorities had to resort to force to put down resistance movements.[8] In more tranquil times, the authorities in Moscow had to deal with a stream of petitions from the regions demanding ethnic rehabilitation and restitution.[9] Largely, however, the Communist Party managed to control the situation.

The Russian Federation is not just a reduced copy of the U.S.S.R., because it includes both non-Russian ethnic republics and ethnic Russian regions or oblasts, which have essentially the same status. In addition, unlike the Soviet Union, there has never been a "Russian Republic" within the federation. Moreover, in most Soviet republics ethnic Russians formed a majority.

In the final years of *perestroika*, the regional interest groups within Russia that were wooed by both Gorbachev and Yeltsin in their struggle for primacy in Moscow emerged as the clear winners. It was at that time, in 1991, that Yeltsin made his famous offer to the regional heads: "Take as much sovereignty as you can swallow." Accompanying this power struggle was a broader public debate about the structure of the post-Soviet Russian state. Some demanded a treaty-based federation, while others favored a constitutionally based one. There was also disagreement between those who regarded Russia as an inherently asymmetrical construction and those who preferred more symmetry, etc. This debate notwithstanding, decentralization continued, largely in a chaotic way.[10]

In 1991-1992, in the wake of the dismantlement of the U.S.S.R., the Russian Federation made serious concessions to its own regions. Like the president of Russia, presidents of the republics and regional governors came to be popularly elected, and thus attained a high degree of independence from the Kremlin. Although the Russian Federation—unlike the U.S.S.R.—had never been a treaty-based federation, the Federation Treaty, signed in March 1992, was made an integral part of the Constitution, adopted in December 1993. These concessions, although much criticized, probably saved the Russian Federation from following the path of the U.S.S.R.

By 1993, massive separatism had ceased to be an imminent threat. The federation saved Russia. The Constitution made the republics and the regions equal, and proclaimed the supremacy of federal law and the unity of state power in Russia. The country's territorial integrity was particularly stressed. No part of the Federation was allowed to seek secession. In reality, however, relations between the Kremlin and the regions were largely regulated by special deals struck between the presidential administration and the regional authorities.

When powerful regions, such as Tatarstan, declined to sign that treaty, a special bilateral agreement was concluded between Kazan and Moscow in 1993, which averted a potentially disastrous confrontation. Later that practice became commonplace, with over half the regions having established "special" relations with the federation. The Yeltsin administration tolerated discrepancies between republican constitutions and the basic laws of the federation. Tatarstan, Bashkortostan, Yakutia, and Buryatia all proclaimed themselves "sovereign states," and Karelia announced its "economic sovereignty." In certain instances, the regions, such as Tatarstan, Yakutia/Sakha, and Bashkortostan refused to pay taxes to the federal government, with impunity. This system was characterized as "feudal federalism."[11]

A number of new frontier regions have emerged, oriented toward commercial relations with their immediate neighbors across the border. Kaliningrad, Vladivostok, Khabarovsk, Blagoveshchensk, and even Murmansk and St. Petersburg are opening up to the outside world. Places deep in central Eurasia such as Astrakhan, Orenburg, Omsk, Novosibirsk, and Irkutsk are all situated in border areas and have to cooperate closely with their neighbors. Along Russia's western border, regional and local authorities, businesses, community leaders, and ordinary citizens cultivate close contacts with their peers in Belarus and Ukraine. It is too early to talk about the formation of frontier communities along the lines of Euroregions: a miracle borderland region is yet to emerge, but the trend is unmistakable. In 1980, there was only one international airport in the whole of the U.S.S.R., twenty years later there are dozens of them in Russia alone.

Those Russians who are looking hard for a niche to be filled by a future Russia point to the country's potential role as a land bridge between Europe and East and Central Asia, as well as the Caucasus. The proposed projects involve rail and road links, oil and gas pipelines, telecom cables, and the like. Russia, however, will not be able to monopolize that role. The proposed transport corridor linking East Asia with Europe through Central Asia and the Caucasus (TRASECA) as well as the Silk Road, and pipelines running west, south, and east of the Caspian pose fierce competition. Still, Russia has the potential of eventually getting a fair share of that traffic. If it succeeds, central Eurasia will be opened up more and more. For the first time in modern history, the influence of the rimland is stronger than the influence of Russia, the region's core state.[12]

This opportunity hides a serious danger. Ironically, this is related to the notion of multipolarity, which had been

Russia's official foreign policy doctrine during Yeltsin's second presidency. Russia, which has no chance of becoming a global pole itself, is being increasingly affected by the two real poles, the European Union and China, whose rise and expansion puts the neighboring Russian regions, the country's northwest and the Far East, in the gravitation zones of Europe and China. At the same time, Russia's southern periphery, especially in the North Caucasus, is feeling the effects of rapid Islamization, which raises an important issue of identity. Unless the central government devises and implements an imaginative regional policy, Moscow may eventually turn into a mere negotiating place where the governors come to strike deals.

Regionalization is an objective and healthy process, cutting at the root of the Russian autocratic tradition, which has stifled regional and local potential. For the first time since the mid-16th century, Russia has a chance to build from the bottom up. In theory, a regionally oriented Russia offers a far better chance of the emergence of a civil society, democratization, and economic reform than an overly centralized Russia. However, like so many other elements of the new order in Russia, this movement toward regionalization has been instituted by various vested interests seeking to expand their power and property holdings.

By 1996-1998, with the majority of presidents and governors elected by popular mandate, power became consolidated at the regional level. With the collusion of the Kremlin, which bought loyalty at the price of non-interference, the federation turned into a de facto feudal-type system in which the local governors and presidents of republics inside Russia emerged as the authoritarian rulers of their territorial fiefdoms. The boundaries of the regions and the republics thus came to denote different political and, to some extent, even economic regimes.

By the end of the Yeltsin presidency, Russia was an extremely weak federation. To take one extreme example, Chechnya was first allowed to proceed on its own, then was invaded in the name of constitutional order, then virtually recognized as independent, and then neglected until a new war began. The question that was asked at the start of the Yeltsin era—"will the Russian Federation follow the path of the U.S.S.R., and break up?"—was reformulated into: "will the steady decline of the central authorities lead to a de facto confederalization of Russia?" These are very serious questions. They demand that factors contributing to Russia's territorial unity and those undermining that unity be carefully analyzed.

Factors of Stability and Instability

Both sets of factors exist side by side, and their relative strength constantly varies. The prime factor of instability is the political implosion of central authority, which rested on the peculiar function of the Soviet Communist Party as the only and omnipresent power structure. The dismantlement of the Communist machine was not compensated in the Yeltsin period by the formation of effective democratic institutions, in particular a functioning federal center. This was especially destabilizing in conditions where vertical (Moscow-to-the-regions) relations traditionally dominated, and horizontal inter-regional links were extremely weak. From a purely economic point of view, once Russia's formerly fortress-like external borders turned into frontiers allowing exchanges of various kinds, there was not enough interest to prioritize the domestic links. The state, which was held together by military force and a centralized bureaucracy, is becoming increasingly vulnerable to the forces of economic globalization. Russia's economic crisis, with which the central government was unable to cope, and the resulting degradation of inter-regional links in such a vast country formed the material basis for economic separatism. One of the most serious practical obstacles to communication within this vast country has been high railroad tariffs.[13] Cultural and personal contacts among the people have deteriorated, and emotional links to such symbols of national unity as Moscow, the capital, and the Black Sea resorts, where many ordinary people used to spend their vacations, even the Armed Forces, which have become much more locally recruited, have slackened. The result was the semi-disintegration of Russia, where weak regions co-exist uneasily with an even weaker center.

Other factors of instability include the still high degree of ethnic, confessional, and civilizational heterogeneity. The Russian Federation counts several republics whose indigenous population is Muslim or Buddhist. The revival of Islam (and potentially Buddhist fermentation) has real implications for those republics and poses a major challenge to Russia. This challenge is only exacerbated by the largely successful work of the Russian Orthodox Church hierarchy aimed at winning a privileged position for itself in society and securing a permanent political role. If the new Russian identity will heavily draw on Slav ethnicity and Orthodoxy, the unity of the country even beyond the North Caucasus can not be guaranteed.

The principal stabilizing factor is the much higher degree of ethnic homogeneity enjoyed by present-day Russia in comparison to the U.S.S.R. The population of the Russian Federation is 82 percent ethnic Russian, compared with the Soviet Union's 50 percent. Another 4 percent (5.6 million) is made up of ethnic Ukrainians and Belarussians who are more or less evenly dispersed around the country and, more importantly, are virtually de-ethnicized.

The Russian people themselves have a strong attachment to the unified state. They have no modern experience of living in separate political entities. The old Russian principalities, the last of which ceased to exist nearly 500 years ago, are distant and vague memories. There are no signs of the revival of regional political loyalties of this kind. In the popular mind, political fragmentation is seen as a calamity, inseparably linked to the turmoil of a civil war or to foreign intervention. The only "separatist" Russian state in recent history to be of some relevance is the Far Eastern Republic, which was (a) artificially created by the Bolsheviks as a buffer against Japan; (b) extremely short-lived (1920-1922) and left few traces; and (c) existed in a remote borderland.

Even in the national homelands, ethnic Russians mostly form a majority. This is a result of the Soviet Communist Party policy of assimilation, which manifested itself in endowing the ethnic homelands with Russian-populated areas, and directing migration flows. As a result of these and earlier imperial efforts, most non-ethnic Russian peoples that have their homelands, such as Tatars, Bashkirs and other peoples of the Volga-Urals basin, or the Buryats and Yakuts in Siberia, are sufficiently russified. Also, these ethnic groups are sufficiently dispersed around the country. Most Tatars, for example, live outside of Tatarstan—where, incidentally, the ethnic Russian population roughly equals the Tatar one.

Altogether, Russia is composed of 89 regions, most of which are relatively small and cannot exist on their own. The existing eight inter-regional associations are nothing but governors' conferences, without an ambition to become even lobbying groups vis-à-vis Moscow. Typically, links between the regional administrations and the federal government are much stronger than between the neighboring regions. Ironically, plans to enlarge the regions and reduce their number to 10-20, rather than making the country more manageable, could even increase the potential for separatism, if the central authority remains weak.[14]

There is also a new fear of being overwhelmed by neighbors, which creates a paradox: while economically the Russian Far Eastern provinces are being willingly integrated with the far more powerful and dynamic China, politically the population there is becoming increasingly defensive. They might wish to become a joint protectorate of America, Japan, and South Korea, but they see absolutely no future for them as part of a Greater China. In these circumstances, the continuation of the status quo is a much lesser evil.[15]

Under these conditions, the case of the North Caucasus, and especially Chechnya, discussed in an earlier chapter, is an atypical one. It must also be noted that the demonstration effect of the two wars in Chechnya and armed conflicts in the CIS states, and in the Balkans, has not been missed by the regional elites within the Russian Federation and is not to be underestimated. The scale of devastation in Chechnya makes all talk of independence sound hollow.

The secessionists, always a small minority except in Chechnya, have become marginalized. Most regional elites in power now are pragmatically oriented. They value the kind of autonomy that they currently have, and though some of them want a better deal with Moscow, none intends to break away from the Russian Federation. For its part, the federation passed a law on national-cultural autonomy, which was downplayed in Soviet times, overshadowed by the notion of territorial autonomy.

In both ethnic Russian regions and national homelands, it is economic not political particularism that is the
main problem. In the same way as during the severe food
crisis in 1990-1991 when many regional authorities closed
their boundaries to food exports, some regions and republics
have had to act independently in the economic sphere simply to fill the vacuum of state authority. This is especially
true of faraway or exposed territories as Primorye or Kaliningrad. In both cases, the level of corruption is extremely
high, even by current Russian standards. The financial crisis
of 1998 briefly raised the specter of Russia's de facto disintegration on purely economic grounds. Similarly, the poor
state of the Armed Forces and their growing dependency
on local authorities led some Russian and foreign observers
to explore the potential of Russia's coming apart at the
seams of its military districts.[16] Still, with only 10 out of 89
regions being net contributors to the federal budget, the
level of dependency on the central government continues
to be very high. In addition, about 80 percent of the nation's
private capital is concentrated in Moscow. As for the regular military, even before the second Chechen war they
would never have supported secession by a region.

Thus, the federal center will probably not be challenged abruptly or *en masse*; but it may well lose gradually
and by default. A semi-dissolution of Russia is more of a
real danger, though at present a remote one, than the country's outright dismantlement. Moreover, the beginning of
the long-awaited economic upturn and modest but sustained economic growth as well as the improvement of the
system of governance in Russia is likely to depress trends
toward secession and disintegration even more.

Thus, with the important exception of Chechnya, separatism is not a current issue. The more relevant question

is the degree of centralization that Russia will have and what the implications of such centralization will be for the territorial and political composition of the country. Traditionally, periods of decentralization in Russian history were followed by periods of recentralization. However, Eurasia in its internal form of an empire has also ceased to exist. Even allowing for discontinuities, Russia is in search of a new regional order within its borders.[17]

With the end of the Yeltsin era, one of the more prominent themes in the public debate has become the restoration of what is called the power vertical, i.e., the central political authority. Proposals included appointment and dismissal of governors by the president, reducing the status of national homelands, and enlargement of the regions.[18]

Putin decided against enlarging the regions themselves, which would possibly increase the potential for autonomy, if not separatism, if the central authorities remained weak.[19] Instead, Putin decided to group the 89 regions, whose boundaries remained intact, into seven federal districts, ruled by presidential representatives. This initiative is laden with consequences. Endowing the president's men with authority over federal officials in their territory, giving them a measure of control over money flows, ordinary and tax police, procurator's offices, and the military can effectively turn the seven regions into proto-states, provided that the center remains unconsolidated. The extent to which this can be implemented, and the manner of implementation, will be of crucial importance. In this context, attempting to affect the status or boundaries of national homelands can be very risky. Defining the status and role of the national homelands within the Russian Federation will be critical to the country's future.

Administrative measures from above can only achieve so much. Russia will only become integrated when there is a single market for goods, capital, and labor, and a common legal space.

Even under the most propitious circumstances, the Russian Federation will in many ways remain asymmetrical, owing to the country's imperial heritage. Its structural elements may be equal as subjects of the federation, yet they are very different because of the continuing multi-ethnic nature of the state. Whatever the future of the territorial makeup of Russia, the national homelands are not to be wished away. Each of them presents very special challenges.

The National Homelands

The non-Russian territorial homelands can be grouped as follows:

- the Muslim republics of Tatarstan and Bashkortostan;
- the republics of the North Caucasus;
- the Buddhist republics of Kalmykia, Tuva, and Buryatia; and
- the Finno-Ugrian republics.

The challenge of Tatarstan and Bashkortostan is two-fold. One part relates to their elites' confederalist aspirations; the other, to the two republics' position as parts of the Muslim world, integrated deep within the core territory of the Russian state.

In 1991, the two republics proclaimed themselves "sovereign states," which is enshrined in their constitutions. A national rebirth is doubtless taking place. In the case of Tatarstan, the historical sources of statehood are traced to the Kazan khanate, which was formed in the 14th century and existed until it was overrun by Ivan the Terrible in 1552 and annexed to Muscovy. The present Kazan leadership regards Tatarstan to be in free association with the Russian Federation.[20] It jealously protects its authority within Tatarstan's borders, and pragmatically emphasizes economic and cultural, rather than political ties with foreign countries. Tatarstan President Mintimer Shaimiyev became a key figure in the Russian Federation Council, taking an independent stance on such issues as Chechnya and integration with Belarus, but on other important occasions, acting as a valuable ally of the Kremlin. The factors responsible for the compromise political solution, which averted confrontation in 1992, are still present.[21] However, the decisive element remains the consistent but moderate approach of the Tatar authorities and the willingness of the federal government to accommodate Tatarstan's special status, neither of which can be taken for granted in the future.

Bashkortostan also declared itself a sovereign state and subject of international law. In defiance of Moscow's official stance, Ufa recognized Abkhazia as a sovereign state. Like Kazan, it has regularized links with fellow Turkic nations such as Turkey and Kazakhstan. Given that both republics are landlocked, Bashkortostan proposed a territorial exchange with the neighboring Russian region of Orenburg to establish a direct border connection with Kazakhstan, only 50 kilometers away. The area in question has a high percentage of Tatar and Bashkir populations. This would have provided Bashkortostan and, indirectly, Tatarstan a land link with the outside world. Despite Moscow's refusal to allow for a change in internal boundaries, the issue has not been put to rest. In both Tatarstan and Bashkortostan, the old idea of creating a confederacy of 8 million people is enjoying support at the top level, where the enclave status of both repub-

lics and the artificiality of their current borders are vehemently resented.[22]

The two Volga republics also experienced a rapid revival of Islam. This process can be best described as *Nachis-
lamisierung*, for the original process of Islamization was
abruptly stopped after the Bolshevik Revolution before it
could be completed. The continued existence of the two republics as Muslim enclaves well inside Russia underlines a
key point: for Moscow, relations with the Muslim world are
not only a foreign policy issue, or a peripheral problem of
its borderlands (as in the North Caucasus), but also very
much a matter of internal cohesion and the territorial integrity of the federation.

Russia's most serious problems with internal cohesion
are concentrated in the North Caucasus. There, certain
ethnic groups such as the Chechens, Ingush, Balkars, and
Karachais were banished to Kazakhstan and Siberia in the
mid-1940s, to be rehabilitated and repatriated in the late
1950s. Whole republics were abolished and then restored,
and the boundaries were constantly changing. After the
end of the U.S.S.R., territorial claims, pent up for a long
time, have led to violence.

The first armed ethnic conflict in Russia occurred in
October 1992 between the Ingush and the Ossetians over a
piece of ethnically mixed territory that used to be Ingush
and is now part of Ossetia. This conflict, although brought
under control, remains essentially unresolved, for the return of refugees has been extremely slow, and relations between the two communities have remained largely hostile.
The Ingush republic constitutionally demands the "restoration of territorial integrity," while the Ossetian republic
defends its territorial integrity. The federal center has been
trying to mediate, but the conflict remains simmering. The

situation is complicated by the wars in the neighboring Chechnya. There are many in Moscow, and among the Russian military, who see the Ingush President Ruslan Aushev as essentially anti-Russian and pro-Chechen, and at the same time regard Ossetia as the mainstay of Russia's entire position in the North Caucasus. In South Ossetia, about two-thirds of the Ossetian population would favor unification with the North within the Russian Federation.[23]

The case of Chechnya is discussed in Chapter IV. Ingushetia, which broke away from Chechnya in late 1991, has decided to stay within Russia, although it has felt a constant need to accommodate Chechnya. Its border with Chechnya is not formally defined, which led to Russian-Chechen and Russian-Ingush clashes before and during both Chechen wars.

The paradox of Dagestan is that despite a very high number of ethnic groups living in its territory, it has always been a single cultural and geostrategic area.[24] In the 19th century, during the Caucasian wars, Dagestan, under Imam Shamil, led the Chechens against Russian rule. Fragmented, yet of one piece, it managed in the 1990s, against all odds, to preserve the precarious internal balance among its 34 nationalities. One of the more serious challenges to that balance was the rise of the Wahhabists, who in 1997-1999 organized a virtually independent enclave uniting three villages in the Buinaksk district, which was becoming the center of the anti-Russian movement in the North Caucasus.[25] Those who supported the creation of an Islamic republic in Dagestan or its confederation with Chechnya were revealed in 1999 to be a small minority. The problem of Dagestan is conflict over land between the highlander and lowlander ethnic groups as a result of massive migration from the mountains into the plains.

Each group attempts to stake out and protect its "ethnic territory."

There are two types of processes in the area: separation and unification. The remaining twin republics of Karbardino-Balkaria and Karachaevo-Cherkessia have developed serious tensions between the two major ethnic groups arbitrarily grouped together in Soviet times. Small ethnic groups, such as Abazins and Nogais, claim the right to territorial autonomy. There is a parallel movement to unite ethnically close peoples, e.g., within a Greater Circassia, which would embrace Kabarda, Circassia, Adygeia, Abkhazia, and the lands claimed by the Abazin and the Shapsug.[26] The federal authorities have been resisting both processes, as any change of existing borders would inevitably open a Pandora's box.

In the areas where the Don and Kuban Cossacks live, they are an indigenous ethnic group. Their leaders insist on their group's distinct identity within the Russian ethnos. The radicals among the Cossacks call for the restoration of the semi-autonomous Territory of the Don Host, abolished by the Bolsheviks. Much of that territory coincides with the current Rostov Region, but parts of it are in the neighboring Voronezh Region and across the border in Ukraine (Lugansk and Donetsk regions). Terek Cossacks have long been demanding the return of two districts that were included into the Chechen-Ingush Republic in 1957. When those districts were overrun by the Russian federal forces in the course of an "anti-terrorist operation" in Chechnya, ideas were put forth about a possible partition of the republic, giving its northern third to the Cossacks. Other Cossack groups raised territorial claims to parts of North Ossetia, Kabardino-Balkaria, and Dagestan.[27]

The Cossacks and their allies among Russian nationalists, accusing the government of inaction and cowardice, have been insisting on pro-active policies or, failing that, on taking the law into their own hands. However, despite these loud claims and resolute and warlike appearance, the Cossacks have been generally docile, unable to organize themselves either within Chechnya, or on its periphery, even to repel frequent Chechen incursions. In the rest of southern Russia, their leaders have been more interested in lucrative business practices than in politics. Thus, the central government, despite its weakness, has not found it hard to buy off the Cossacks by means of token concessions. The regional authorities in Krasnodar, Rostov, and Stavropol, having legally prohibited the creation of Cossack enclaves in their regions, succeeded in quickly domesticating the local Cossack leaderships. As a result, no real paramilitary organizations sprang up outside of government control. If this were to change, however, the situation could quickly get out of hand.

The three nominally Buddhist republics present a very different set of challenges.

Tuva is the only part of present-day Russia that was nominally a sovereign state in modern times (1921-1944). It is also the only Russian republic whose Constitution contains a clause about the right of secession. However, the virtually total reliance on Russia in all areas and the lack of external support makes the Tuvinians unlikely separatists. Inter-ethnic relations in the republic, volatile in the early 1990s, are stable, though the conflict is in a latent stage.[28]

Buryatia, whose indigenous population is close to the Mongols (the republic's first name was Buryat-Mongolia), did not develop pro-independence or secessionist leanings. In any event, unification with Mongolia was hardly an attractive option. However, there is the latent issue of Buryat reunification, since two Buryat autonomous districts are located outside the boundaries of the republic.[29]

Kalmykia, although bordering on the North Caucasus, has been generally quiet. Its ruler, President Kirsan Ilyumzhinov, is reputed to be one of Russia's most undiluted feudal autocrats. His brief defiance of Moscow in the late 1990s did outwardly resemble separatism, but more probably it was an example of blackmail designed to receive more subsidies from the federal budget.

The Finno-Ugrian Republics Are the Least Restive

Karelia, a republic that in 1940 was given by Stalin the status of a constituent Soviet republic and the formal right of secession—in anticipation of a then apparently imminent Soviet takeover of Finland—has been the only one in the history of the U.S.S.R. whose status was demoted. Ethnic Karelians, whose relatives in northern Karelia live across the border in Finland, are a minority in the republic; after the U.S.S.R. broke up, only marginal though vocal groups called for a confederacy with Finland.

Other fellow Finno-Ugrians, Komi, Mordovians, Udmurtians, and Mari, live in their republics well inside the territory of the federation. When Soviet-era controls were abolished, only in the Komi Republic did a moderately nationalistic party gain ascendancy. Ingrians (or Ingermanlandians, as they are called in Russia) and Vesps, who are both very close to the Finns and live in the borderland Leningrad Region, are very small in number and have not requested territorial autonomy. Rather, many of the 200,000-strong community fled to Finland after the Bolshevik revolution, and the rest were deported. After 1990, some of the few survivors chose to emigrate to Finland as *Aussiedler*.

The Pull of the West

It is sometimes argued that the continuation of Russia's transformation and Westernization could lead to the country's splitting along a new East-West divide *inside* Russia. In this scenario, Kaliningrad would be the first "convert" to Europe, but St. Petersburg followed by Novgorod and other regions of the Northwest could form a major EU-oriented bloc inside Russia. Moscow would remain cosmopolitan, but less relevant as a power center, whereas southern Russia would look to the Caspian and the Black Sea and beyond to Turkey, Iran, and the Mediterranean. It will be up to Russia east of the Urals to form a new East.[30]

This scenario seems to be more than flawed. Westernization is happening in a non-linear fashion. It is not necessarily the places closest to Europe that adopt Western-like lifestyles and consumption habits first. Moscow is the undisputed leader, ahead of St. Petersburg, the historical locus of Russia's Westernization.[31] Both capitals are then followed by the principal cities across the country, from Nizhni Novgorod to Novosibirsk to Khabarovsk. The port cities, wherever they may be, from Kaliningrad to Vladivostok, and the regions with substantial foreign capital investment also belong in the leading group. The process then radiates from the capitals, major cities, ports, and investment centers further and deeper into the hinterland. Siberia's vastness should not mesmerize observers: in reality, Russia east of the Urals resembles a wedge that is becoming ever narrower as one moves eastward. Most cities and towns are located in the vicinity of the Trans-Siberian Railroad, which is the principal conduit for impulses originating in the country's metropolitan cities. There is simply no option of an Eastern Russia should its European part become more closely intertwined with the rest of Europe. The most likely result would be a more rapid Westernization of the territories lying between the Urals and the Pacific.

The "Russian Question" and the Chances of Ethnic Russian Separatism

The break-up of the Soviet Union resulted in some 25 million ethnic Russians and 4 million people belonging to other ethnic groups with a homeland in the Russian Federation living beyond Russia's new borders. This has created a long-term problem. The Russians' situation, of course, is by no means unique: at least 50 million other ex-Soviet citizens fall into the same category. The "divided nations" complex, although not yet a majority view, is certainly present. The Russian Federation itself is the home to several million people whose homelands have become independent states with the demise of the U.S.S.R. The difference is that the Russians are not only Europe's largest ethnic group, but also the only ones who are not used, historically, to such a situation.[32]

This situation presented the Russian government with a challenge. It needed to find a formula for managing that problem without raising a specter of imperial restoration abroad while at the same time being careful not to allow the domestic opposition to exploit the issue of ethnic Russians.[33]

The Yeltsin government's stand was ambiguous. Initially, it chose to ignore the problem altogether, but soon began to suggest that it was prepared, under the circumstances, to use military force to help "compatriots" in the "near abroad." In most cases, this was bluster, and very unhelpful at that. It is a moot point as to whether this may have deterred mass anti-Russian pogroms in the new states.

There has never been any official recognition of the meaning of the term "compatriot." A very broad definition includes former citizens of the U.S.S.R., who, for whatever reason, did not receive new citizenship after 1991; persons born in the territory of the Russian Federation, but living outside of it (between 3 and 5 million); Russian citizens living in CIS countries or the Baltic States; and those who possess dual citizenship.[34]

To be sure, nationality in the post-Soviet world is still very closely linked to ethnicity—nowhere among these new states will one find a citizenship-based nation. Still, the long-term trends, working very unevenly in each of the new states, are eroding both the imperial and the local mentality.

The Russian Federation automatically granted its citizenship to all its residents who held Soviet passports at the time of the dissolution of the U.S.S.R. Ukraine, Belarus, Moldova, and Central Asian countries did the same. Of the Baltic States, only Lithuania, with its 9 percent Russian population, felt confident enough to follow suit, which is known as the "zero option." Latvia, on the contrary, reneged on the promises its leaders made in 1990-1991 to grant the resident Russians equal citizenship rights.

In fact, Latvia and Estonia have enacted legislation that automatically recognized as citizens only those who had those countries' citizenship at the time of their incorporation into the U.S.S.R. in 1940, and their descendants. All others have to go through naturalization procedures, and some categories of professions, such as former Soviet military and security officers, have been totally disqualified. Russia, admitting formal conformity of these acts with the legal documents operating in West European nations, was quick to point out that the special situation of the Baltic Russians had not been taken into account. The Russians who settled down in Estonia and Latvia at the time when those were constituent entities of the U.S.S.R. were not to be compared to Turkish guest workers who actually had to cross borders to arrive in Germany, etc. The Russian government called this blatant discrimination, and the various Russian commentators suggested that the true reason for such treatment was to secure political and administrative power in the hands of the titular ethnic elites and to exclude the Russians from the process of state property privatization.

The nationalist groups in Russia, which continue to be very strong in the State Duma, have fashioned themselves as the prime champions of the Baltic Russians' cause in the face of the government's "inaction." The government, which briefly toyed with the idea of using the schedule of the troop withdrawal or the threat of economic sanctions as leverage vis-à-vis Tallinn and Riga, has opted for seeking international support in the OSCE, the Council of Europe (which Russia joined in 1996, well after the Baltic States), and the United Nations. Although the OSCE and the Council of Europe recommendations fall short of what Moscow believes should be changed in the Baltic States' legislation, Russian officials privately suggest that they would be happy to see these recommendations fully implemented.

There is also a widely shared view that the Baltic Russian issue is becoming less acute, with most people adapting to the situation, and the governments, seeing their independence secured and immediate political goals fulfilled, are easing up. The prospect of membership in the European Union is offering the Baltic Russians the prospect of becoming the first "Euro-Russians."

For Moscow, helping Russian "compatriots" fully establish themselves as rightful citizens of the new states has always been a declared priority; turning them into Russian citizens has never been its preferred policy in the Baltic States. Bowing to a wave of requests by the people who needed a document to travel, it had, however, to grant citizenship to some 120,000 residents of Estonia and a far smaller number of those living in Latvia. When the Russian consular officers proceeded to do the same in the Crimea in 1995, this provoked Kiev's anger, and Moscow had to backtrack.

Meanwhile, Russia urged other CIS states to allow dual citizenship, which is legal under Russian law. This proposal was rejected by all Russia's partners, with the sole exception of Turkmenistan: all the rest remained fearful of erosion of their own citizenship corps.

In all the new states, the Russian language has been quickly replaced by indigenous tongues as the state language. The language laws were adopted from 1988; their enactment significantly accelerated the republics' march to independence and thus the disintegration of the Soviet Union. Independence from Russian is both the first outward sign of independence from Russia and a key element in the construction of a new national identity. The first step to achieving that identity was de-Russification. This turned out to be most difficult in the two Eastern Slav republics, Belarus and Ukraine.

In Belarus, during the first post-Soviet decade, the Russian language preserved most of its previous functions. The efforts by the Belarussian National Front and its supporters among the national intelligentsia to promote the indigenous language brought only limited results. Russian remains both the official language and the language of the urban population, while the use of Belarussian is confined to the villages, Catholic masses, and the obligatory slots on television. The language situation in Belarus closely reflects political realities and relations with Russia.

Ukraine offers a different paradigm. Nationalist feelings there have always been far stronger than in Belarus, and the language was considered a prime vehicle of identification. Sweeping Ukrainization was first attempted by the Central Rada government in 1918, and was repeated from 1991 under Ukraine's first president, Leonid Kravchuk. His successor, Leonid Kuchma, who during the 1994 presidential campaign vowed to give Russian an official status (which helped him defeat Kravchuk), had later to renege on his promises, bowing to the pressure of his more powerful allies in Western Ukraine. It must be especially noted that in Ukraine, the number of Russian speakers is substantially higher than the share of ethnic Russians in the population (20 percent). According to one analysis, the cultural breakdown of the Ukrainian population is as follows: 40 percent Ukrainian-speaking Ukrainians, 33-34 percent Russian-speaking Ukrainians, 20-21 percent Russian-speaking Russians, 1-2 percent Ukrainian-speaking Russians (in Galicia), and 4-5 percent Russian- and Ukrainian-speaking Jews, Poles, et al.[35] It is interesting to compare this data with the Ukrainians' attitude to Russia (61 percent positive), their stand on the desirability of a political union between the two countries (one-third positive), and the overwhelming support for keeping the Ukrainian-Russian border transparent.[36]

While fully committed to a policy of Ukrainization, the government in Kiev has been careful to proceed incrementally, easing the Russian language out from the various spheres step by step. Central government bureaucracy was the first to be Ukrainized, but in the economic agencies and in the military this process is more drawn-out. Universities are a more distant goal, while secondary schools are an immediate priority. Regional differences are also very important. Whereas in Galicia, which never belonged to the Russian Empire, and spent only 50 years within the U.S.S.R., Russian has never been the preferred means of communication, eastern Ukrainian provinces, such as Donetsk and Lugansk, held referenda in which close to 90 percent of the voters spoke in favor of making Russian a second official language. In the Crimea, this is in fact the case already.

Meanwhile, Ukrainian is gradually establishing itself as the only official language in the country. In the first seven years after independence, the number of purely Russian schools decreased seven times. Access to Russian electronic and print media in the Ukrainian market was sharply curtailed. In the long run, it is probable that Ukrainian will finally assert itself, but Russian will remain a second language in a country that, even as it remains fully independent, will preserve close ties with its neighbor to the east.

The Russian language has met a very different fate outside of the Eastern Slav countries. The number of Russian schools has dramatically decreased in Transcaucasus, the Baltic States, and Western Ukraine. Local Russian-language newspapers have survived, but their circulation is rather limited. Newspapers from Russia reach only the capitals and some of the major cities. Russian television went off the air in the Baltic States; its re-broadcasting has been reduced in eastern and southern Ukraine, and discontinued in Galicia altogether. In Lviv, public airing of Russian songs was formally banned in 2000. However, Russian-language radio broadcasting is still common, and Russian pop and rock music has many fans among the youth of the new states.

The living standard of the Russian population of all the Baltic and the new East European states is generally comparable to majority ethnic groups in those countries. The non-citizens are discriminated against, however, economically (for example, with respect to their property-owning rights) as well as politically, but some of the richer people in Latvia and Estonia are ethnic Russians or "Russian-speaking" Jews. Still, the plight of Ukrainian and Estonian heavy industries, concentrated in either country's eastern region, has dealt a blow to the living standard of the regions' mostly Russian blue-collar workforce. The exception is the ethnic Russian intelligentsia, which suffers from the loss of many teaching positions and the impossibility of getting a job in the state-run sector.

A few Russian politicians, opinion leaders, and academics, taking their cue from their Serbian colleagues, maintained that the Russian state should include all territories where the Russians constitute a majority from northeastern districts of Estonia to the northern provinces of Kazakhstan. Unlike in Serbia, however, this has never become a dominant trend even within the Russian political elite. As to the "compatriots," they never fell for it. For the latter, the key factor was that unlike the Serbs in Croatia, Bosnia, and Kosovo, the Russians in the Baltic and Ukraine did not have to fear physical violence. Since 1989-1990, the local Russians have accepted the reality of the Baltic States where they live. Initially, most of them were passive, not bothering to defend the disintegrating Soviet Union, and a strong minority voted for independence. Most of these then became bitterly disillusioned when Latvians and Estonians breached their promises. A decade later, virtually no Russian has rebelled against the Baltic States, and all are glad to be moving to the European Union, but few regard Latvia or Estonia as *their states*. In other words, there is no loyalty lost, or yet gained, for that matter. There is a distinct prospect that

Latvia and Estonia will become cleft societies, with permanent tension between their two communities.

In Belarus, "integration" with Russia has been the dominant political theme anyway. In the eastern, southern, and central regions of Ukraine, Russians have not been the only ones advocating closer ties between Ukraine and Russia. Only in the Crimea, which since early 1991 has been a republic within Ukraine, have there been moves to separate and either join Russia or continue as an independent political entity.

The relationship between Kiev and Simferopol, the Crimean capital, became especially tense in early 1994 when a pro-independence candidate, Yury Meshkov, was elected Crimean president. Soon, however, factional strife within the Crimean elite, lack of popular mobilization, and Moscow's abstention from the crisis allowed Kiev to gain the upper hand. The successful work of an OSCE conflict-prevention mission and the deterring effect of the war in Chechnya, which began in late 1994, helped calm the situation, and the 1997 Russo-Ukrainian Treaty, complete with an agreement on the Black Sea Fleet, further normalized it.

Still, the Crimea remains a potentially explosive issue, and not only because of the Russians. The Crimean Tatars returning from banishment in Uzbekistan, and numbering 250,000 at the end of 1997, are turning the ethnic situation into a three-corner one. Many Tatars are not yet Ukrainian citizens. They often lack decent housing and permanent work. Tatar organizations are demanding the restoration of Crimean autonomy, with Tatars as the titular national group. A triangular Russian-Tatar-Ukrainian conflict over power-sharing and the return of property confiscated when the Tatars were banished to Central Asia are major potential problems.[37] Should this situation reach the level of an open conflict, it could draw in other countries, first of all Russia and Turkey.

The only case of real separatism in the new Eastern Europe was in Moldova, where an armed conflict broke out in 1992 along the Dniester River. This was only partly ethnic in nature. The self-proclaimed Dniestrian Moldavian Republic has a mixed population of Ukrainians, Moldavians, and Russians. While it has an ethnic Russian president, other leaders come from different ethnic groups. The conflict, which in 1992 threatened to suck in the Russian troops in the area, was succeeded by a long impasse when Russian peace-keepers, alongside the belligerents, policed the ceasefire, and no progress was made in resolving the political dispute. The political process became more intense from 1996 when the OSCE, Russia, and Ukraine started to coordinate their efforts to move the parties to a solution that would preserve Moldova's unity. The situation was ameliorated by Bucharest's final repudiation of the notion of restoring a Greater Romania and its formal rejection of any territorial claims to Ukraine, resulting in a 1997 treaty fixing the existing borders de jure. A similar agreement has been negotiated between Romania and Moldova, which reaffirmed its desire to remain an independent state. A decade after the armed violence, the issue is not only the implementation of the formula of a common state, but perhaps equally so the fate of the Transdniestrian leadership.

In Kazakhstan, Russians complain about the ethnocratic character of the government at all levels, but the great majority of them have chosen not to protest publicly, let alone call for autonomy of the northern regions, where Russians form a majority. Secessionist proclamations have been made by several Cossack leaders, and the alleged conspiracy to start an armed rebellion to create an independent Russian Altai republic in eastern Kazakhstan is an odd and isolated development, but the problem is potentially fraught with the gravest of consequences. Initially after independence, Russians began leaving Kazakhstan, but most of them have so far preferred to stay. With so many of them remaining, it is difficult to expect that the problem will go away by itself. A failure of civic integration in Kazakhstan would lead to a very severe conflict in that republic and possibly to a confrontation between Kazakhstan and Russia along the world's longest border.

Finally, there were declarations of intent by the unrecognized separatist states, such as Abkhazia, Transdniestria, South Ossetia, as well as the Azeri Lezghins, to join the Russian Federation. Some Russian political, economic, and security quarters responded favorably, hoping to strengthen their hand. The Russian government, however, never officially flirted with the idea, and from the start of the second Chechen war has strongly repudiated separatism.

Conclusion

As far as its internal composition is concerned, Russia is likely to preserve its territorial integrity, and rein in some of those regions—both "ethnic," such as Tatarstan, and "Russian," such as Primorye, that have been exercising an inordinately high degree of autonomy, at the sufferance of the federal constitution. This recentralization will have its limits. Abolition of national homelands, which can bring about serious and potentially violent conflicts, is unlikely to be attempted. Eventually, a new structure of regions, fewer in number and more adequate to economic and social realities, will be established as a result of the central government's drive for more uniformity, and the regions' desire to play a more prominent role in the affairs of the state. This new more genuinely federal Russia will not be a "Russia of the regions" in the sense that it won't be a treaty-based federation. Moscow probably won't become another Brussels, a place for negotiations among the still largely sovereign entities. By the same token, Russia won't be a unitary state, and its regions, fewer in number but larger and potentially more powerful, will be important players on the domestic and the national scenes. If mishandled, the recentralization effort could have explosive consequences, especially in Tatarstan and parts of the North Caucasus.

One consequence of the Russians' close attachment to their state is that they generally lose their identity relatively quickly and easily once they are no longer citizens, or subjects of Russia. In Russia, they assimilate others; once outside of Russia, they are eager to be assimilated themselves. There are, for example, no Russian lobbies in America or France, although both countries in the course of the 20th century absorbed millions of Russian expatriates. (There is, ironically, a very powerful "Russian lobby" in Israel, but it is anything but ethnically Russian.) As to the ethnic Russians now outside of the federation, they face very different futures.

Unlike Western Europe or the United States, newly independent states of the former U.S.S.R., where most of these Russians live, exhibit various forms of ethnically based and often anti-Russian nationalism, which the indigenous elites use as a basis for state- and nation-building.

In the Baltic States, the Russians will coexist with the indigenous majority groups, gradually acquiring citizenship, but not becoming fully integrated for a long time to come. All-inclusive Baltic civic societies are a long way off, and the Russians' best hope lies in their resident countries' accession to the European Union, which is expected to level the playing fields in Latvia and Estonia somewhat. The two countries, however, are likely to become divided societies with calm but tense relations between the ruling ethnic majority and the sizeable Russian minority. This uneasy relationship will remain a permanent factor in Russo-Baltic and, by extension, Russian-Western relations.

By contrast, Russians will continue to live largely without any problems in Belarus, where Belarussianization has failed. This creates a wholly different kind of problem. Belarus has not been able to establish its national identity, and its leaders have opted for a union with Russia. This logically makes Belarussian nationalism anti-Russian and pro-Western, and binds the fate of the union to the political future of President Lukashenko.

In most of Ukraine, with the notable exception of the Crimea, the Russians' problems are confined to the language issue, and are fully manageable over the long-term.

In the Crimea, the Ukrainian government is facing a serious test over its ability to avert a potentially explosive conflict involving the Crimean Tatars and the ethnic Russian majority.

Moldova, on the other hand, appears ready for conflict resolution with Russia and Ukraine, with the help of the OSCE, and perhaps the European Union joining forces to achieve it. As in Ukraine, there are reasons to believe that the Russian community in Moldova can find a modus vivendi with the Moldovan majority.

In the South Caucasus, the Russian minorities, decimated by ethnic conflicts and wars, will survive in tiny niches, devoid of major political or economic significance, within the ethnically defined local societies.

Across Central Asia, the emerging situation will be very uneven. In Tajikistan, Turkmenistan, and Uzbekistan local Russians realize that the future holds no hope for them. The younger people will try to migrate to Russia, with only few remaining in the region. The prospects for those living in Kyrgyzstan are only slightly less grim, but they depend on the viability of a somewhat looser political regime in that country, which is fragile domestically and vulnerable externally.

The hardest problem is Kazakhstan, where the future of the local Russian community depends on the economic success and political and social tolerance of the new state, which cannot be guaranteed with any certainty.

With the end of the Yeltsin era, the attitudes of the federal government in Moscow and the Russian public to the Russian diaspora in the newly independent states has undergone a subtle but significant change. During much of the 1990s Moscow paid lip service at best to the problems of ethnic Russians, and the public remained passive and uncaring. By contrast, even in his first pronouncement as prime minister, in August 1999 Vladimir Putin highlighted protection of the rights of Russian citizens and Russian compatriots as a major task of his government. On a visit to Uzbekistan the following December, he met with representatives of the local Russian community. As acting president, Putin personally intervened in the case of a Soviet war veteran facing trial in Latvia. In early 2000, Dmitri Rogozin, long-time leader of the Congress of Russian Communities, a champion of Russian rights, was elected chair of the Duma International Affairs Committee.

In the years to come, the Russian government can be expected both to be more assertive on the issue of the Russian diaspora abroad, and to calibrate its actions more carefully than was done under Yeltsin. There is no single Russian Question. Rather, the Russian questions are many, many more than there are solutions.

NOTES

[1] Only the Grand Duchy of Finland enjoyed real autonomy toward the end of the Romanov empire; Polish autonomy was minimized after the uprising of 1830-1831, and finally abolished after the next major uprising of 1863. As to Bukhara, Khiva, and Uryanhai Territory (Tuva), they were Russian protectorates, formally outside of the empire.

[2] Khiva and Bukhara (from the second half of the 19th century), Outer Mongolia (from 1911), and Uryankhai Territory (now Tuva, from 1914).

[3] *Kontseptsiya natsionalnoi bezopasnosti Rossiiskoi Federatsii*, p. 1.

[4] The Central federal district (capital: Moscow) includes Moscow City and Moscow Region; Belgorod, Bryansk, Ivanovo, Kaluga, Kostroma, Kursk, Lipetsk, Oryol, Ryazan, Smolensk, Tambov, Tver, Tula, Vladimir, Voronezh, and Yaroslavl regions. The Northwestern federal district (capital: St. Petersburg) includes the republics of Karelia and Komi; Nenets Autonomous Region; Arkhangelsk, Vologda, Kaliningrad, Leningrad, Murmansk, Novgorod, and Pskov regions, and the city of St. Petersburg. The North Caucasus federal district (capital: Rostov/Don) is composed of the republics of Adygeia, Dagestan, Ingushetia, Kabardino-Balkaria, Kalmykia, Karachaevo-Cherkessia, North Ossetia-Alania, Chechnya; Krasnodar and Stavropol territories; Astrakhan, Rostov, and Volgograd regions. The Volga federal district (capital: Nizhni Novgorod) includes the republics of Bashkortostan, Chuvashia, Mari El, Mordovia, Tatarstan, Udmurtia; Komi-Permyk Autonomous Region; Kirov, Nizhni Novgorod, Orenburg, Penza, Perm, Samara, Saratov, and Ulyanovsk regions. The Urals federal district (capital: Yekaterinburg) is made up of Chelyabinsk, Kurgan, Sverdlovsk, and Tyumen regions and Khanty-Mansi, and Yamalo-Nenets autonomous regions. The Siberian federal district (capital: Novosibirsk) includes the republics of Altai, Buryatia, Khakasia, Tuva; Altai and Krasnoyarsk territories; Chita, Irkutsk, Kemerovo, Novosibirsk, Omsk, and Tomsk regions; Aginski Buryat, Evenk, Taimyr (Dolgano-Nenets), and Ust-Ordynski autonomous regions. Lastly, the Far Eastern federal district (capital: Kha-

barovsk) includes the Republic of Sakha (Yakutia), Khabarovsk and Primorye territories; Amur, Kamchatka, and Sakhalin regions; Jewish Autonomous Region, and Chukotka and Koryak autonomous districts.

5   See the Winter 2000 issue of *Pro et Contra* dedicated to "The Center and Regions of Russia."

6   The Russian Federation within the U.S.S.R., one of the 15 constituent entities of the Soviet Union, contained 16 autonomous republics, 5 autonomous regions, 10 autonomous districts.

7   For instance, in Tatarstan.

8   The Chechens, in particular—up until the German invasion of 1941—but also the Don and Kuban Cossacks in the early 1920s.

9   For example, from the Chechens, the Ingush, the Karachais, and the Balkars banished by Stalin to Kazakhstan and Central Asia, and the Crimean Tatars.

10 See Nikolai Petrov, *Regiony Rossii*, Carnegie Center, Moscow, 1999.

11 Alexander Uss (Chair, Krasnoyarsk legislative assembly), "Rossii—imperskuyu federatsiyu," *Nezavisimaya gazeta*, April 6, 2000, p. 8.

12 Sherman W. Garnett, "A Wedged Bear . . . in the Great Tightness," *Pro et Contra*, Vol. 2, No. 1 (Winter 1997), pp. 5-20.

13 Gavriil Popov, a prominent economist and a former mayor of Moscow, quoting Sergei Witte's phrase that the issue of rail tariffs is the issue of national unity, argues that should tariffs stay high, they will make Kaliningrad turn to the EU, and orient Siberia toward China. Economic separatism, he warns, logically leads to a change in political loyalty. See Gavriil Popov, "Transport," *Nezavisimaya gazeta*, March 15, 2000, p. 8. A similar point was made by another noted economist, Nikolai Shmelyov, the director of the Institute of Europe within the Russian Academy of Sciences. See Nikolai Shmelyov, *Rubezhi*, No. 12, 1997, p. 38.

14 At present, there are eight inter-regional associations (Northwest, Central Russia, Black Soil Lands, North Caucasus, Greater Volga, Greater Urals, Siberian Accord, and the Far East/Transbaikal) that are nothing but fora for limited economic and social cooperation.

[15] This observation is based on the author's own conversations with the repre-sentatives of regional elites in Khabarovsk and Vladivostok in 1998-1999.

[16] Thomas Graham writes: "Military commanders are known to cut deals with regional and local governments in order to ensure themselves uninterrupted supplies of energy and provisions. Some military garrisons are supported with money from local entrepreneurs. . . . As a result, the loyalty of the military and security forces to the central government—even the elite units around Mos-cow—is dubious. This does not mean that they would carry out the will of the local leaders—there is little evidence that they would—but rather that they would not necessarily defend the central government in a crisis" (Thomas Graham, "A World Without Russia?"). This is a fair assessment. It is interesting to note that in Kazan, the capital of Tatarstan, the local officers' club and the gates of some Russian military units fly both the federal and Tatarstan flags—Kazan certainly did learn a lesson from a near-confrontation with the central authorities in early 1992, and has been trying to co-opt and cultivate the lo-cally-based Russian military personnel.

[17] See Nikolai Petrov, "Otnosheniya 'Tsentr-regiony' i perspektivy territo-rialno-gosudarstvennogo pereustroistva strany," in *Regiony Rossii v 1998 g.*, Gendalf, Carnegie Moscow Center, 1999, p. 57.

[18] See, for example, *Strategiya dlya Rossii: Povestka dnya dlya Prezidenta-2000*, Vagrius, Moscow, 2000, Chapter 7, pp. 227-262; Andranik Migranyan, "Natsionalny vopros v Rossii," *Nezavisimaya gazeta*, April 28, 2000, p. 8.

[19] See endnote 14.

[20] It is legally possible, from a Kazan point of view, to be a Tatarstan citizen without being at the same time a citizen of the Russian Federation.

[21] For a recent summary of official Tatarstan views, see Farid Mukhamet-shin (chairman of the State Council, or parliament), "Kazan za realny federalism," *Nezavisimaya gazeta*, February 15, 2000, p. 4.

[22] Bashkortostan President Murtaza Rakhimov, as quoted by Igor Rotar in "Natsionalnaya politika Ufy vygodna Kremlyu," *Nezavisimaya gazeta*, December 31, 1997, p. 3.

[23] *Bulleten seti etnologicheskogo monitoringa i rannego preduprezhdeniya konf-liktov*, No. 25, May-June 1999, p. 82.

[24] *Mezhetnicheskiye otnosheniya i konflikty v postsovetskikh gosudarstvakh,* Annual report 1998, Institute of Ethnology and Anthropology, Russian Academy of Sciences, Moscow, 1999, p. 38.

[25] Ibid., p. 44.

[26] The Adyg-Abkhaz group has a numerous diaspora in the Middle East, numbering 2 million people in Turkey, Jordan, Syria, and Lebanon.

[27] *Mezhetnicheskiye otnosheniya,* p. 92.

[28] Ibid., 1999, p. 108.

[29] From 1923 through 1937, Aginski and Ust-Ordynski enclaves were part of the Buryat-Mongol Republic, and then transferred respectively to Chita and Irkutsk regions. In 1993, Buryatia's Supreme Soviet called this decision illegal and claimed back parts of its historical territory. This, however, had no immediate consequences. Attempts to put this item on the agenda of the State Duma have invariably failed. Of the combined population of the two enclaves, about 220,000, just over 50 percent, are Russians.

[30] See Igor Yakovenko, *Rossiyskoye gosudarstvo: natsionalniye interesy, granitsy, perspektivy,* Sibirsky Khronograf, Novosibirsk, 1999, p. 60.

[31] It is interesting to note that Muscovites and Petersburgians have lately become accustomed to celebrating Western Christmas along with the Orthodox one (although the functions of the two events are different, and the latter one is the only religious celebration).

[32] Stalin, ironically, was a great "unifier" of nations, especially the Ukrainians and Belarussians. He insisted on the annexation of the Ukrainian lands which had never belonged to the Russian Empire, such as Galicia, Ruthenia, and North Bukovina. Bjalystok, which was assigned to Belarus in 1939, was only reluctantly returned to Poland in 1945. He supported Azeri nationalism in northern Iran, and the Uigur national movement in Xinjiang.

[33] "Protection of their interests by methods of traditional diplomacy is practically impossible on a long-term basis and requires other, integrated strategies," concluded a report by the Council on Foreign and Defense Policy (*NG—Stsenarii,* May 23, 1996, p. 4).

34 Alexei Miller, "Ukraina kak natsionaliziruyushcheyesya gosudarstvo,"
    Pro et Contra, Vol. 2, No. 2 (Spring), 1997, p. 88.

35 See *Rossiya na poroge XXI veka,* RAU-Korporatsiya and Obozrevatel Pub-
    lishers, Moscow, 1996, p. 259.

36 See V.A. Kolosov, R.F. Turovsky, "Geopoliticheskoye polozheniye Rossii
    na poroge XXI veka: realii i perspektivy," *Polis,* No. 3, 2000, p. 44.

37 *Nezavisimaya gazeta*, December 11, 1997, p. 3.

CHAPTER 7

Fitting Russia In

The change of Russia's traditional identity, as has been observed, is not a new phenomenon. Already in the late 19th century it was becoming evident that the old "Russian idea" had outlived its usefulness. The search for a new identity was cut short by the Bolshevik Revolution which deformed Russia and did not provide any lasting solutions to the crisis. The search has resumed. Key components will be fitting Russia into the wider world, defining its new place and role, and examining the supranational identities that the country can consider in the changing global environment.

The fundamental fact about Russia is that it lies on the periphery of several of the world's civilizations. Often it is credited (by the Slavophiles, Toynbee, and Samuel Huntington) with being a distinct civilization in its own right. For a long time this argument appeared credible. In the 10th century, Russia embraced an Orthodox version of Christianity and the Byzantine model of government, which set it apart from Germano-Roman Western Europe. Russia was effectively separated from the rest of Europe by Mongol rule; much more than a mere physical separation, this changed Russia's identity. The Russian political system—the ways, habits, physical appearance, and ethnicity of the people itself—were heavily affected.

Later on, Russia experienced no Reformation. Its religious schism of the 17th century was a totally different phenomenon. Modernization ("Westernization") under Peter the Great provided the country with a powerful modern military, an industry, and a Westernized upper class, but it failed to reach deeper into the masses of the people who were progressively more and more alienated from both the upper classes and the state. European Enlightenment gave an impetus to the flowering of Russian literature and the arts but again failed to liberate the spirit of the people, the majority of which remained slaves until 1861. When slavery was finally abolished and capitalism could develop in Russia, this capitalism was unable to manage the myriad conflicts within Russian society and was swept away by the Bolshevik Revolution.

The Communist rule by definition set Russia apart from the rest of the world. "Eurasia" was never so big and self-contained as under Stalin's rule, extending from East Germany and Albania to China and North Vietnam. The Communist Party did claim that the U.S.S.R. and the socialist community represented a new civilization radically different from that of the capitalist West and the backward feudal East. This Soviet civilization was deemed to be universalist in nature, but in practice, although it rejected Russian traditionalism, it nevertheless displayed many uniquely Russian features.

"The U.S.S.R.," a thoughtful American analyst once observed, "had the world's longest borders but no real frontiers."[1] The end of the U.S.S.R. had a revolutionizing effect not just on the day-to-day operation of the border, but first of all on society, which used to be confined within that border. Freedom of travel was immediately considered to be among the principal human freedoms. Most Russian people cross the border for profit (however small), not pleasure. Short shopping trips help them to survive inside Russia. There has been an exponential growth in the number of border crossings. While in the final years of the U.S.S.R., 5 million people (out of a population of 280 million) crossed its borders, almost exclusively on government business, in 1996, 60 million people crossed Russian frontiers both ways.[2] On average, one Russian in five traveled abroad in 1996. The government and its agencies were anything but prepared for this sudden and massive change. The number of border crossings barely doubled, and there was an acute shortage of personnel, equipment, and expertise to manage the new situation. As a result, the undesired effect of globalization quickly came to be felt.

The explosion of contacts with the outside world came together with the fall in intra-Russian communication, which was no less dramatic. Whereas before the 1990s to fly from Vladivostok to Japan or from Tallinn to Helsinki one had to go to Moscow first, now many Far Easterners, having made many trips to China and Japan, have yet to visit European Russia, which has suddenly become a very distant and expensive destination.

The end of the Soviet Union again raised the question of Russia's identity as a civilization. With Communism marginalized, and the Communist Party of the Russian Federation espousing a traditionalist ideology, the main protagonists were again those who thought of Russia as a Western country and those who believed in its *Sonderweg*.

Russia-as-Part-of-the-West: A False Dawn

The first attempt to fit Russia within the boundaries of Western civilization was a failure. The reason for this was the over-abundance of optimism on both sides, and the refusal to see the formidable difficulties involved. When in the late 1980s Mikhail Gorbachev started his calls for a common European home, he hardly reached in his thinking beyond the uppermost layer of international politics and strategy. When at the turn of the 1990s the phrase was coined of a common security space from Vancouver to Vladivostok, little effort was made to explain its nature and to develop the architecture of such a "space." When in 1991-1992 Moscow played with the idea of applying for NATO membership, or even later when senior Russian figures casually mentioned their "vision" of Russia in the European Union,[3] no attempt was made to think through even the most obvious implications of either membership.

Somehow it was believed that Russia was a Western country by birthright; that it had only been held hostage by the Bolsheviks for more than 70 years, had liberated itself and others whom the Bolsheviks had also held hostage, and deserved the warm embrace of the rest of the Western community and eternal gratitude from its co-hostages. This elite "Westernist" desire to gain access to the prestigious clubs was strengthened by the popular expectation that joining the community of the world's most prosperous nations would soon make Russia itself prosperous and successful.[4]

The elites soon realized that they had received far less than what they had bargained for. Russia was to be treated according to the realities of its economic, political, social, and legal systems, not the inflated ideas that its leaders had of themselves. Russia acceded to the North Atlantic Cooperation Council, later renamed the Euro-Atlantic Partnership Council, but the idea of a Euro-Atlantic area did not become popular, for it failed to confer a special status on Russia. Joining NATO as "the United States of Eurasia" was out of the question. The Partnership for Peace program, which put Russia into the same category as Estonia and

Moldova, was perceived as a calculated slight. A world condominium of America and the newly democratic Russia was immediately exposed as a chimera, and playing the role of a junior partner to Washington brought accusations of toadyism against then Foreign Minister Andrei Kozyrev. Membership in the G-8, when it came at last in 1998 at Birmingham, was regarded as a mere sop.

NATO enlargement was the turning point. Its effect on the Russian elites cannot be explained merely in terms of threat perceptions.[5] Above all, there was bitter disappointment with the West in general. As a well-known historian put it, while Russian idealists fell for the abstract ideas of "new thinking" and the "common interests of humanity," the rest of the world (meaning the West) remained loyal to the "old thinking" and the reality of national interests. The West did help Russia get rid of its imperial possessions, but it was not a disinterested facilitator.[6] Having emerged from the Cold War, Russia was allegedly thrown 70 years back to the times of hostile foreign encirclement. In the words of an eloquent exponent of that view, it was as if the Berlin Wall had been transported to the borders of the 17th-century tsardom of Muscovy.[7]

The notion of Russia's becoming isolated as a result of NATO admitting new member states in Central and Eastern Europe is a closer description of a deeper truth, but it also fails to explain the vehemence of Moscow's reaction. Most members of the new Russian elite, having shed Communism, have preserved a keen interest in traditional geopolitics. They see the aim of the West in extending its sphere of influence to the former socialist countries and ex-Soviet republics.

Central and Eastern Europe in NATO means not just the removal of the hope that sometime in the future when

Russia emerges from the crisis and grows economically strong and powerful, it will be able to restore its "natural" sphere of influence. The problem that Russia has with NATO enlargement is a problem of its own international identity. The harsh reality is that, with Poland already in NATO, the Baltic States aspiring to join, and the GUUAM countries leaning toward the Alliance, there is no Eurasia left for Russia to return to. Russia simply cannot withdraw again into some kind of "splendid isolation," à la the U.S.S.R. It can decide to become marginalized, but even then it can no longer hope to have a protective shell around it.

Russia-as-Eurasia Revisited

In the words of a witty Russian scholar-turned-politician,[8] some people in the country have been so much offended by the West spurning them that they became patriots. This reaction gave support to the alternative, but otherwise highly traditional vision of Russia-in-the-world, namely, Russia-as-Eurasia.

This vision has many variations. The official concept appeared under the rubric of the multipolar world that regarded Russia, flanked by its CIS neighbors, as an independent pole of power and influence. This concept was first developed by the Chinese, but it became known as the Primakov doctrine. Officially described as ensuring equal proximity with all other power centers[9], and aiming at non-entangling interaction with them, it was gradually evolving into a primarily anti-American, or even anti-Western concept.

What mattered most to Primakov was constructing a global system of checks and balances to constrain an over-assertive United States, which emerged from the Cold

War as the most powerful nation in the annals of world history, and which was also for the first time becoming the dominant power in Eurasia. The accompanying "Eurasianism" of many in the military industrial complex, whose early hopes of doing business with the United States and NATO were soon thwarted by Western defense companies' ruthless pursuit of their interests, was based on the dual need to maintain NATO as a necessary bogey to build up arms against, and to keep countries the United States regarded warily, such as China, India, and Iran, as customers. Against this highly pragmatic background, the various political forces were much more parochial in their outlook.

The Communist Party favored the restoration of the Soviet Union as a political slogan whose message was to contrast Soviet "normalcy" with the post-Soviet chaos. Vladimir Zhirinovsky's supporters and a number of splinter groups,[10] playing on the feelings of national humiliation, came out in favor of the restoration of the Russian Empire. The surviving reactionary romantics[11] toyed with the ideas of pan-Slavism or a spiritual community based on Orthodoxy. Despite the different ideological packaging, the idea was basically the same.

Eurasianism, as Alexander Solzhenitsyn wrote, is a reaction of Russians slighted by the West.[12] There is nothing new in its current reappearance. The grudge against the United States now was historically preceded by the acute feeling of betrayal by Europe after World War I and the Russian revolution. The most poetic description of this disappointment was given in 1920 by Alexander Blok in his famous poem *Scythians*. Read today, it captures all the spirit and fury of, for instance, Russian opposition to NATO enlargement, but does this infinitely more vividly and elegantly.

Disappointment with Eurasianism, however, is certain. No Russian-led Orthodox bloc surrounded by a buffer of Muslim states, as envisaged by Huntington, is likely to emerge.[13] Of all the former Soviet republics, only Belarus, which has had problems with establishing a distinct national identity, has indicated its desire to integrate closely with Russia. No other newly independent state is leaning in that direction. Ukraine is slowly but steadily avoiding violent conflicts and emerging as a nation-state within Europe. Its elites have made their choice, and the public is ultimately likely to follow. The situation in Moldova is aggravated by the internal conflict that tore the country apart, but it also gravitates toward Europe. The Baltic States, outside the CIS, identify themselves as Western and stand a good chance of becoming integrated within Western structures in the medium-term.

After a decade of conflict in the Caucasus, Georgia and Azerbaijan have come to view Russia with deep and permanent suspicion, and Armenia looks to it largely as an outside protector. The Armenians have an essentially national project. Many Russians, for their part, have developed phobias against *all* "Caucasians," whom they regard as likely criminals, religious fanatics, or unwanted immigrants. Russia and the Central Asian states are becoming ever more distant, and more peripheral in each other's thinking. The one exception is Kazakhstan. Even in this case, however, few in either Russia or Kazakhstan imagine full-fledged integration. The presence of 6 million ethnic Russians, mostly in Northern Kazakhstan, is a factor that warrants close bilateral cooperation, but it is also a major irritant for the relationship.

Ten years after the demise of the U.S.S.R., the notion of the external border of the CIS is becoming less and less relevant. On the contrary, borders are hardening within the CIS. Few things are done involving all 12 members. The Customs Union includes Russia, Belarus, Kazakhstan, Kyrgyzstan, and Tajikistan. The Collective Security Treaty also includes Armenia. The Russo-Belarussian Union is a bilateral affair. On the other hand, some combinations exclude Russia, namely the GUUAM group and the Central Asian Union. From 1999, the transparency of intra-CIS borders ceased to be universal. Turkmenistan has totally ended its visa-free regime, Uzbekistan has made an exception only for Russia. Moscow itself threatened to impose visa requirements on the citizens of Georgia and Azerbaijan.

Occasional attempts to go beyond the borders of the former U.S.S.R. in search of territories to be integrated within a Greater Russia have a long tradition but are plainly pathetic now. Konstantin Leontiev discussed at length how Russia would manage relations among Slav nations in its own way, which would be the most impartial one, of course.[14] The most likely candidates for this remain Bulgaria and Serbia.[15] In the former case, it is conveniently forgotten that non-Communist Bulgarian elites were traditionally Western-oriented. In both world wars, Bulgaria sided with Germany against Russia. It now longs to be in NATO and the EU, despite Moscow's disapproval. Sofia took a staunchly pro-Western position during the 1999 Kosovo crisis. By contrast, the desire to join the Soviet Union is regarded as part of the legacy of the Bulgarian Communist Party, which has always been loyal to Moscow to the point of national self-negation.

Another problem, of course, would be to have Bulgaria *and* Serbia as part of the new union in view of their historical competition in the Balkans. Stalin himself had to drop his plan for a Balkans federation, unable to reconcile

differences among the local Communist leaders. The resolution of the Serbian parliament in the spring of 1999 to seek
accession to the Union of Russia and Belarus illustrated the
potential dangers for Russia of engaging too seriously in
the hopeless pursuit for a time long past. Surprised by this
move by President Milosevic, Moscow had to postpone the
consideration of that request until after the end of NATO's
air war against Yugoslavia. This option was never considered, of course, for Belgrade's purpose was to get Russia
involved in its conflict with NATO.[16]

Russia and the World of Islam

There is a tradition of regarding the Slavic-Orthodox and
the Turkic-Muslim worlds inside Russia as an example of
inter-ethnic and inter-confessional integration. It is certainly
true that Russia has produced a highly original and still
extremely useful model of ethnic relations, which is exem-
plified in creation of a durable supra-ethnic identity. This
is one of the most important and useful pieces of imperial
heritage to be carried over into the post-imperial age.

What is more doubtful is the notion that this affinity
can be a solid basis for new integration within the boundaries of the former Soviet Union. Reintegration of the econ-
omies and harmonization of the political systems of the
Soviet successor states versus their common fall into barbarism pose a false dilemma. The post-Soviet experience of
Russia and the newly independent Muslim states of Central
Asia and Azerbaijan is vastly different. Their historical
paths are diverging fast.

Thus, despite the intellectual constructs of those who
see Russia as a Slavo-Turkic empire and the rightful descen-
dant of the Eurasian realm of Genghis Khan, there is very

little at present that would make this construct possible, let alone stable. Moreover, it is a major historical challenge to the Russian Federation to learn to live with the revitalized world of Islam both on Russia's southern periphery and *within* its own boundaries.

The southern borders of Russia do not follow any clear civilizational boundaries. Both Georgia and Armenia are Christian, while most of the Russian republics in the North Caucasus are Muslim. Russia's Dagestan and Azerbaijan are populated by Muslims. Bashkortostan and Tatarstan, reaching almost from the Kazakh border into the very heart of European Russia, are Muslim, while Northern Kazakhstan is mostly Russian. The alarmists, however, talk about an "Islamic wedge" that would tear Russia apart from the North Caucasus to the Arctic Ocean.

Russian commentators and even politicians occasionally fall victim to the temptation to regard Russia as the ultimate barrier between the world of Christianity and Europe and that of Islam or Asia. This follows in the tradition of the cliched self-characterization of Russians as the "saviors of Europe" from the Mongol hordes. In the early 1990s, this was the tune sung by both Russian Westernizers, such as Andrei Kozyrev, and some military figures, such as General Pavel Grachev, who sounded the alert over the threat of "Islamic fundamentalism" emanating across the Afghan border into Tajikistan and capable of provoking a domino effect all across Central Asia. In the mid-1990s, the Russian military presence in Tajikistan was described in terms of erecting a barrier to a large-scale drug trade that provided resources for Muslim extremists. Some analysts saw the conflict in Dagestan and the second Chechen war in the late 1990s as a threat to Western civilization, against which Russia was fighting on its own territory, and as international terrorism sponsored by Muslim extremists.

Russia's physical weakening has invited Islamist activists into the areas that had heretofore been closed to them. Occasionally the Islamic world is perceived in Russia as a more or less coherent power center, one which, like the West, may be tempted to capitalize on Russia's weakness and to change the balance in its favor.

Alternatively, there are conspiracy theorists who see Russia's problems with militant Islam as the result of a plot hatched by the United States which in its turn is trying to divert the anger and fury of the Muslim world away from American actions in Iraq and Washington's longstanding support for Israel. According to the Russian "discoverers" of such a plot, the goal was to turn two of the West's potential adversaries, Russia and the Islamic world, into mortal enemies, so that their long border became a permanent battlefield.

Turkey is seen by these same conspiracy theorists as another trouble-maker allied to the United States while pursuing its own agenda of imposing Turkish domination over the whole of the Turkic world, from the Balkans to the Crimea to the Caucasus, the Volga region to Central Asia, and even reaching as far as Sakha (Yakutia) in eastern Siberia. What is not publicly recognized is that America's persistent effort to get the European Union to accept Turkey as a candidate for membership also meets the Russian interest of confirming that country's secular identity and directing the Turks' energy toward European integration, and away from the ghosts of the Ottoman Empire and the mirage of Pan-Turkism.

The hard fact remains that since 1979 the Soviet and Russian military have only had one enemy on the battlefield: a rebel or a guerilla fighting under the green banner of Islam in Afghanistan, Chechnya, Dagestan, and Tajikistan. In the Balkans, Kosovo Albanians give the Russian peacekeepers a hostile reception. The likely future military contingencies point in the same direction. The fighting in Kyrgyzstan in August-September 1999 highlighted the rising Islamist challenge to the Central Asian regimes, especially that of Uzbekistan, which have been turning back to Moscow for military support.

Thus, restoring Russian domination over Turan or even a symbiosis with it, cannot be considered in principle as a viable proposition. Russia's prime task is integrating its own Muslims and making them feel like Russians. This is a tall enough order.

The Far Eastern Europe

In contrast to Russia's southern periphery, its easternmost one does represent a clear civilizational divide. The Sino-Russian border and, to a smaller extent, the Russian-Mongolian one, are real dividing lines. There is virtually nothing in the Russian Far East borderlands that would remind one of the proximity of China or Japan. Indeed, the areas around Lake Baikal, and along both the Amur and the Ussuri rivers, as well as the Sakhalin and the Kuril islands were sparsely populated by various indigenous tribes, which were later russified. A heavy and steady influx of ethnic Russians and Ukrainians from European Russia throughout most of the 20th century gave the region its strong East European flavor.

However, since the time of the Russo-Japanese war in the early 20th century Russia has perceived the demographic pressure from across the border as a threat. The forcible expulsion or resettlement in the 1930s of several hundred thousand ethnic Chinese, Koreans, and, in 1945, Japanese further increased that perception. The Mongolians were hardly a problem. First, they were small in number. Second, Mongolia itself had been a Russian protectorate since 1911. Third, the Russian/Soviet political, economic, and cultural influence in Mongolia was overwhelming. Ironically, the Russian-speaking Mongolian elites identified themselves with Eastern Europe rather than Asia. All this had serious implications for the region.

It was as if the Russian Far East was turning its back on neighboring Asia. Its role was that of a fortress, an outpost of Moscow. Its lines of communication with the countries just across the border—which often were merely a few dozen kilometers from the region's principal cities—lay, via Moscow, five to eight thousand kilometers away. This was abruptly ended in 1991. The explosion in contacts with the outside world and the simultaneous dramatic weakening of contacts inside the country that immediately followed the collapse of the Soviet Union brought mixed results.

On the one hand, the Russian provinces established lifelines to China, Japan, and South Korea, which have guaranteed the provinces uninterrupted supplies of foodstuffs and cheap consumer goods. Shopping tours to the neighboring Chinese cities and Japanese ports provide economic opportunities to thousands of local Russians. On the other hand, there are fears that, should the borders remain open and transparent, and the police regime lax and prone to corruption, the Chinese and the Koreans will establish a permanent presence in the area, which could spell the end of the *Russian* Far East.

Russia's exposure to Asia has rapidly grown in the last decade, but its economic role there is negligible. In

1998, Russia became a member of the Asia-Pacific Economic Conference (APEC), but it is not seen as either an Asian country or a power in Asia. Russia is virtually absent from the region, with the partial exception of its immediate Asia-Pacific neighbors.

The pressure from its more competitive neighbors promises the Far East interesting times. At the beginning of the 21st century, Russia faces a stark choice on the shores of the Pacific—either it will transform itself into a modest but viable economic player or it will continue to lose ground figuratively, and later start losing it literally.

As with the continuing turmoil in the south, the mounting challenge in the east pushes Russia toward Europe. Finding its proper place there, however, is not an easy task.

Toward a Europe Without Dividing Lines?

As previously discussed, the principal challenge that Russia perceives in Europe is the growth of the West, both through its internal consolidation and outward expansion, despite the obvious tensions between the two. Virtually all countries in Eastern and Central Europe and the South Caucasus are gravitating to this organized West at least politically and economically. The European Union, NATO, and the United States have become poles of attraction so powerful that there are practically no countries that wish to opt out or drop out of its institutions. Ukraine is proceeding cautiously, but its elites have basically made their choice. Even Serbia, once President Milosevic leaves the stage, is widely expected to fill in its applications in Brussels.

Thus, the buffer zone separating Russia from the organized West is shrinking fast. Already in the medium-term, Russia's only neighbor in the West will be the European Union (and the EU-leaning Ukraine). The union's presence to the south of Russia's borders will be much less pronounced but clearly discernible. All of this will be a powerful political, economic, financial, information, and military reality. As to NATO, it will probably not expand that far afield, but its capabilities for intervening anywhere in the Euro-Atlantic area will have increased substantially with America's increasing technological lead confirming it as a global military power in a class of its own. What, then, should Russia be doing?

A leading Russian commentator characterized NATO enlargement as the beginning of a new geopolitical epoch for Europe, America, and Russia.[17] This statement may be right, but the implications drawn from it are often wrong. A confrontation with NATO is something Russia cannot afford and should never attempt. Vacillation between half-hearted partnership and token confrontation is a waste of both resources and good will. It is also frustrating and disorienting. Rather, it is in Russia's supreme national security interest to strive toward full demilitarization of its relations with the West. This cannot be done through expanding the relationship with NATO alone. The demilitarization of relations, however, cannot be done without closer ties. At some point, Russia will need to seriously consider applying for NATO membership.

Raising the hypothetical possibility of Russian membership in NATO provokes criticisms on two fronts. One is that this would remove the last obstacles, in the form of objections from Moscow, to the accession to the alliance of the former Soviet republics, the Baltic States, Ukraine, and even Georgia and Azerbaijan, all of which have indicated their willingness to join. The second is that this would lead to long-term tensions with China, which would perceive Russia's membership in NATO as an element of America's encirclement policy.

The issue of NATO enlargement all the way to the borders of Russia calls for new thinking about both NATO and Russia. Poland, the Czech Republic, and Hungary have been members of the alliance since the spring of 1999, and so far little has changed in that strategic direction for Russia. None of the dire predictions about the consequences of membership has come true.[18] If anything, the Poles and other Central Europeans have grown more confident about their national security, and more ready for building a new lasting relationship with Russia, from the position, of course, of a Western country.

References to the new military imbalance in Europe, where Russia is outnumbered and outgunned by NATO by a ratio of 4:1 or 3:1, are not very convincing. The modified treaty on conventional forces in Europe (CFE) provides material reassurances, through its system of national and regional ceilings and ceilings on the deployment of foreign forces as well as an elaborate system of verification, that there can be no massing of forces that would threaten any country in Europe.

References to the new possibilities for power projection deep into European Russia are more serious on the face of it, but they totally ignore the nuclear deterrence factor. This factor does not work along Russia's southern periphery, but it is as present as ever in Russia's relations with the West.

The Baltic membership in NATO is believed to be an extremely difficult and painful issue for Russia. A decision to invite the Lithuanians, Latvians, or Estonians would bring the alliance across the former Soviet border, thus eliminating a highly sensitive psychological barrier.[19] Owing to their geographic position, Estonia, Latvia, and Lithuania are considered the ideal staging area for air and cruise missile attacks deep inside Russia. Also, since they are difficult to defend, their security within NATO would have to be guaranteed by some kind of trip wire mechanism, whether by means of symbolic U.S. troop deployments or in the familiar form of nuclear weapons. Last, while Estonia's membership would bring NATO to the doorstep of St. Petersburg, Lithuanian membership would turn Kaliningrad into a latter-day version of West Berlin.

The hard truth is that, Russia's objections notwithstanding, the Baltic States are more likely than not to be invited to join the alliance during the first decade of the new century. One lesson from the previous campaign to stop the Central Europeans from becoming members of NATO is that, if Moscow tried and likely failed to prevent this, a major political crisis with the West would follow. Russia would then either have to resort to token and costly "counter-measures" or enter into a more serious confrontation that would seriously compromise or distort its domestic reform agenda. While some Russians think they can still prevent the Baltic States from entering into NATO, they must admit that they are powerless to bar Sweden and Finland from accession, should these countries make such a decision. Seen from whatever angle, membership of all of Scandinavia in NATO would be a far more significant development than the issue of the Baltic States.

Russian traditionalists perceive "NATO's expansion to the Baltics" as a dangerous provocation, and see the prospect of Ukraine's joining NATO almost as a *casus belli*. Having advanced so far, the alliance, they argue, will be in a position to finish Russia off, which they see as the West's ultimate goal.

Ukraine's prospects as a potential member are remote at best, but its willingness to cooperate with the alliance is real, and growing. Although the Charter of Distinctive Partnership between NATO and Ukraine is a much-reduced-size model of the NATO-Russia Founding Act, the relationship has been vibrant and expanding. To recognize that fact, in February 2000 the North Atlantic Council held its first-ever meeting outside Brussels, in Kiev. Even if Kiev remains a partner rather than a member, the NATO issue will weigh heavily on Russo-Ukrainian relations.

There is the potential for a crisis to threaten the internal stability of Ukraine. To some in Russia this would be a golden opportunity to "liberate" eastern, southern, and central Ukraine, as well as the Crimea, all deemed to be pro-Russian, from pro-Western "Galician rule." Afterward, the Uniate, anti-Russian province of Galicia would be amputated for the sake of the remaining Orthodox Ukraine. Such a crisis, however, could lead to large-scale violence, and even war, into which Russia and the West would probably be drawn. This is where the Balkans-type scenario, feared by Russian military planners and some civilian strategists, may actually become a reality.

Many of Ukraine's problems with its military and more broadly with its political institutions, the economy, and society are similar to Russia's. It is as far as Russia is from meeting NATO standards. Its advantage over Russia lies in the fact that it has made its basic choice, while Russia hasn't. If Russia, however, were to decide in favor of joining the alliance, it would make a lot of sense for Moscow and Kiev to agree that the two largest East European nations seek NATO membership jointly and simultaneously. This plan is obviously risky. However, although a breach of faith by either partner can not be ruled out later on, nor can the temptation in Brussels to play off the differences between Moscow and Kiev, there are enough incentives to keep the process on track and come to a final conclusion. A NATO that included both Ukraine and Russia would be a new NATO indeed.

It cannot be emphasized more strongly that NATO enlargement is a relatively peripheral matter, both for the alliance and Russia. What has been and remains of central importance is the nature and quality of the relationship between the two. An *equal* relationship coveted by the Russian leadership can be more readily achieved within a partnership framework than by means of some version of a critical dialogue.

The Russia/NATO-China issue was first raised in 1994 when Moscow was considering joining the Partnership for Peace program. It is not difficult to see China's interest in Russia's staying outside of NATO, and even in opposition to it. On the other hand, throughout the 1990s Russia has been more than a loyal neighbor to China, providing it with modern arms and technology and supporting it politically on such issues as Taiwan and Theater Missile Defense. By itself, Russian-Western reciprocal demilitarization of relations should not be a problem to China. At the same time, Russia is even less interested than China in the resumption of military confrontation along the long border. Russia should by all means avoid becoming a pawn in a U.S. geopolitical game. By the same token, however, Russian foreign and security policy should not be held hostage to Beijing.[20]

Finally, Russia has reached a moment of truth in its relations with the West. It faces the hard question of which external threats are realistic in the near and medium-term: a Balkans-type air invasion from the West; the multiple contingencies along the southern perimeter; or a very vaguely, and never officially defined, large-scale conventional threat in the Far East. At present and in the foreseeable future, Russia will not be able to man concurrently three strategic fronts. Or even two. Thus, the issue of Russia's strategic boundaries, potential allies, and partners has to be re-examined.

The EU-Russia relationship, while it is less controversial than the Russia-NATO one, equally calls for hard thinking and bold decisions.

Some already see the internal consolidation and enlargement of the EU as a potential threat to Russia. Europe's foreign and security policy objectives may occasionally conflict with Russia's. The emergence of a common European security policy and a separate defense identity could ultimately make the original trading bloc into a more traditional geopolitical player, and a formidable one at that. The European Union has also indicated, in the case of the second war in Chechnya, that it can be an even harsher and more consistent critic of Russian human rights practices than the United States.

The European Union is not merely the largest Russian trading partner and potentially its principal foreign investor. It is the only political-economic "large space" into which Russia can integrate once its "large space"—Eurasia—has ceased to exist.

The European Union, currently consisting of 15 members, is already considering applications from 13 other countries, many of them in Central and Eastern Europe. Other countries, such as Ukraine and Moldova, would like to be in that category, but are being disqualified for the time being for obvious economic reasons. This means eventually creating an uninterrupted boundary line between Russia and the EU from the Barents to the Black Sea.

This potential enlargement changes the very character of the European Union, born as a Western Protestant/Catholic, Roman-Germanic institution. Within the next ten to fifteen years, the union will include several Slav states, new Orthodox members, and a few former Soviet republics with several hundred thousand ethnic Russians living there—Europe's first *Euro-Russians*. A Europe that includes Bulgaria and Turkey as future candidates cannot close its doors to Russia—at least not on cultural grounds.

The enlargement of the European Union has the double effect of making Europe both closer to Russia geographically and more distant in terms of the widening economic and social gap. Under these conditions, Russia faces the prospect of progressive marginalization. This process can be arrested and later reversed only by a conscious Russian decision in favor of Europe.

Russian membership in the European Union, of course, is not on offer at present, and will not be in the foreseeable future. Russia, however, should make its basic choice now. It should make accession to the European Union a long-term policy goal. Achieving this goal may well take the efforts of two generations, but 50 years is too long a period to be meaningful to those who are active today. Thus, a 30-year time frame should be advised instead. The decision to seek accession would have to be a unilateral one, not predicated on the European Union's stated willingness to consider the idea some time in the future. No effort should be wasted, for Russia will need to adapt to the reality of the expanding union anyway.

Even a 30-year period is not waiting time, but time to be used to harmonize Russia's economic, political, legal, and humanitarian practices with those of the European Union. Traditionally, Russians have viewed integration as a process of making an ever larger Russia. This process is now over, and in its place there is a need to integrate Russia into something that is much larger than Russia. Russia will also need to recognize that its place in Europe will rest on its ability to integrate, not on its political-military influence beyond its borders.

The notion of Russia's joining Europe is criticized as capitulation and betrayal of its unique identity. Whereas the Central European countries may aspire to become part of "second-tier Europe," Russia can only hope to get a third-class ticket, which is where the West sees its proper place.[21] From Nikolai Danilevsky on, there has been a Russian tradition of blaming Europe for its anti-Russian bias, its "civilizational rejection" of Russia, which was allegedly an obstacle to Europe's and the world's progress. Nowadays, both Communist and nationalist ideologues in Russia refer to the increasingly closed, exclusive nature of the contemporary West as a *golden billion* of people."

To other thoughtful observers there is no realistic alternative to joining the expanding West other than Russia's being the proverbial *ostrov nevezeniya*, an island of bad luck.[22] Joining Europe, however, will have to be based on accepting post-Cold War realities, such as America's current global preponderance, and observing the rules of the game, which Russia didn't write but will have to honor. At the same time, Russia's identity and its culture will not suffer. What passes for "Western" values has a universal ring to it. On the other hand, core national identities, while transformed, are not being abolished.

This pro-Europe choice, *Europa-Bindung* (an analogy to West Germany's post-1945 *Westbindung*) is likely to be supported by the bulk of the population of Russia. It is among the elites, not the electorate, that anti-Americanism is strong.[23] Tatarstan and Bashkortostan, both staunchly secular, will move toward Europe economically rather than toward some Islamic economic model. So will Sakha and Buryatia, which are not "pro-Asian." For its part, Europe's overriding idea (next to human rights) is diversity. This pluralism—not only *nach Innen*, but *nach Aussen* as well—is not being diminished. Together with the Muslim populations of Britain, France, Germany, and other EU countries, Western-leaning countries such as Turkey, Albania, and Bosnia will constitute Muslim elements of a Greater Europe, which the rest of the continent can and will accommodate.

Becoming part of a Greater Europe can only be the result of a sustained long-term effort. In geopolitical terms, stress will have to be laid on trans-border cooperation. At the micro level, Kaliningrad is a natural laboratory for Russia-EU integration. Other Euro-regions could include St. Petersburg and the areas around the Gulf of Finland; Murmansk and the northern regions of Norway and Finland; parts of Karelia; and Finland. Sub-regional cooperation in the Arctic Barents region and in the Baltic and Black Sea basins already provide useful frameworks at the middle level.

Russia as part of Europe does not contradict other national projects, such as the development of central Russia, the inclusion of Islam within Russia, and the development of a formula for good relations with the Muslim world outside of it, or the reversal of the erosion of Russia's position in the Far East and Siberia. There are also special projects for the North Caucasus and the Russian North. For Russia at the beginning of the 21st century, the domestic agenda is incomparably more important than the foreign policy one. Russia's new frontier is not Europe; it is Russia itself.

The Russian word *derzhava* is difficult to translate, because it is not easy to define. If its meaning is indeed "a

state that is self-sufficient," as Gennady Zyuganov succinct-
ly put it,[24] then the epoch of *derzhava* is definitely over.

NOTES

[1] Sherman W. Garnett, *A Wedged Bear in a Great Tightness: Understanding the Constraints of Russian Power*, Russian version in *Pro et Contra*, Vol. 2, No. 1 (Winter 1997), pp. 5-20.

[2] Alexei Arbatov cited the figure of 80 million. See *NVO*, No. 10, March 15-21, 1997, p. 1.

[3] Such as Prime Minister Viktor Chernomyrdin.

[4] For a very thoughtful analysis of this historic disappointment, see Alexander S. Panarin. "'Vtoraya Yevropa' ili 'Tretii Rim'? Paradoksy yevropizma v sovremennoi Rossii," in *Voprosy filosofii*, No. 10, 1996, pp. 19-31.

[5] Immediately following the end of the Cold War, the Russian leadership considered its western borders to be secure. Serious questions began to be asked in Moscow only in 1993 after the Clinton administration decided in principle to open the North Atlantic Alliance to new members. This was perceived as an attempt at "isolating" Russia, which Moscow unsuccessfully sought to prevent. The Russian military argued that the enlargement of the alliance would fundamentally upset the strategic balance in Europe. The situation on Russia's borders, it was thought at the time, would drastically change. Some military analysts even suggested that new members of NATO would be encouraged to display "intolerance and aggressiveness" vis-à-vis Russia. Not only would NATO's "war-making military pressure assets" be moved closer to Russia's borders. Norway might drop its self-imposed restrictions regarding military deployments and exercises in the vicinity of Russian territory. Emboldened by the collective support of the West, the Baltic States would press their border claims even harder. Kaliningrad would not only be an isolated enclave: Germany may ultimately claim it back. Similar, but even more acute and complicated problems, it was argued, would arise from NATO's enlargement "in the direction of the Black Sea." In general, the situation along the borders would become more tense, so that border incidents and even conflicts could not be ruled out. The proposed military countermeasures along the border predictably included strengthening the

border troops; beefing up the armed forces units deployed near the western border; ensuring closer coordination between FPS border districts and MOD military districts, with the FPS gaining operational control over MOD forces and assets, such as army and tactical aviation, and motor rifle units. Lastly, more intra-CIS military coordination was urged. (See Lieutenant General Sergei Bogdanov, Chief, Center for Operational-Border Studies, ex-General Staff analyst, "Problemy, kotorie nado reshat uzhe seichas," *Nezavisimaya gazeta*, May 28, 1996, p. 2.)

[6]   Natalia A. Narochnitskaya, "Politika Rossii na poroge tretyego tysyache-letiya," *Mezhdunarodnaya zhizn*, No. 9, 1996, pp. 26-40. Quoted from *Vneshnyaya politika i bezopasnost sovremennoi Rossii,* A Reader, Vol. 1, Book 1, p. 249.

[7]   Sergei Kortunov, op. cit., Reader, Vol.1, p. 130.

[8]   Vladimir Lukin, a Yabloko leader and a former ambassador to the United States and long-serving chairman of the International Affairs Committee of the Russian State Duma.

[9]   For instance, in the *Presidential Address on National Security to the Federal Assembly*, June 25, 1996.

[10]   Including Alexei Podberyozkin, a one-time Zyuganov adviser-turned-monarchist and head of the Spiritual Heritage movement.

[11]   For example, Oleg Rumyantsev, a leading deputy in the first Russian parliament.

[12]   Alexander Solzhenitsyn, *Rossiya v obvale,* Russki put', Moscow, 1998, pp. 44-45.

[13]   Samuel Huntington, *The Clash of Civilizations and the Remaking of World Order*, New York, Touchstone, 1997, pp. 163-168.

[14]   Konstantin Leontiev, *Vostok, Rossiya, Slavyanstvo,* Respublika, Moscow, 1996, p. 158.

[15]   Not only Podberyozkin, but also Yeltsin mentioned Bulgaria as a possible future member of the Russian-led confederation.

[16]   It has been reported that during a 1999 meeting with the Russian Duma's delegation in Belgrade, Slobodan Milosevic asked Sergei Baburin, a Deputy Duma Speaker and a leading supporter of the Russian-Belarussian-

Serbian unification, what he thought the name of the new state should be. "Why, Great Russia, of course," replied Baburin. "Well, *I* was thinking of Greater Serbia," Milosevic retorted.

[17] Alexei Pushkov, "Novy yevropeisky poryadok," *Nezavisimaya gazeta*, October 24, 1997, pp. 1, 4.

[18] The only really unpleasant surprise for Moscow was the sudden expulsion by Warsaw in February 2000 of nine Russian diplomats accused of espionage.

[19] Two Russian authors, Sergei Kortunov and Natalia Narochnitskaya, repeat in their writings *verbatim* the same thesis: the entire territory of the U.S.S.R. with its 1975 borders is the zone of Russia's responsibility and security, the military strategic space that Russia inherited from the Soviet Union as its successor state. These authors insist on Russia's unique succession right regarding all arms control treaties and agreements, and thus Moscow's *droit de regard* with respect to third-party presence on the former Soviet territory. (See Sergei Kortunov, Reader 1, p. 135; Natalia Narochnitskaya, Reader 1, p. 257.)

[20] Periodic crises over Taiwan (such as in 1996 and 2000) indicate to Moscow the need to display some caution and avoid unnecessary and dangerous involvement.

[21] See Alexander S. Panarin, "'Vtoraya Evropa' ili 'Tretii Rim'?"

[22] See Alexei Arbatov, *Bezopasnost: rossiisky vybor,* EPI Center, Moscow, 1999, pp. 32-42; Anatoly Adamishin, "U nas net soyuznikov, no net i vragov," *Nezavisimaya gazeta,* February 6, 1999.

[23] A public opinion poll held by the All-Russia Public Opinion Research Center (VTsIOM) in late January, 2000 showed that more than a third of Russian citizens (37%) favor the development of cooperation with NATO, or even Russia's membership in the alliance. Despite the government's highly critical attitude toward NATO following the air raids in the Balkans, this is the highest indication of support over the previous four years. Only half that number opposes cooperation with NATO. Only 6% favor building an anti-NATO bloc led by Russia. Over one-quarter (28%) of the respondents prefer neutrality. To the question about their attitudes toward the United States, 66% replied "positive or mostly positive," and only 22%, "negative or mostly negative." The ratings for their attitude

toward the American *people* are even higher—78% responded "very positive and mostly positive," versus 10% who said "negative or very negative." See *Trud*, March 7, 2000.

24 Gennady Zyuganov, *Rossiya—rodina moya: ideologiya gosudarstvennogo patriotizma*, Informpechat, Moscow, 1996, p. 50.

Conclusion

AFTER EURASIA

After Eurasia

Borders define a country on a map, but there is much more to the contemporary world than borders, especially those between nation-states. "No torment is deeper than that of being a former superpower—unless perhaps it is that of being a fallen superpower which also undergoes the transition to a market economy," wrote a leading American expert on Russia.[1] One should add to that the transition from autocracy to democracy, civil society building, and the creation of a genuine federation. In the past decade, Russia has gone through an unparalleled catastrophe, which changed both its shape and much of its substance. Russia-Eurasia is over, suddenly but finally.

The end of Eurasia came about for several reasons. First of all, the international environment changed profoundly. The relative importance of the principal factors of state power was altered, with the economy and technology coming to the fore, and culture (the "civilizational factor") becoming more salient. Russia, "a nuclear giant but an economic dwarf," discovered that its resources are vastly inadequate for continuing its traditional role.

Nearly as important, the internal crisis in Russia has eliminated the internal prerequisite for extending the life of the transcontinental empire. In the political sphere, it is safe to say that not only autocracy and totalitarianism but also rigid authoritarianism are things of the past. In the year 2000, Russia, which passed the crucial test of the transfer of power from the first freely elected president to the second one, is not yet a full-fledged democracy. However, it is genuinely pluralistic and, for all its ups and downs, continuing along the path toward democracy. An important dimension of this pluralism is the rise and consolidation of regional interests, which spells the end of the unitary state structure. Russia will probably not turn into a loose confederacy, but it can become, over time, a true federation. In the economic sphere, property ownership is also crudely pluralistic. Thus, the mobilization of all available resources for some government policy project cannot be guaranteed. To both the populace and the elites, the idea that the outside world is hostile and poses the threat of permanent insecurity is receding. Russians are getting used to the country's unprecedented openness, with all its positive and negative implications. What the bulk of the electorate wants is the improvement of its economic and social conditions, not the return of imperial greatness, which is still on the minds of the traditional political elite.

While the disintegration of the Eurasian empire came suddenly and as a shock to most people, this was the natural result of a long process. The Soviet Union helped modernize and develop nations along Russia's borderlands, and raised the self-consciousness of their fledgling elites. This had predictable consequences. Even within the U.S.S.R., "real socialism" within different Soviet republics had its distinct characteristics. The Communist Party's nationalities policy created national-territorial units that were given the status of proto-states. In principle, the formal dissolution of the U.S.S.R. was the final and logical step, although it could have come in different forms, and had vastly different results. Neither the elites nor the people in the newly independent states can be expected to try to reverse the process.

Even as Russia grew exceptionally weak, its neighbors were becoming stronger and more active. The United States emerged as the only truly global power, with incomparable capability to influence developments anywhere in the world, including the former Soviet space and Russia itself. The countries of the European Union, which emerged as genuine welfare states, proceeded to form both a more cohesive and more inclusive union, which challenged Russia's position in Europe much more than NATO enlargement. China made a great economic leap forward in comparison with Russia, breaking an essentially Moscow-dominated pattern of relations and outstripping Russia's gross domestic product, and soon surpassing its per capita GDP. The decline of Russia's population and the migration from the Far East to European Russia, compared with China's huge demographic "overhang," is another development with serious long-term implications. Lastly, Russia faces a historical revival of Islam both as a religion and as a political doctrine. Brought about first by Chechnya, then Central Asia, and finally by the September 11 events and their aftermath, this challenge is of double significance for both Russia's external and internal environment. None of the factors listed above is trivial, or of short duration. All have a direct impact on Russia.

Last but not least, globalization has opened up Russia-Eurasia to powerful forces operating at the world level. These forces do not originate from states. They are forming an international environment in which the primacy of the state may survive (in the much watered-down form of *primus inter pares*) but in which the state will no longer have a monopoly over international relations. The impact of globalization has been tremendous throughout the former Soviet Union, but it was very specially felt in the formerly tightly closed Russo-Eurasian borderlands such as the Caspian basin, the Russian Far East, and Kaliningrad.

As a result of these profound changes, it has become clear that "Eurasia" was never a symbiosis of "Europe" and "Asia" within some cohesive and well-integrated large space. Rather, it was the extension of Russia and a function of its power at any given historical moment.[2] Its fate depended on Russia, and its borders would move to and fro. In its prime, when it stretched from the Elbe and Danube in the west, Mount Ararat and the Hindukush in the south, and was washed by the waters of the Yellow Sea and the Sea of Japan in the east, it was monolithic in military strategic terms, reasonably united politically and economically, but extremely diverse culturally. It was these forces of diversity, in Moscow as well as in the borderlands, that eventually brought about the demise of the empire, and will block its reconstitution.

Even if this much is accepted, questions remain. Is the geopolitical earthquake over, or will there be more, and equally powerful, tremors? Has the current period of reshaping and restructuring Russian territory reached its end in this historical cycle? Or, alternatively, will the current Russian borders move again in the near- to medium-term? Will the Russian elites adopt revisionist policies out of sheer frustration? If so, in which direction, and under what circumstances? Is there substance to the notion of a *Weimar Russia*, which suggests that its own brand of national socialism is getting ready to engulf a humiliated and bitter country? Most importantly, the way Russia's borders are eventually drawn will provide an answer to the fundamental questions, "What is Russia *now*? Where will it fit in?"

Basically, there are three kinds of options for post-imperial Russia as it enters the 21st century: revisionism, disintegration, or creative adjustment. Each of these options has implications for Russia's emerging political system and its international role, both in the vicinity of Russia's borders and further afield.

Options for Russia

Revisionist Russia?

The pain that Russia has endured from its transformation has been so excruciating that nationalism and revisionism are widely feared to be just around the corner, waiting for the right moment to step forward and engulf the entire country. The revisionist credo is that Russia is "doomed" to be an empire; the failure to hold on to it is tantamount to national suicide.[3] It confidently postulates that "Russia will rise again." To the adherents of this view, even regional power status for Russia would be no less than "suicidal."[4] In simple policy terms, Eurasianism means the restoration of Russian domination over the entire Soviet/imperial space and the adjacent traditional spheres of influence. The union with Belarus is thus viewed as only the first step, to be followed by a "trilateral union" with Yugoslavia, an eventual "second reunification" with Ukraine, and new "voluntary" accession by Armenia, Kazakhstan, Kyrgyzstan, and potentially other post-Soviet states.[5] A more "intellectual" and decidedly romantic version of revisionism is pan-Slavism with its delusion of creating a "second Constantinople," a new eastern Orthodox empire.[6] A much scaled-down version is a Russia-plus, i.e., the Russian Federation absorbing parts of the neighboring states where the ethnic Russians form a majority (the Crimea, Northern Kazakhstan), or where the local separatists align themselves with Moscow (Abkhazia, South Ossetia, Transdniestria).

This model implies competition and conflict with the West in the former Soviet space, the Balkans, and Central Europe. To counter the immense capabilities and resources of the West, revisionists propose creating a new Eastern bloc made up of Russia and the CIS, China, India, and Iran. For these geopolitically conscious thinkers and actors, this "Eurasian dream" should be realized by confronting America with what it fears most: the nightmare of a Eurasia united by a single power structure. This would mean the reincarnation of both the Mongol empire and the short-lived Sino-Soviet alliance. The first task of this alliance would be to wrestle away the rimlands from U.S. domination and turn them into anti-American allies.[7]

Revisionism's irrational response to a very real challenge carries the danger of trying to reach the impossible at the cost of suffering an even more crushing defeat. Such an attempt cannot be ruled out. In the 20th century, it took Germany two successive defeats to leave the well-trodden track of militarism and aggression.

A less extreme version, reconstitution rather than revisionism, is embodied in the concept of multipolarity, and calls for strategic independence without confrontation. It views America, Europe, and China as both competitors and partners, and is prepared to enter into an ad hoc coalition with any other power center, following the balance of power pattern of 18th century Europe. Thus, humiliated in the West through NATO enlargement and Western intervention in the Balkans, Russia, according to this logic, can and should turn to the East—in the manner of the 19th century foreign minister Alexander Gorchakov[8]—and not only build alliances with China, India, and Iran, but also promote ties with the former Soviet republics. Moscow's multipolarity naturally views the Commonwealth of Independent States, this "non-Russian Eurasia," as the building site of a new integrationist project. Without a Russian leading role within the CIS, there can be no Russian "pole."

Unfortunately for the authors and supporters of this idea, it assumes a capacity that is simply lacking in today's Russia. A medium-sized country with a mediocre level of development is saddled with the mentality of a great power and world leader. The country's principal macroeconomic measurements are too modest for such an ambitious project. Russia's natural resources are vast, but they demand substantial investment to extract and deliver to the market. More importantly, they are not crucial to the nation's standing in the post-industrial age. The option of "reimperialization of Russia," a term coined by Henry Kissinger,[9] is virtually foreclosed.

This notion equally overstates the willingness of the newly independent states to harken back to the former imperial power. Intra-CIS trade flows have been steadily declining throughout the 1990s. Political regimes in the 12 countries are diverging, and so are the economic systems. The security challenges they face call for very different responses. Examples to the contrary, be it Russian-Belarussian integration, the Customs Union, or, in other words, closer cooperation between the remaining members of the Collective Security Treaty, merely confirm the futility of a Eurasia-wide integration. It is highly significant that the failure of the last attempt at reintegration occurred on the watch of the thoughtful and pragmatic Yevgeny Primakov, Russia's most enlightened and exceedingly experienced Eurasianist. And the failure was not due to his lack of effort.

Multipolarity also attaches undue prominence to traditional geopolitics, to the detriment of geoeconomics. The more far-sighted members of the Russian political, economic, and intellectual elites increasingly look to the CIS as a collection of individual states of very different importance and value to Russia. Thus, they strongly support a bilateral approach to any pretense of integration "of the twelve."[10]

It is not difficult to see that multipolarity is a precarious concept, especially for a country in Russia's position. Given that it is not a first-level pole itself, and is incapable of reintegrating its former borderlands, Russia finds itself in the field of attraction of several major and active power centers. It could well be that if central authority in Russia continues to be "privatized" by selfish vested interests, parts of the Russian Federation could gravitate in different directions, making the unity of this country a very tenuous concept.

Thus, traditional territorial thinking is unlikely to yield positive results. It is possible to elevate geopolitics to a new mantra, but impossible to restore imperialism. This, however, carries an unexpected bonus with it: Russia has lost ground, but simultaneously its expanse has ceased to be a source of strength the way it was before the mid to late 20th century.

Russia's Disintegration

Usually, there is no shortage of dire predictions concerning Russia's ultimate fate. In a characteristic exchange of views on the eve of the year 2000, a prominent Russian intellectual predicted Russia's disintegration within 10 to 15 years. His European counterpart's vision of Russia was that of Muscovy west of the Urals, with Siberia under Chinese control.

The American scholar limited himself to the vision of a Sino-Russian war.[11] If a doomsday scenario were to become a reality, this would be the result of a major economic catastrophe. If Russia became a loose confederation, its borderlands would gravitate in different directions, and governing Russia would require the art of managing these very different orientations. In other words, Russia would still join the world, but it would do so in less than one piece.

Disintegration along the boundaries of the Russian regions, of course, is a scenario, not an option. An Ataturk solution—salvation through substitution of failed imperialism by vigorous nationalism—is not a credible option for Russia. It is at best naïve to believe in "liberation" through self-diminution. There is no basis for a complete de-imperialization of Russia. The notion of an "(ethnic) Russian republic within the Russian Federation," which was debated in the late 1980s and early 1990s, made the map of Russia appear like Swiss cheese. In terms of culture as well as territory, there is no such thing as an ethnically purified Russia.

Creative Adjustment

A creative response is based on an honest assessment of the lessons of the past 10-15 years, including the end of the Cold War, the dissolution of the U.S.S.R., and the experience of the Yeltsin era, and—equally importantly—the impact of globalization. More broadly, it must include the Russian/ Soviet imperial experience.

One notable lesson is the need to do away with the obsession for territory. This does not mean giving out more chunks of Russian territory to any potential claimant, but rather ceasing to bemoan territorial losses related to the break-up of the U.S.S.R. Even more importantly, it means dropping territorial reconstitution as an important foreign policy goal—which, although not supported officially, is still lingering in the minds of many elite figures. The oft-repeated analogy with the Federal Republic of Germany misses an important point: Russia was not defeated in a war; its territory was not occupied by the forces of the East and the West; and its historical capital was not divided into several sectors. No historical injustice took place. Moscow acted freely, and its choice can't be reversed.

This adaptation will be made easier by the diminishing importance of geopolitical factors at the beginning of the 21st century. It is often small-sized countries without substantial natural resources that emerge as the most successful and prosperous: Japan, Singapore, Iceland, etc. On the other hand, certain large countries face mounting problems: Russia, India, Brazil. Space and territory, which used to be a major resource of national wealth and national power, are exhibiting their inadequacies and weaknesses. Russia's long lines of communication along the West-East axis, its vast underdeveloped north, and its long borders all require a significant investment of the national treasure.

The much-overused notion of great power should best be rejected or at least downplayed in view of the change in the world environment. Russia will probably find it hard to stop being an empire internally, in the sense of being an amalgam of a variety of ethnic groups, cultures, and confessions, and keeping within its federal body a number of national homelands. It must, however, drop any pretence to an imperial role beyond its borders.

The role of the economy in foreign policy is the way of the future. Russia will survive and develop, or fail and stagnate, depending on its performance in such fields as economics and information technology. Even if it is difficult to expect Russia to emerge in the foreseeable future as a great country—which implies a measure of economic and social progress well beyond Russia's capacities—its ambition to become a successful country, with all the attendant qualifications, can be realized.

Such an approach demands making foreign policy a resource for the country's internal development, rather than following the opposite historical pattern of using Russia itself as a resource base for some grand design on the world arena. The early Bolshevik promoters of the world proletarian revolution have grossly erred in this direction, but the Soviet Union's global competition with the West cost Russia even more. Even the traditional territorial expansion of the Russian Empire demanded a redistribution of resources away from core Russian territory toward the borderlands. Today and in the foreseeable future, Russia will need to concentrate intently on its own domestic development.

This necessitates looking for Russia's comparative advantages, and exploiting them. It means understanding globalization and finding the right niche for the country. It means stressing culture, education, and science, and finding ways to revitalize them.

Russia stands on the boundary between the post-modern and modern and even pre-modern world. It must make its choice. The only rational option is to fully stress Russia's European identity and engineer its gradual integration into a Greater Europe. Even then, Russia will not immediately become, of course, a member of Europe's core. However, it could avoid isolation, and, most importantly, a clear pro-Europe choice would facilitate the country's modernization, its adjustment to the 21st century world. Still, joining the European Union will not be on the agenda for the foreseeable future. Russia should first "build Europe" within its own borders. In parallel to this, it should seek to build a common economic space with the EU, progressively strengthening that association. A failure to integrate would spell Russia's marginalization and possibly its disintegration. There is no longer an option of withdrawing into "Eurasia."

Russia should practice openness as a European country in Asia, but it should not aim to be either a bridge or a barrier. Moreover, in order to keep its position on the Pacific, it will need to keep its Far Eastern doors open to foreign investment, foreign technology, and foreign workers. Integration of the latter will be an important but not an impossible task. That is where Russia's past imperial experience can help.

Across Eurasia—and this may be the only case where the notion could survive—Russia could continue to be a cultural magnet. There is a chance that the Russian language will be an important means of communication in business, culture, and even politics. Russian classical and popular culture, including Pushkin and Tolstoy, as well as rock music, is a major vehicle of cross-cultural exchange. Russian-language radio and TV stations are thriving and highly competitive, from Riga to Bishkek. Even the Chechen separatists have preferred to use Russian for official papers and documents.

However, following Samuel Huntington's notion of Russia as the core state of Orthodoxy is risky, for this can easily compromise Russia's multicultural character, which is the principal pillar of its internal stability.[12] This would immediately raise problems with the Russian Muslims, and could exacerbate relations with fellow Orthodox countries, which will probably see this as a thinly veiled attempt at restoring Moscow's domination over Eastern and Southeastern Europe. Moreover, an Orthodox Russia may be more easily manipulated by the states and groups pursuing extremist policies, which would ultimately set Russia on a collision course with both the West and Islam. It must also be noted that the level of religious devotion among ordinary Russian people is much lower than the political prominence of the top hierarchy of the Russian Orthodox Church.

Along Russia's European façade, the main immediate challenges will be related to Belarus and Ukraine. It will be in the Russian interest to help Belarus survive as an independent state closely integrated with Russia economically and allied politically. If, however, there is a merger, the only reasonable option is for the six Belarussian regions to join the Russian Federation. Otherwise, Russia's fragile internal balance will be jeopardized.

It must be fully understood that Belarus is a special case among the post-Soviet states. The maturity of the Russian political class and society will be demonstrated by their ability to fully internalize Ukrainian "separateness" and independence, and develop a constructive and satisfying relationship. So far, things have gone far better than expected. There is a need to turn the Russo-Ukrainian border into a model of close and vigorous interaction, a European analogue of the U.S.-Canadian boundary. In the medium-to long-term future, Moscow and Kiev will probably have another chance to test the maturity of their relationship on the Crimea issue.

Moldova has overcome an early temptation to erase its border with Romania, and will keep its sovereignty. Erasing the former frontline along the Dniester will be a difficult long-term task. Satisfied that Moldova will not fall into Romania's lap, Moscow has been acting as a broker between

Chisinau and Tiraspol. With the progressive reduction of Russian forces in the area and the new activity in Ukraine's foreign policy, Russia's role in conflict resolution is likely to diminish. Any solution that would give certain rights to the Dniestrians, however, would have Russia among the prime guarantors. Thus, even when the last Russian peacekeeper goes home, the boundary between Transdniestria and the rest of Moldova will continue to require the attention of Moscow's diplomats and politicians. The standoff between Chisinau and Tiraspol should not be left to run its course without intervention. If Russia and the European Union are serious about future strategic partnership, then helping solve the conflict in Moldova can be a good test and, if successful, a model of their security cooperation.

Border problems with Estonia and Latvia are more than ripe for final resolution. There is no reason for postponing the signing of border treaties with both countries, and ratifying the one concluded with Lithuania as far back as 1997. Linking the border issues with the minority question is no longer useful. From the Russian point of view, supporting Baltic membership in the EU while letting Europe (i.e., the European Union, the OSCE, and the Council of Europe) take care of the minorities problem in the Baltic States is the most sensible approach.

Kaliningrad is Russia's geographical stepping-stone to joining the core of EU-Europe. To the extent that the borders of the exclave remain uncontested, and NATO membership for Poland does not lead to a massive military buildup, as is very likely, Fortress Kaliningrad has no *raison d'être*. On the other hand, Kaliningrad as a laboratory for EU-Russian integration has everything going for it.

Along the western façade, the boundary of the most interest is the one between Russia and the European Union.

It is in Russia's interest to do whatever necessary to keep it open for progressively closer interaction. Economic cooperation and combating new security threats, such as organized crime, will be of crucial importance. The degree to which the union's eastern border will turn into a deep divide, or a high wall, will be a measure of Russia's failure.

Along the southern flank, Russia needs to work to stabilize its periphery, both within its borders and in their direct vicinity. Internal borders in the North Caucasus and the land rights disputes, which undermine many of them, will remain among Russia's main security worries, at least for the medium-term, but the phenomenon of the inner abroad must be dealt with for the sake of the stability of the Federation as a whole. Reconstructing Chechnya is the main problem, the solution to which can be neither independence nor military rule *per se*. Such a solution has to satisfy Russia's main interest—security (at regional and national levels)—and Chechnya's key interests, namely, self-government and access to legitimate economic opportunities. Avoiding the fragmentation of Dagestan and stabilizing the power-sharing mechanism in that republic are other long-term problems. Elsewhere in the North Caucasus, an effort to redraw the internal borders could only destroy whatever stability there is in the area. For quite a while, ambiguity, constructive or otherwise, will continue to be *faute de mieux,* the awkward tool of all conflict managers. A major region-wide economic program is needed at least to de-emphasize territorial issues in the political discourse over the North Caucasus.

During the 1990s, Russia has been pushed from the concept of a double border toward the reality of virtually no border in the south to the need to construct such a border. In the South Caucasus, Russian border troops are stationed only in Armenia, and their role should be seen in the context of Armenia-related issues. As a result of the Chechen wars, Russia's instinct has been to follow a policy of *Abgrenzung* vis-à-vis Azerbaijan and especially Georgia, closing borders and threatening or actually imposing visa requirements. While the need to erect barriers to organized crime, terrorism, religious extremism, and other threats to stability is obvious, Russia does not have the option of shutting itself out of the region. On the strength of the Chechnya example, Russia should have realized that conflicts north and south of the main Caucasus range are closely linked. An enlightened self-interest approach would call for further steps toward conflict resolution in Abkhazia, South Ossetia, and Nagorno-Karabakh. It is in Russia's interest to continue to support the domestic stability and territorial integrity of its neighbors.

In Central Asia, Russia will have to decide where to draw the line in the sand as it defines its security perimeter. The forward position in Tajikistan has long remained important in view of the proximity to Taliban-ruled Afghanistan, as well as Kyrgyzstan and Uzbekistan, both of which are seriously threatened by Islamists and terrorists. Abandoning the Tajik base would leave Russia without resources to make a direct impact on the political-military situation in the region. As to the fallback positions, there are several options available. One is a line along the southern borders of Kazakhstan, with Kyrgyzstan as a flank buffer, which makes a lot of strategic sense, but requires a long-term and costly commitment. Another one is along Kazakhstan's northern frontiers, which makes very little sense, strategic or otherwise. The big question is, however, whether Kazakhstan—even with Russia's support—will be able to survive over the medium-term within its present borders.

While before the U.S. war against terror was started, to much of the outside world Central Asia had appeared to be the arena for great power competition, a sort of Great Game II, it is not only that and the terrorist threat that require attention. There are also problems between the new states in the region that can become sources of future violent conflicts. Borders between them, such as in the Fergana Valley, are ill defined. Disputes over land rights and water supply can get out of hand, fanning inter-ethnic hatred and provoking international crises. As recent examples demonstrate, Russia will neither be able to act as the supreme arbiter nor to stay out of the conflicts altogether. In this context, the internationalization of conflict prevention and of conflict management will be required. One set of partners is the Shanghai Cooperation Organization, with China, Russia, and all the Central Asian states except Turkmenistan. Another one is India and Iran. Finally, there is America and, to a much smaller extent, the European Union. Contrary to the popular perception, Central Asia had long offered a good opportunity for cooperation between Russia and several sets of outside partners to ensure security and stability. This view was fully vindicated in 2001, when a broad anti-terrorist coalition came into being.

No matter how serious the threat from the south, it is in the Far East that Russia's fate will be decided in the next several decades. The challenge is primarily of domestic origin, and Russia will need to concentrate on the development of its resource-rich, but backward and increasingly degraded, borderlands. External challenges, however, are not absent either.

The Russian government prides itself on finally reaching agreement on the border with China. Although some outstanding issues pertaining to islands on border rivers remain, they are unlikely to lead to serious problems in relations. Over the medium-term, however, Russia will increasingly be worried about several things: (1) Chinese migration into the Russian Far East and southern Siberia and (2) the growing economic attraction of China. Over the long term, the fundamental change in the balance of power between Russia and China could lead the border issue to re-surface in a totally different way. A more assertive China, wielding commanding influence in the region, could mean returning to the problem of the "unequal treaties" that gave Russia control over Primorye and Transbaikal.

Until now, Mongolia has been transformed into a neutral buffer between China and Russia. As China becomes the pre-eminent power in the region, Ulan Bator will have to navigate carefully between Moscow and the much closer Beijing. Russia will need to take this possibility into account as it develops its border strategy in the Far East.

The territorial issue in Russia's relations with Japan is unlikely to go away soon. Sophisticated plans to engage in joint development of the islands are important and potentially advantageous, but they will at best make the resolution of the dispute smoother, and not act as a substitute for such a solution. Eventually, Russia will probably agree to hand over all the disputed territories. This may come as the final stage of a fairly long process, symbolizing a fundamental turn-around in Moscow's relations with Tokyo. However, a weak Russia can't be a generous Russia, and the direction of the change is more important than any deadline.

Options for Russia's Neighbors

The CIS has virtually never existed as a unit, a superregion. The former Soviet Union has gone the way of the U.S.S.R.

itself, breaking up into a number of subregions—the new Eastern Europe (Russia, Ukraine, Belarus, and Moldova), the Baltic States, the South Caucasus, and Central Asia. In their turn, these subregions are drifting in different directions, gravitating toward organized Europe or the Greater Middle East. Already, parts of the former Eurasia are joining Europe, while others become part of the Muslim world. Despite their apparent weakness and vulnerability, all CIS countries not only have survived, but have retained a certain freedom of maneuver.

For Russia and its neighbors, territorial status quo is a must. All CIS countries feel the need to hold on to the territories that they received when the U.S.S.R. broke up, no matter how strong separatist claims may be. They also believe all countries should refrain from making claims on the territory of their neighbors. The alternative would be chaos. The only exception to the general rule is the Karabakh conflict, where Armenia does in fact favor a change of the status quo.

Except Russia, all CIS countries immediately defined themselves as unitary states. Still, this will have to be changed in several cases (Georgia, Moldova, Azerbaijan) if there is to be a solution to their internal conflicts. On the other hand, Ukraine and Kazakhstan see federalization as a last resort for averting secession, should they be threatened with it in the future. Both countries refused the option of becoming federations when they became independent out of fear of Russian separatism. In fact, quite opposite policies have been adopted.

Kiev has been steadily solidifying its control over Simferopol and Sevastopol. In 1997, President Nazarbayev, despite the dismal economic condition of Kazakhstan, transferred the capital to the north, from Almaty to Astana, closer to the Russian border. The Moldovans and the Georgians demand the complete withdrawal of the Russian Army from their territories, and have received pledges from Russia that it will do so under the modernized CFE agreement of 1999. National consolidation centered on raising the status of the countries' main ethnic group (ethnic Moldovans and Georgians respectively), however, creates problems for their relations with Russia.

Unfortunately for the new states, the ceasefire lines that divide Georgia, Azerbaijan, and Moldova will be difficult to overcome, even within a common-state approach proposed by international mediators. In all cases, they have to admit, Russia will have a role in either stitching together the split states or keeping them permanently divided, even fanning the conflicts. Thus, they can ill afford to seriously challenge Russia. During the second Chechen war, Moscow issued a clear warning to its neighbors that aiding or abetting the Chechen separatists by Russia's neighbors will not be tolerated.

Having secured their sovereignty and independence from Russia, the new states will need to learn to live next to Russia, each in its own way. There will be no common pattern. The remaining border issues, mostly of a technical nature, are likely to be tackled at the negotiating table. Until Russia creates a viable modern economy and achieves domestic stability, economic associations with other CIS states will be loose, and political alignments ad hoc. Aligning themselves closer to Russia is an option that several countries will exercise if that suits their national agendas. The Customs Union, while less than perfect, has admitted Tajikistan as its fifth member. Armenia, Belarus, Kazakhstan, Kyrgyzstan, and Tajikistan, all members of a revitalized Collective Security Treaty, have been joined by Uzbekistan as Russia's bilateral security/military partners. The larger CIS will probably survive as another commonwealth.

Options for the West

Even as the notion of a "world without Russia" is gaining currency, prominent American authors celebrate their country's accession to the status of the principal and virtually unrivaled power in Eurasia. True, from an American global perspective it is *now* possible to describe "Eurasia"—the way Zbigniew Brzezinski does, for example, as a continent defined by its geographical boundaries. This, however, is not how this term is used in this book, or the way "Eurasia" was commonly understood heretofore, except by theorists of geopolitics. From a political, economic, military, and cultural view, Eurasia traditionally meant the Russian Empire and the U.S.S.R. One can argue, however, that even in a narrow sense, Eurasia has recently witnessed the arrival of massive American power and influence. In fact, this U.S. activism has been made possible by the demise and disintegration of the historical Eurasia. The Americans arrived at its funeral feast.

There are two pitfalls to watch, from a U.S. perspective. One is concentrating on preventing a Russian imperial renaissance. Although the dissolution of the U.S.S.R. was never a Cold War goal, restoration of a Russia-led union is generally believed to be contrary to Western, as well as Muslim and Chinese interests.[13] Although Russia has ceased to be seen as a threat in Washington's eyes, Russian moves toward integration are being carefully, and often suspiciously analyzed for their potential neo-imperialist implications. However, the more insightful Russia-watchers have recognized early on that it is now Russia's weakness, rather than its strength, that is the problem for the West.[14]

Another trap is becoming too closely involved in Eurasian disputes. In the eyes of the newly independent nations across the former U.S.S.R., Washington replaced Moscow as the ultimate referee, protector, and donor. In various ways, from seeking NATO membership to offering to host a U.S. military base to staging peacekeeping exercises in some desert oasis, they have been trying to create permanent and privileged relationships between themselves and the only global superpower. For its part, America is certainly interested in non-proliferation, regional stability, access to important resources, democratization, and countering terrorism across Eurasia. Following these goals intermittently, by means of remote control, is hardly possible, but an entanglement there would heavily tax U.S. resources and make America, itself, more vulnerable. A failure to match promises with action would lead to bitter disappointment and a reversal of loyalties.

Despite America's predominance in Eurasia, it can't do everything by itself, or even arbitrate effectively. Even more importantly, Americans may not support a high level of Washington's activism across the continent. Anyway, the United States will need allies and partners with whom it can cooperate on the basis of common interests. In Europe, there is at present NATO and the EU; in the Caucasus and the Caspian, Turkey and to some extent the EU; in Northeast Asia, there are Japan and South Korea, and in a few cases, China. Russia is largely missing from this list. There is even a theory that three Russias are better than one.[15]

This reminds one of the original approach taken by the likes of Henry Morgenthau in the U.S. and some people in France, like François Mauriac, toward Germany at the end of World War II. They loved Germany so much that they preferred to see several of them. Had they been successful in seeing their plans through, Europe would probably look entirely different today, with nationalism hardly confined to its fringes. Stalin, after all, had a point on the destructive potential of pent-up nationalism. By the same token, a weak and humiliated, truncated and divided Russia would do no one any good, including itself.

The alternative, of course, is to integrate Russia into the West (which as a result could become "the North"). This calls for a bold decision and a sustainable long-term strategy, supported by careful and imaginative tactics. The 2001 anti-terrorist coalition has led to Russia's alliance with the Western alliance. The challenge is to deepen it and turn this relationship into a vehicle for Russia's integration within the American-European security community.

Ways must be found to bring about mutually satisfying cooperation between Russia and the United States in those regions where their interests are closest. The fight against terrorism is an obvious rallying element. Central Asia, threatened by the spillover from the civil war in Afghanistan, domestic Islamic extremism (though foreign-inspired and financed), and the international drug trade are also good candidates. America's interests in the region are not limited to oil. Neither are Russia's. They could join forces to help themselves by helping each other. If such an attempt at regional interaction were a success, a very important precedent would be created. There is one outstanding feature in the Russian political psyche that can be especially valued by the Americans—Russians can think globally. Not all U.S. allies can.

For Europe, the worst option would be enclosing Russia in the West. As in the case of West Germany, strategic integration by the United States needs to be supplemented by economic, political, social, and cultural integration *within* Europe. As the European Union deepens and expands, it must keep the door open to eventual Russian membership. A Europe separated by a high wall or a deep moat from its easternmost point would not only be incomplete and unstable, but would miss a historic opportunity. It is precisely the human resources of Russia *and* its geographical reach rather than the country's proverbial raw materials deposits that can provide Europe with an important comparative advantage in the 21st century. With Russia embedded into it, Europe can become secure, "whole" and internally much better balanced. It would be at that stage that an Atlantic/Pacific security arrangement "from Vancouver to Vladivostok" would finally become a reality.

That, of course, is a long-term proposition, but it could serve as a guide. Keeping the barriers as low as possible as the union moves closer to the Russian border and engaging the immediate hinterland is a thoroughly sensible approach. One also needs to reach out beyond the doorstep of Russia, and think big—reaching, all the way to the ultimate and natural frontier of Europe, which lies on the Amur River and off Sakhalin Island.

The strategic dimension of this relationship could emerge as a result of a joint effort to heal the internal division of the European countries torn apart by ethnic conflict. A good place to start would be Moldova. The European Union would also be wise to make sure that Russia is actively engaged in the implementation of its Stability Pact for Southeastern Europe, and Russia would be equally wise and forward-looking to cooperate with the EU and the United States in looking for ways toward conflict resolution and reconstruction of the Caucasus, including both South Caucasus and Chechnya.

This won't be easy, as evidenced by the international community's behavior during the Chechen war. Although the Western countries, as well as virtually all countries, recognize the territorial integrity of the Russian Federation, they abhor Russian methods and do not necessarily wish Russia to succeed. The idea is to "nip Russian revisionism in the bud." Since outright support for the rebels could be dangerous, invoking direct confrontation with Russia, the preferred role is that of a mediator, which is resolutely rejected by Moscow.

The Chechen problem will probably not be solved even in the medium-term, but it needs to be managed in the interim. Should the West wish to bring that solution closer, it must accept some responsibility for the reconstruction and rehabilitation of the war-ravaged republic. The Chechen war underlies the importance of addressing the larger issue of the Western-Russian relationship in the Caspian region, which is laden with mutual suspicions, recriminations, and other attributes of the Great Game.

For Japan, the relationship with Russia is not limited to the territorial issue. Russia is an essential element of the balance of power in Northeast Asia, which hopefully can be transformed into some kind of a security framework. A stable democratic and market-oriented Russia with a vibrant civic society is the best guarantee of Japan's security.

On its territorial dispute with Russia, Japan has been disappointed twice before, with Gorbachev and Yeltsin. It has made a great effort after 1997 at enveloping the border dispute within a wider and less one-sided agenda. In the early 21st century, Tokyo's true objective should be a stable and sufficiently broad-based relationship with Russia, to which it could serve an eastern anchor alongside with Germany, its principal European point of contact. In return, a friendly and well-disposed Russia would add to the strength of Japan's position in East and Central Asia. In this much-improved climate, it would be easier to finalize the border between the two countries that, instead of being "distant neighbors," could indeed become much closer.[16]

Borders and Ethnicity

The question "Who is a Russian?" still has many competing answers. The concept of a citizenship-based Russian nation is spreading, but it cannot yet prevail. The idea of a "multinational Russian people," similar to the previous Soviet notion, lives on. Ethnic Russian nationalism remains a minority view: the Russians have a long imperial tradition, which cancels out or at least greatly mitigates narrow ethnic nationalism. This helps to explain why the "Russian Question" has failed to arouse much enthusiasm.

The idea of using "Russian compatriots" for geopolitical purposes is doomed.[17] A more reasonable approach is to promote civil societies in Russia and the countries with the largest ethnic Russian populations—Ukraine, Kazakhstan, and Belarus, and to work to move Estonia and Latvia to speed up the process of internal integration there.

The Russian diaspora has demonstrated very different reactions to the geopolitical developments responsible for their new condition. The Russians in the Baltic States are on the way to becoming, through self-differentiation, "Baltic Russians," very distinct from their brethren in the federation. With Estonia's entry into the EU, the union will receive its first installment of Euro-Russians. In the context of the Baltic nations themselves, assimilation will proceed, but will remain incomplete, and the development of bicommunal societies, in everything but name, is probable. Kaliningraders, though "Russian Russians," will develop a Euro-centered regional mentality.

It may appear that Belarus is more Russian-conscious than Russia itself. President Lukashenko was not silent about his ambitions to assume a pan-Slavic (i.e., Russian) role. Russian national patriots became accustomed to making regular pilgrimages to Minsk, creating in the minds of liberals' uneasy historical parallels.

Ukraine is only at the beginning of its Long March of nation-building. Its Russian population is gradually becoming assimilated with Ukrainians, but the process will be drawn-out and patchy, reflecting the different orientations of Ukraine's diverse regions. If Russia becomes economically more successful, however, it will again act as a cultural magnet.

Most Russians in Moldova, who live outside of the Transdniestrian Republic, are becoming assimilated. The Transdniestrians, meanwhile, are becoming a small regional community that is unlikely to fully integrate itself with the rest of the country.

In the Transcaucasus, the Russians have become a small minority and keep a low profile. Now that most Russians have left, Russian language and culture, such as they have survived, are what has remained of the empire.

The exodus of ethnic Russians will be most pronounced from Central Asia. In Uzbekistan, Tajikistan, Kyrgyzstan, and Turkmenistan this may mean a marked change in the social environment. There will remain isolated pockets of ethnic Russians, who, because they are too poor or too old, will be unable or unwilling to move north. These small pockets of ethnic Russians will be all that is left from a century of Russian rule. As the local elites try to become westernized, the masses will turn to Islam. It is in Kazakhstan, however, that the "Russian Question" may have the most dramatic consequences. If Russians are not fully integrated within a uniquely "Eurasian" society, they may develop separatist trends. In the early 21st century, Kazakhstan will be highly vulnerable from within.

* * *

Thus, at the close of the 20th century, one can claim that "eternal Russia," which, in the form of the U.S.S.R. reached a climax of territorial and cultural expansion, has run its full course. With enormous difficulty and pain, Russia is slowly overcoming the "gravitational pull of its own history."[18] Modernization of the Russian state and of Russian society requires non-traditional answers to the twin questions about Russia and the Russians. Before modernity finally takes root, however, Russia and its neighbors will have been through many crises over borders and ethnicity. One can only hope that they all survive in one piece.

Russia-Eurasia is over. To the west of its borders, there lies an increasingly unified Europe, a natural place for Russia's own integration as a European country in an appropriate form. To the east lies an increasingly interconnected Asia, where Russia must either establish itself as a country in Asia or face the mounting pressure to withdraw west of the Urals. To the south, there is the challenge of Islamic activism whose source is both internal and external. All of this places Russia in a highly uncomfortable position, demanding vision and the capacity for action, which is not very much in evidence at the moment. Yet, the end of Eurasia, a real catastrophe, is no tragedy. It is merely the end of a long era. But it is not the end of Russia, for which a new and potentially happier era can now start.

NOTES

[1]   Steven Sestanovich, "Geotherapy," *The National Interest,* Fall 1996, p. 3.

[2]   Thus, the Transcaucasus joined Eurasia in the early 19th century, North Caucasus in the middle of it, and Central Asia in the second half of the century, while Poland, Finland, and the Baltic States have been "in and out."

[3]   Alexander Dugin, *Osnovy geopolitiki. Geopoliticheskoye budushcheye Rossii,* Arktogeya, Moscow, 1997, p. 197.

[4]   This is one of the reasons why so many Russian commentators found Zbigniew Brzezinski's suggestion of precisely such a role for Russia "offensive."

[5]   These motifs are recurrent in the speeches and writings of Zyuganov, Zhirinovsky, and Sergei Baburin.

[6]   This idea is promoted by Alexei Podberyozkin and his Spiritual Heritage group.

[7]   Alexander Dugin, op. cit., p. 168.

[8]   Prince Alexander Gorchakov, Russia's Foreign Minister from 1856 through 1882, who after Russia's defeat in the Crimean War (1856) pursued a policy of "concentration" while promoting the conquest of Central Asia and the Far East.

[9]   Henry Kissinger, *Diplomacy,* Simon and Schuster, New York, 1994, p. 80.

[10] See Sergei Karaganov, "Strategy for Russia — IV. Report of the Council on Foreign and Defense Policy" presented at its 8th annual assembly, Moscow, 2000.

[11] Sergei Karaganov, Chairman of the Council on Foreign and Defense Policy; Giullietto Chiesa of *La Stampa,* and Samuel Huntington interviewed by *Obshchaya gazeta,* No. 52/1, December 30, 1999-January 6, 2000, p. 6.

[12] Samuel Huntington, *The Clash of Civilizations and the Remaking of World Order,* Simon and Schuster, New York, 1966, p. 312.

[13] Kissinger warned that partnership with Russia was possible only "if Russia remained within its borders" (Henry Kissinger, *Diplomacy,* p. 825). Presum-

ably, this meant to discourage aggression or coercion by Russia, not voluntary associations, as with Belarus.

14 For example, Sherman Garnett. See his "Granitsy rossiiskoi vlasti," in *Nezavisimaya gazeta*, May 5, 1996.

15 See, for example, Zbigniew Brzezinski, *The Grand Chessboard: American Primacy and Its Geostrategic Imperatives,* Basic Books, New York, 1997, p. 202.

16 This very apt description belongs to Professor Hiroshi Kimura.

17 Roughly one-third of Israel's population are "compatriots" in the sense of the proposed Russian legislation.

18 The phrase is borrowed from Sherman Garnett, "Granitsy rossiiskoi vlasti," *Nezavisimaya gazeta*, May 5, 1996.

Index

Maskhadov, Aslan, 171, 173
Mauriac, François, 322
Mead, Walter, 22n17
media, 257, 312
Mediterranean access, 52
MERCOSUR, 5
Meshkov, Yury, 259–60
migrations, 15, 42, 45, 65
  from Afghanistan, 194
  Central Asia, 113
  CIS membership, 94–95
  Dagestan, 247–48
  ethnic Russians, 84
  Finno-Ugrians, 250
  forced, under Stalin, 266n9
  illegal, 118, 127n63
  Norway, 139–40, 163n3
  peasant resettlements, 211,
    223n28
  from Russian Far East, 303
  Soviet assimilation
    policies, 240
  See also immigration
    policies
Mikhalkov, Nikita, 27–28
military factors, 10–11, 28, 46,
  76n55
  Afghanistan defeat, 83, 87
  Arctic routes, 45
  Baltic States' independence,
    145–47
  Black Sea Fleet, 157, 165–
    66n29, 165n26, 259
  borders, 54, 104–5, 125n35
  breakup of U.S.S.R., 80,
    85–86
  Chechen war, 185, 197n4,
    197n5, 198n15
  Chinese threat, 223n29
  CIS countries, 92, 316, 320
  defeat of the Red Army,
    95–96
  demilitarization of Chinese
    border areas, 205–6
  demilitarization of Federal
    Border Service, 115–18

  demilitarization of Western
    areas, 285
  double border concept, 108–13
  drug trafficking, 280–81
  Eastern Europe, 51–52
  expansion of territories, 72n8
  external threats, 289–90
  Federal Border Service, 112,
    114–19, 192–93, 223n23
  Islamic fundamentalism,
    281–82
  lack of funding, 242
  loss of territories, 61
  loyalty to central government,
    267n16
  Manchuria, 74n29
  naval bases, 50, 215
  Norwegian restrictions, 139–40
  nuclear weapons, 155, 286–87
  occupation of Chechnya,
    177–78
  paramilitary activity, 185, 190,
    249
  patriotism, 66–67
  peacekeeping activities, 160–61,
    182–83, 260, 314
  restoration of territories, 56–57
  Sea of Okhotsk, 215
  Sevastopol, 155
  strategic borders, 46–56
  territorial expansion, 71
  union with Belarus, 103–4
  U.S. troop presence, 194
  withdrawals of Soviet
    troops, 227
  See also separatist movements
Milosevic, Slobodan, 104, 120,
  279, 295–96n16
modernization, 196, 228
  See also Westernization
Moldova, 21n5, 160–62, 278
  CIS membership, 93, 94
  conflict resolution, 324
  double border concept, 108
  ethnic Russians, 260, 263, 327
  future options, 313–14, 320

Index

incorporation by Russia/
U.S.S.R., 57, 60
independence from U.S.S.R.,
123n14
NATO membership, 275
post-Soviet era, 166n35
Molotov, Vyacheslav, 65
Molotov-Ribbentrop pact, 143
monarchy, 37, 295n10
See also Russian Empire
Mongolia, 203, 220–21n4,
221n11, 249, 283
affiliation with U.S.S.R., 48,
60, 72n5, 78
future options, 318
Mongol invasions, 32, 35, 46,
109, 279–82
Monroe Doctrine, 108
Montreux convention, 158
Morgenthau, Henry, 322
Moscow, 33, 37, 54, 82
invasions, 73n12, 74n27
multipolarity, 236–37, 306–8
Murmansk, 45, 163n2, 236
Muslims. *See* Islamic issues

N

NAFTA, 4, 21–22n8, 95
Nagorno-Karabakh dispute,
21n5, 89, 94, 168, 182, 233
future options, 316, 319
Nakhichevan, 186
Napoleon, 9
narcotics. *See* organized crime
networks
Narochnitskaya, Natalia,
296n19
nationalism, 60, 79, 122–23n11,
125n38, 133
anti-Russian, 262–65
Baltic States border disputes,
147–48
border issues, 100–101,
147–48
breakup of U.S.S.R., 86

Chechnya separatism, 170–71
Cossacks, 248–49
Duma, 254
ethnic Russians, 326–28
irredentism, 7–8, 14–15, 258–
59, 305
linguistic aspects, 255–57
revisionism, 305–8, 321
Ukraine, 154
nationalities. *See* ethnicity
National Security Concept of
2000, 229–30
nation building, 177–78, 180–81
nation-states, 64–66, 91, 94,
103, 132
NATO, 47, 51–52, 103, 110, 119
Baltic States, 149
Belarus, 153, 165n24
Charter of Distinctive
Partnership, 288
Eastern Europe, 122n8
expansion, 7, 135–36, 162–63,
228, 272–75, 284–90, 294–
95n5, 303
Kosovo action, 6
Moldova, 162
Norway, 139–40
Poland, 143–44
public opinion, 296–97n23
Russian membership, 272–75,
285–86
Slavic members, 97
Warsaw Pact countries, 142–49
natural resources, 22n12
Arctic ocean, 141, 163n6, 163n7
Barents Sea, 140
Caspian basin, 169,
186–87, 197
development, 317
Russian Far East, 220
Siberia, 201
Nazarbayev, Nursultan, 189–90,
319–20
Nazdratenko, Yevgeny, 206–7
Nazran Agreement, 198n6
neutral buffer states, 52

"new" West, 135–62
Nicholas II, 41, 75n42
Nikolayev, Andrei, 114–19, 184, 192
NIS (Newly Independent States).
    See CIS (Commonwealth of Independent States)
North Atlantic Cooperation Council, 273
North-Caucasus region, 13, 24n29, 167, 169–81
    ethnic conflict, 246–49
    future options, 315
    internal borders, 315
    Islamic challenges, 279–82
    post-Soviet era, 169–81
    See also specific regions
Northern Dimension (Finnish) initiative, 138, 142
Northern Kazakhstan, 13, 41, 42–46
    See also Kazakhstan
Northern Sea Route, 45
North Kuril Islands, 223n30
North Ossetia, 175–77, 179–80
Norway, 119, 136, 139–40, 163n2
Novo-Ogaryovo process, 123n13

O

Oder-Wester Neisse line, 50, 51–52, 144
oil. *See* natural resources
Operation Federal Task Force, 174
Organization for Security and Cooperation in Europe, 185, 259, 260
organized crime networks, 198n10
    Afghan border regions, 193–94, 199–200n32, 199n31
    Chechnya, 170–76
    smuggling, 110, 113, 118, 127n63
    South Caucasus, 184
Orthodox religion, 37, 64, 97, 133, 239, 312–13

future options, 305
Grand Duchy, 165n20
identity issues, 270–71, 276
Ossetia, 98, 100, 168, 175–77, 246–47
    See also North Ossetia; South Ossetia
Ottoman Empire, 281
Outer Mongolia, 265n2

P

Pacific Ocean, 45
pan-Slavicism, 41–42, 276, 278, 295n15, 295n16, 305
    future options, 327
    trilateral union, 104, 305
Partnership for Peace, 273–74, 289
peasants, 42, 65
    resettlements, 211, 223n28
    slavery, 23n20, 271
perestroika, 19, 85–86, 227, 234
Perestroika (Gorbachev), 123n12
Persia, 47
Peter the Great, 22n12, 47, 231, 271
phoenix theory of territory gain and loss, 95–99
Podberyozkin, Alexei, 295n10
Poland, 329n2
    autonomy, 265n1
    border cooperation agreements, 119
    breakup of U.S.S.R., 80
    German possession, 164n11
    incorporation by Russia/ U.S.S.R., 48–59, 65, 75n41
    invasions, 56, 74n30, 143
    NATO membership, 275, 286, 296n18, 314
    post-Soviet era, 143–45
    Red Army defeat, 95–96
    1980 revolution, 105
    Russian Empire, 229, 231–32
    separation from Russia, 229
    territories, 41

About the Author

Dmitri Trenin has been deputy director of the Carnegie Moscow Center for eight years. He retired from the Russian Army in 1993 after a military career that included participation in the strategic arms control negotiations in Geneva and teaching at the Military Institute. He was the first Russian officer to be selected to attend the NATO Defense College, and he is a member of the International Institute of Strategic Studies. Dr. Trenin was a senior fellow at the Institute of Europe from 1993 to 1997, and holds a Ph.D. from the Institute of the U.S.A. and Canada. He is the author of numerous articles and books on Russian security issues.

The Carnegie
Moscow Center

In 1993, the Carnegie Endowment committed resources to the establishment of a public policy research center in Moscow designed to promote intellectual collaboration among scholars and specialists in the United States, the Russian Federation, and other post-Soviet states. Together with the Endowment's associates in Washington, the Center's Russian associates conduct programs on a broad range of major policy issues ranging from economic reform to civil-military relations. The Carnegie Moscow Center holds seminars, workshops, and long-term study groups involving international participants from academia, government, the private sector, journalism, and nongovernmental organizations. The Center also provides a forum for prominent international figures to present their views to informed Moscow audiences.

The Moscow Center publishes books, occasional papers, and monographs based on the work of its associates and other participants in its programs. The Center also publishes a Russian-language quarterly journal, *Pro et Contra*.

Carnegie Moscow Center
Ul. Tverskaya 16/2, 7th Floor, Moscow 103009
7-095-935-8904 • www.carnegie.ru

CARNEGIE ENDOWMENT FOR INTERNATIONAL PEACE

The Carnegie Endowment is a private, nonprofit organization dedicated to advancing cooperation between nations and promoting active international engagement by the United States. Founded in 1910, its work is nonpartisan and dedicated to achieving practical results.

Through research, publishing, convening, and, on occasion, creating new institutions and international networks, Endowment associates shape fresh policy approaches. Their interests span geographic regions and the relations between governments, business, international organizations, and civil society, focusing on the economic, political, and technological forces driving global change. Through its Carnegie Moscow Center, the Endowment helps to develop a tradition of public policy analysis in the states of the former Soviet Union and to improve relations between Russia and the United States. The Endowment publishes *Foreign Policy,* one of the world's leading magazines of international politics and economics, which reaches readers in more than 120 countries and in several languages.